I0729493

# REMBRANDT

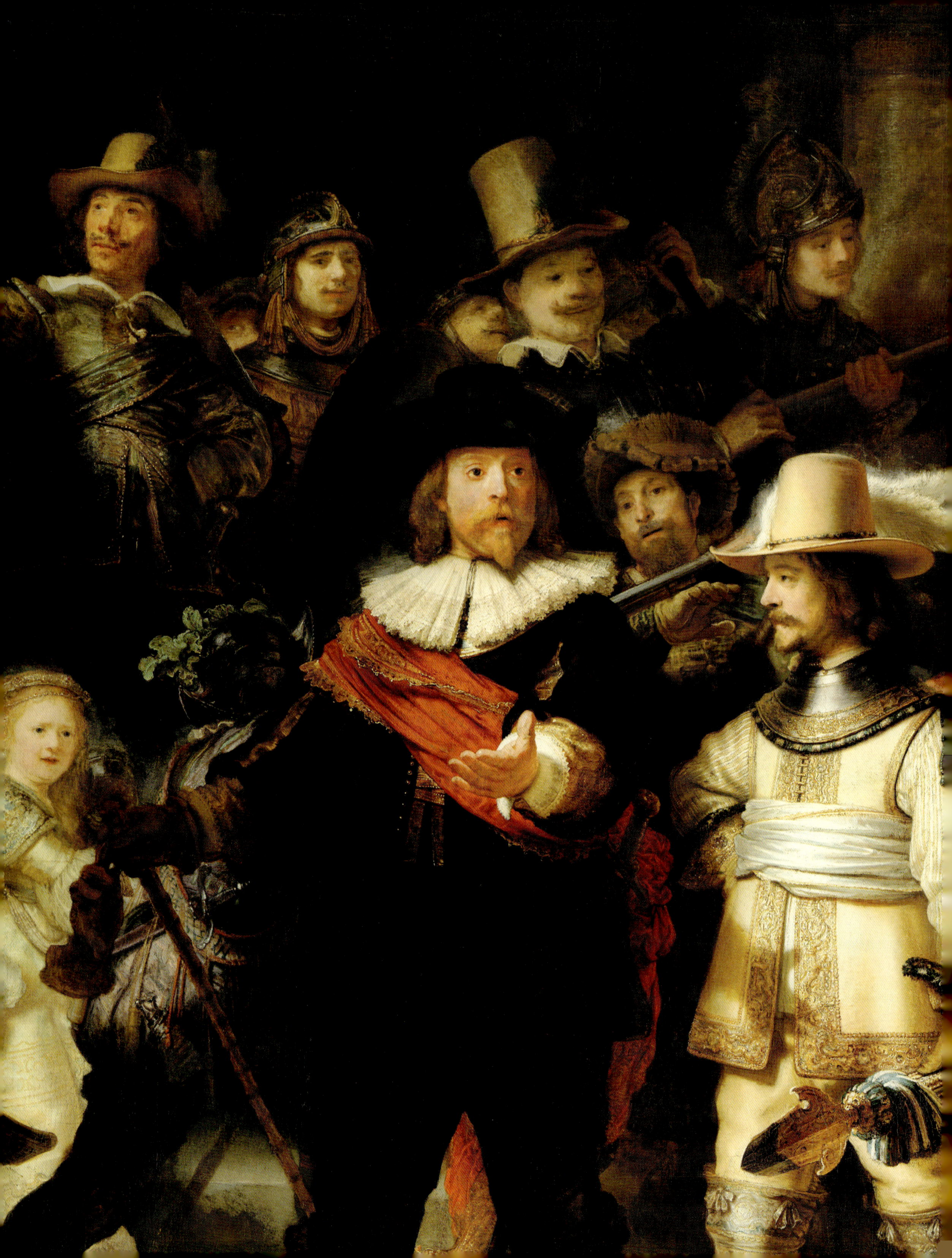

# REMBRANDT

## BETHANY MCINTYRE

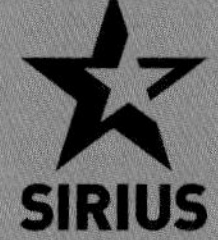

SIRIUS

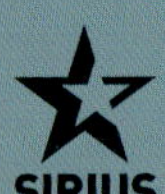

**SIRIUS**

This edition published in 2024 by Sirius Publishing, a division of
Arcturus Publishing Limited,
26/27 Bickels Yard, 151–153 Bermondsey Street,
London SE1 3HA



ISBN: 978-1-3988-5100-9
AD007297UK

Printed in China

# CONTENTS

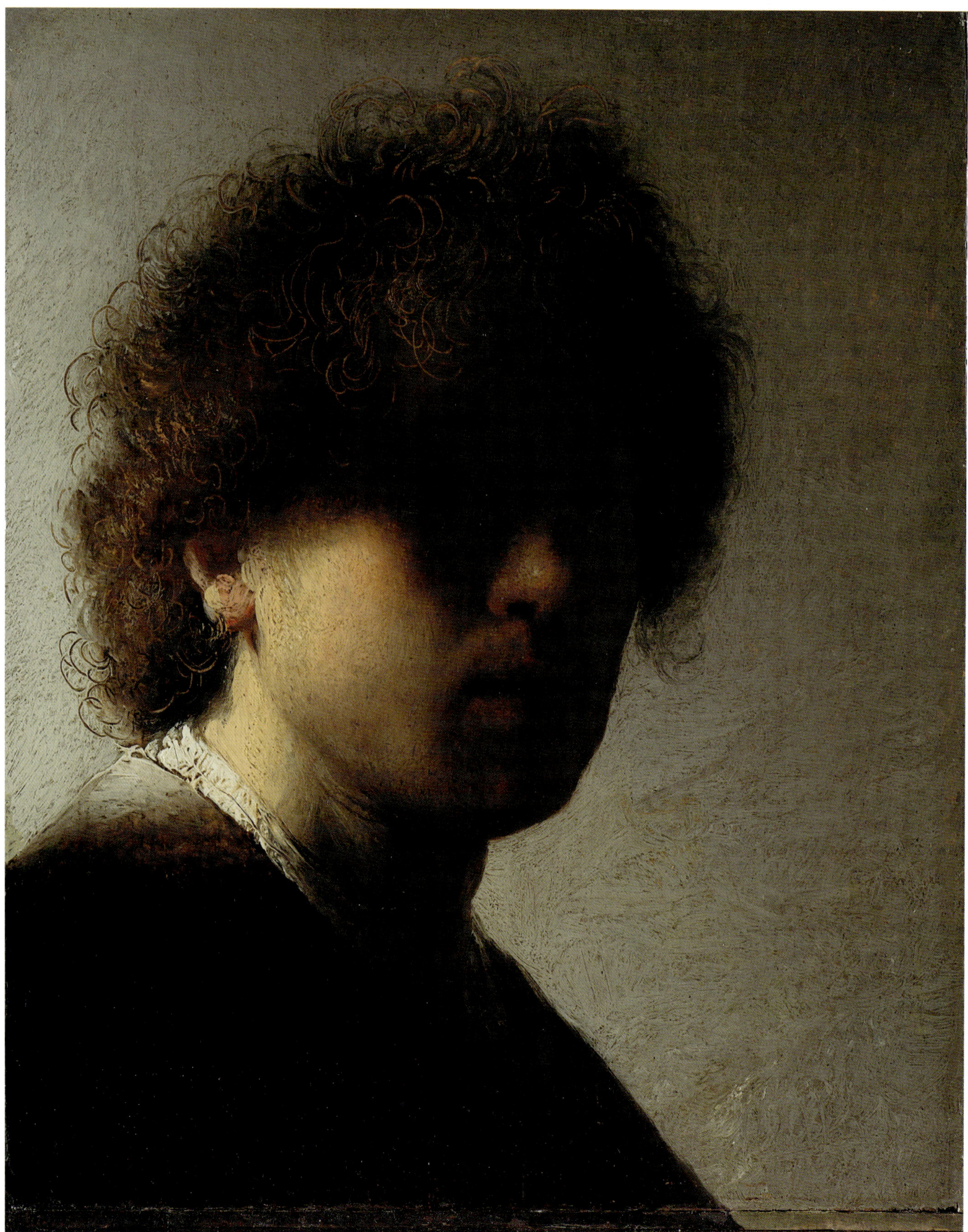

# INTRODUCTION

**R**embrandt is hailed as the greatest painter of the Dutch Golden Age. Not only that, he is also recognized as one of the greatest and most important artists in the history of art. Although he lived over 350 years ago, his paintings are still widely appreciated and surprisingly accessible to a modern audience. His work depicts a wide range of subjects. Rembrandt made his reputation with grand history paintings, a genre that included biblical, mythological or allegorical subjects. However, he also painted hundreds of portraits, including numerous self-portraits, painting himself throughout his life more than any other artist had done previously. He was a draughtsman and a master printmaker too. His work was mysterious and innovative – sometimes too innovative for his contemporaries – and prolific. However, the one feature that links all his work is his ability to portray mood and emotion: he got to the heart of a story and portrayed its soul.

Rembrandt left very few documents written by himself, but through memoirs, early biographies, official documents and the art itself, we can follow his life. It was a life marked by personal tragedies and financial hardships. Through highs and lows, he continued all the while to paint and make prints.

We start in Leiden, where Rembrandt was born, and follow him to Amsterdam, where he achieved fame and fortune and where for a time he was the most celebrated artist in the city. He was continually innovative and his style gradually changed to the characteristic loose, broad brushwork of his later paintings. By the time of his death, he lived almost in obscurity, and financial ruin meant that he was buried in a rented grave.

Today his paintings are displayed all around the world and are treasured by museums and art galleries. If they come on the market, they sell for some of the highest prices in the art world. His art works have a power and beauty that command the viewer to look at them.

*Self-Portrait, 1628. A young Rembrandt wears a simple white shirt and dark overgarment. The strong use of shadow casts shade over the upper half of his face, particularly his eyes, while leaving his ear lobe in full light. This intriguing painting is one of his earliest self-portraits.*

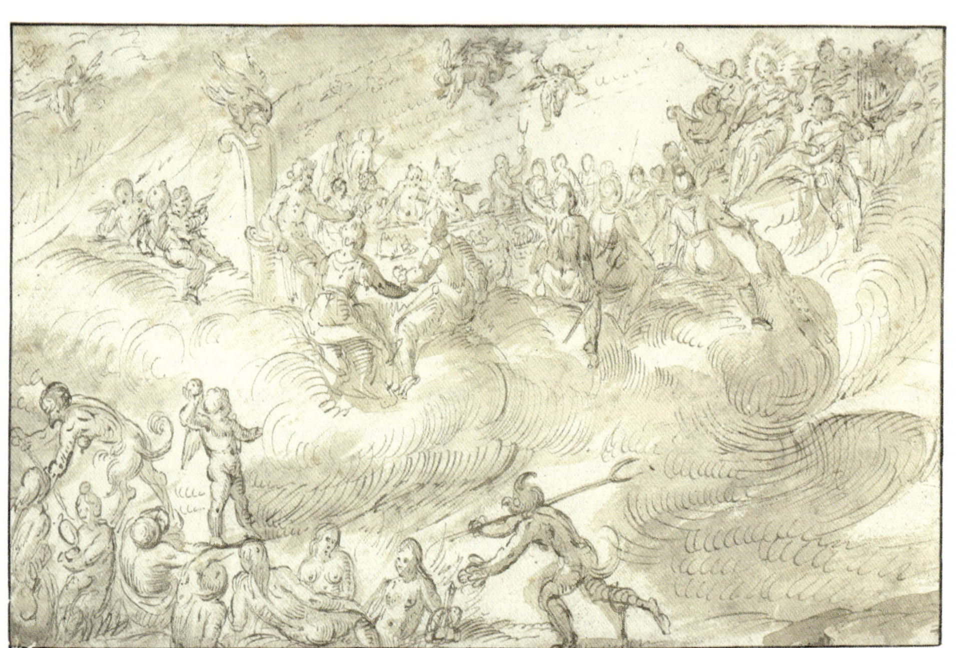

**Above:** A Feast of the Gods (with Seven Deadly Sins) *Jacop Isaacsz van Swanenburg, c.1581–1638. An ink and wash drawing showing a feast with figures representing the Seven Deadly Sins at the bottom being guarded by devilish figures.*

**Below:** The Last Judgement and the Seven Deadly Sins, *Jacop Isaacsz van Swanenburg, c.1600–38. Rembrandt's teacher specialized in such scenes of hell. Naked, damned souls are chased by devils and monsters. On the right the figures represent the seven deadly sins, standing before an entrance to hell.*

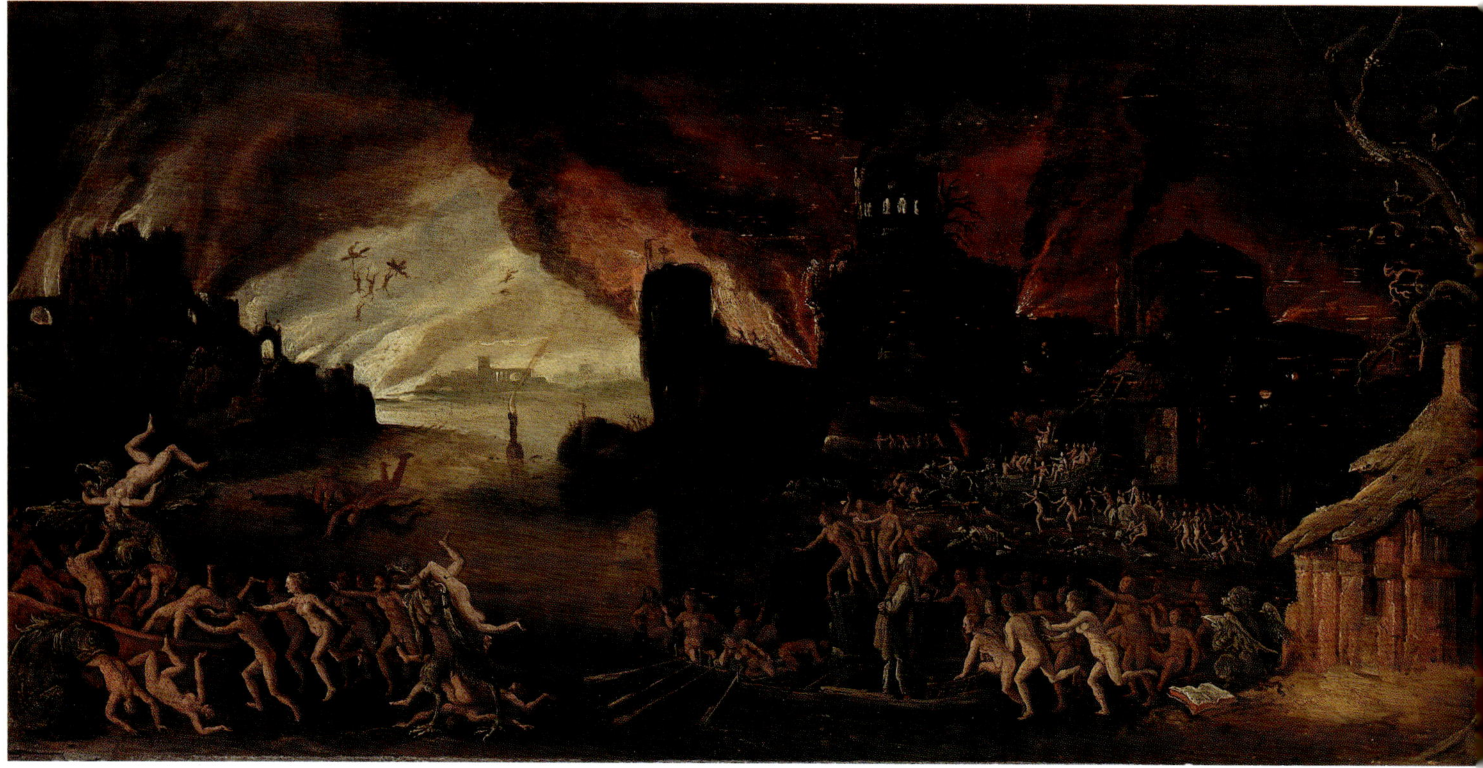

# CHAPTER 1

# Early Life in Leiden

Rembrandt is best known as living and working in Amsterdam, which is where he made his name as a famous, influential artist of the Dutch Golden Age. However, his early life was spent in a different city, Leiden, and it was there that Rembrandt laid the foundations for his career that would later blossom in the artistic centre of Europe, Amsterdam.

Rembrandt Harmenszoon van Rijn was born in Leiden on 15 July 1606. He was the ninth child of Harmen Gerritszoon van Rijn (1567/8–1630) and Neeltgen (Cornelia) Willemsdochter van Zujitbrouck (1568–1640). His parents had 10 children in total, three of whom did not survive childhood.

Rembrandt was not born into a family of artists or craftsmen, the usual background of artists at this time: his father was a miller and his mother was from a family of bakers. Biographers have traditionally described him as coming from very humble beginnings, his parents having lowly jobs and little income. More recent research, however, has concluded that the family had a good income and both Harmen and Neeltgen's estates were of significant value when they died. The family are probably best described as middle class: they were not rich or titled, but they were quite well off, and in the Dutch Republic of the seventeenth century, to be a miller was a respectable job.

The family owned a malt mill, which had been in the family for generations. It was situated next to the river Rhine and the family lived in a house close by. The location of the mill is the reason for 'Rijn' in their

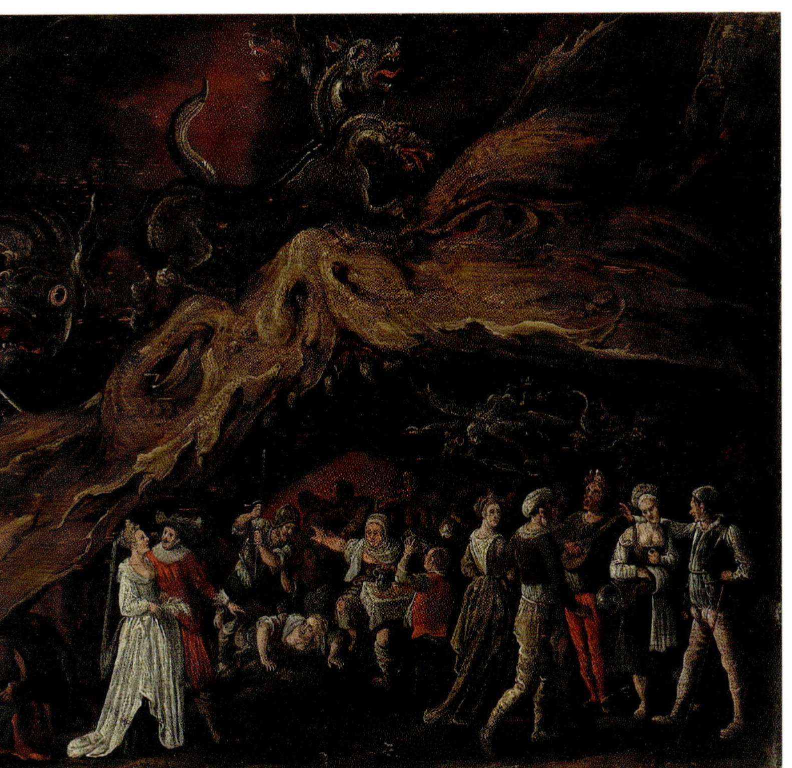

name. The family lived in a town that was booming: in an age of prosperity, the population was growing. Leiden is in the south, close to The Hague and around 48 km (30 miles) from Amsterdam to the north. Rembrandt grew up in the shadow of the Dutch War for Independence against Philip II of Spain, and William I of Orange had established a university in Leiden in 1575, to honour the city's loyalty during the Spanish siege. By the seventeenth century Leiden had a thriving textile industry and was the second largest city after Amsterdam. It was also known for its important printing and publishing businesses.

It was no doubt advantageous for Rembrandt that he was not one of the older siblings in his family, who would have been expected to follow in their father's footsteps and learn the family trade. Rembrandt had four older brothers: Gerrit (c. 1590/5–1631), the eldest, worked in the family mill as did brother Adriaen (c. 1597–1652), and another brother Willem (c. 1604–1655) was a baker's assistant before working in grain warehouses. Nothing is known about brother Cornelis (born c. 1600). Rembrandt also had two sisters, neither of whom married. His older sister Machtelt (*c. 1596–1625*) died in 1625 and his younger sister Lijsbeth (*c. 1606–55*) lived at the family home until her death in 1655.

It is thanks to Jan Janszoon Orler, an early biographer, that we know about Rembrandt's childhood and education. In his book *Description of the City of Leiden*, published in 1641, he included a half-page biography of the artist. Rembrandt attended elementary school before being sent to the Latin school in Leiden, a fee-paying school with an emphasis on biblical studies and Classics as well as maths and history. The lessons were taught in Latin and pupils were encouraged to speak Latin to each other. It is unclear whether he was sent there because he showed academic ability at an early age or whether his parents had ambitions that they wanted him to fulfil.

At the age of 14, on 20 May 1620, Rembrandt was enrolled at Leiden University, but it is unclear to what extent he attended lectures, if at all. It was not uncommon for boys in Leiden to be enrolled at an early age, and it is likely that Rembrandt continued his studies at the Latin school and that attending university was his parents' plan for his future.

Being enrolled at university had its advantages, including tax-free wine and beer, and exemption from military service. In any event, Rembrandt did not continue with his academic studies or attend university because he had discovered a desire to be a painter. It is probable that a teacher at his Latin school had sparked this interest and Rembrandt persuaded his parents Harmen and Neeltgen to take him out of school to begin an apprenticeship with a painter. This most likely happened in 1621, when Rembrandt was 15.

## APPRENTICESHIPS

Rembrandt enrolled on a three-year pupillage with a local history artist Jacop Isaacszoon van Swanenburg (1571–1638) to learn the basics of painting. This was the usual route for training to be an artist. Here, he would have been taught all the knowledge and skills of the profession. Swanenburg was from a family of painters, his father and two brothers were also in the profession. His father, Isaac Claeszoon van Swanenburg (1537–1614), was one of Leiden's most famous artists and had also been mayor of the city. They were a well-established Leiden family with influence and prestige. Swanenburg specialized in scenes of

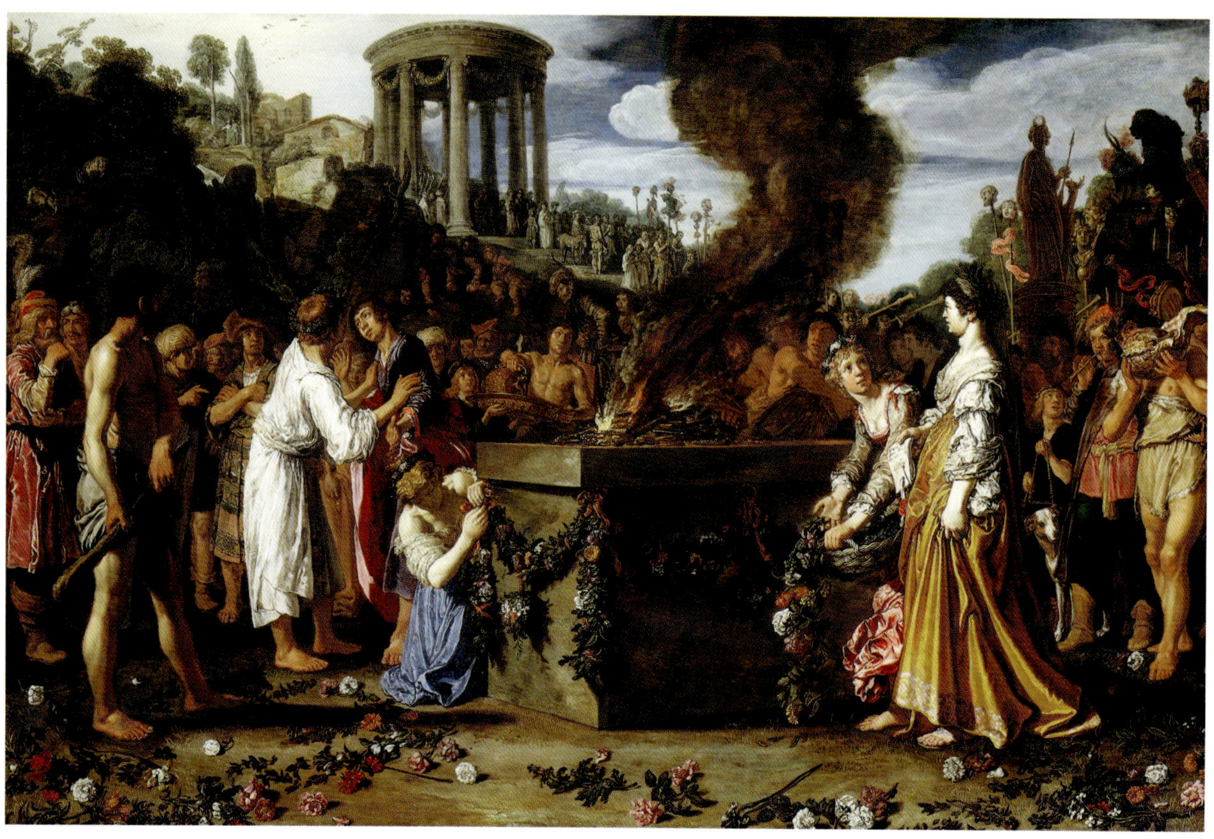

Opposite: Jonah and the Whale, *Pieter Lastman c.1583–1633. Jonah contorts his body as he is spewed from the mouth of the whale.*

Left: Orestes and Pylades Disputing at the Altar, *Pieter Lastman, 1614. Orestes and Pylades dispute which one of them will be sacrificed for stealing a statue.*

Hell and townscapes, but before being allowed to copy his master's work, Rembrandt first had to learn and master the basics of drawing.

Pupillages at this time more or less followed the same teaching. Students initially spent most of their time developing their drawing skills, often repeatedly drawing details such as noses or mouths before moving on to faces and the whole figure. The students also made copies of prints before going on to three-dimensional objects, such as casts and sculptures. They might then move on to painting and copying oil paintings but also worked from nature, outside with a sketchbook and drawing from life. However, to be a successful painter, it was most important that pupils also learned how to compose scenes, to arrange multiple figures together in a mythological setting and to create characters from their imagination. Sadly none of Rembrandt's works from his time with Swanenburg have survived. We cannot know if these early drawings and studies showed the abundant talent and inquisitive mind that is so evident in his later works. In addition to learning these artistic skills, Rembrandt would have also been tasked with duties such as tidying and learning how to prepare canvases, pigments and cleaning paint brushes – all important skills for an artist to be able to run a studio.

## SECOND APPRENTICESHIP

Rembrandt evidently progressed well with Swanenburg – so much so that he was sent to further his development with a more highly regarded artist. He therefore began a second, shorter apprenticeship with the painter Pieter Lastman (1583–1633), who had a successful studio in Amsterdam. This was probably the first time that Rembrandt had visited Amsterdam and spent time away from this family. Amsterdam was a busy, bustling city and the excitement of being there and all the opportunities it offered must have made a lasting impact on the young artist. Lastman was a well known and important history painter, and Rembrandt's time with him helped him to develop his skills for that particular genre of painting. In the Dutch Republic of the seventeenth century, art was divided into different genres and artists usually specialized in one field, sticking to their specialism for the whole of their careers. History painting, which included allegories and religious subjects, was regarded as the most prestigious art form. Next in status was portrait painting, then genre scenes of everyday life, landscapes and seascapes, and finally still lifes. History painting required an artist to combine a full command of many painting skills, including landscape, architectures and figures as well as being able to tell a story and express meaning and emotion.

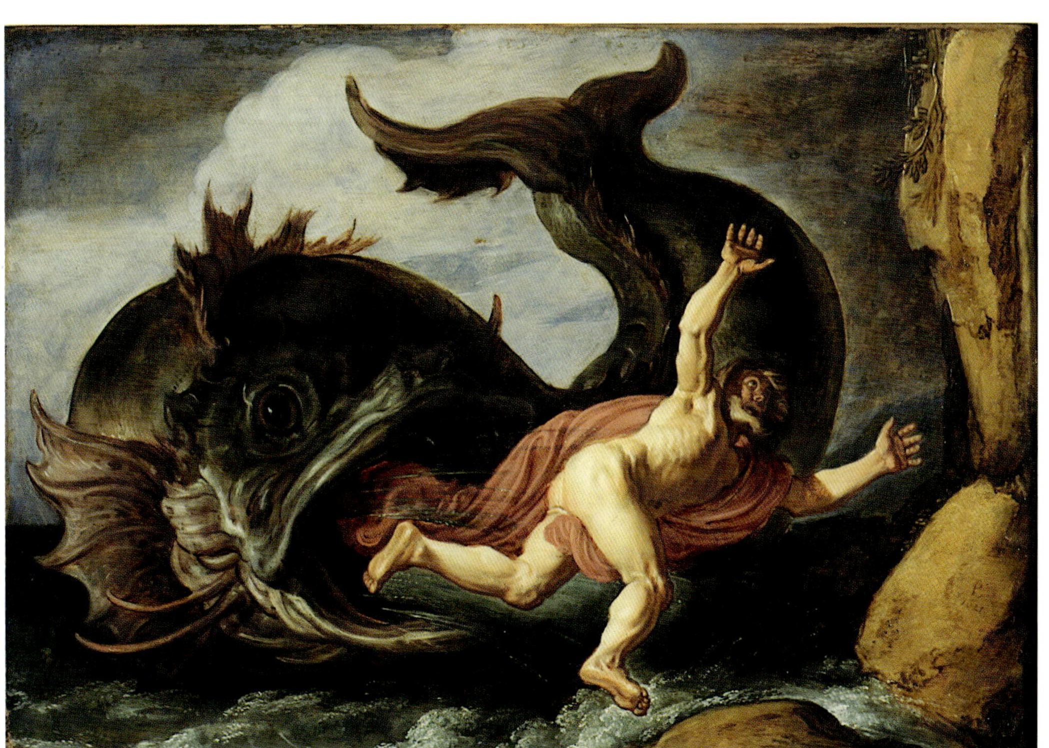

Rembrandt was with Lastman for only about six months, which may indicate how advanced his painting skills were already. He then returned from Amsterdam to Leiden, ready to set up his own studio. Around this time he painted his first known paintings: genre paintings of the five senses, Touch, Hearing, Smell (The Leiden Collection, New York), Sight (Lakenhal Museum, Leiden) and Taste, still undiscovered. They are painted somewhat crudely but are full of human character and emotion.

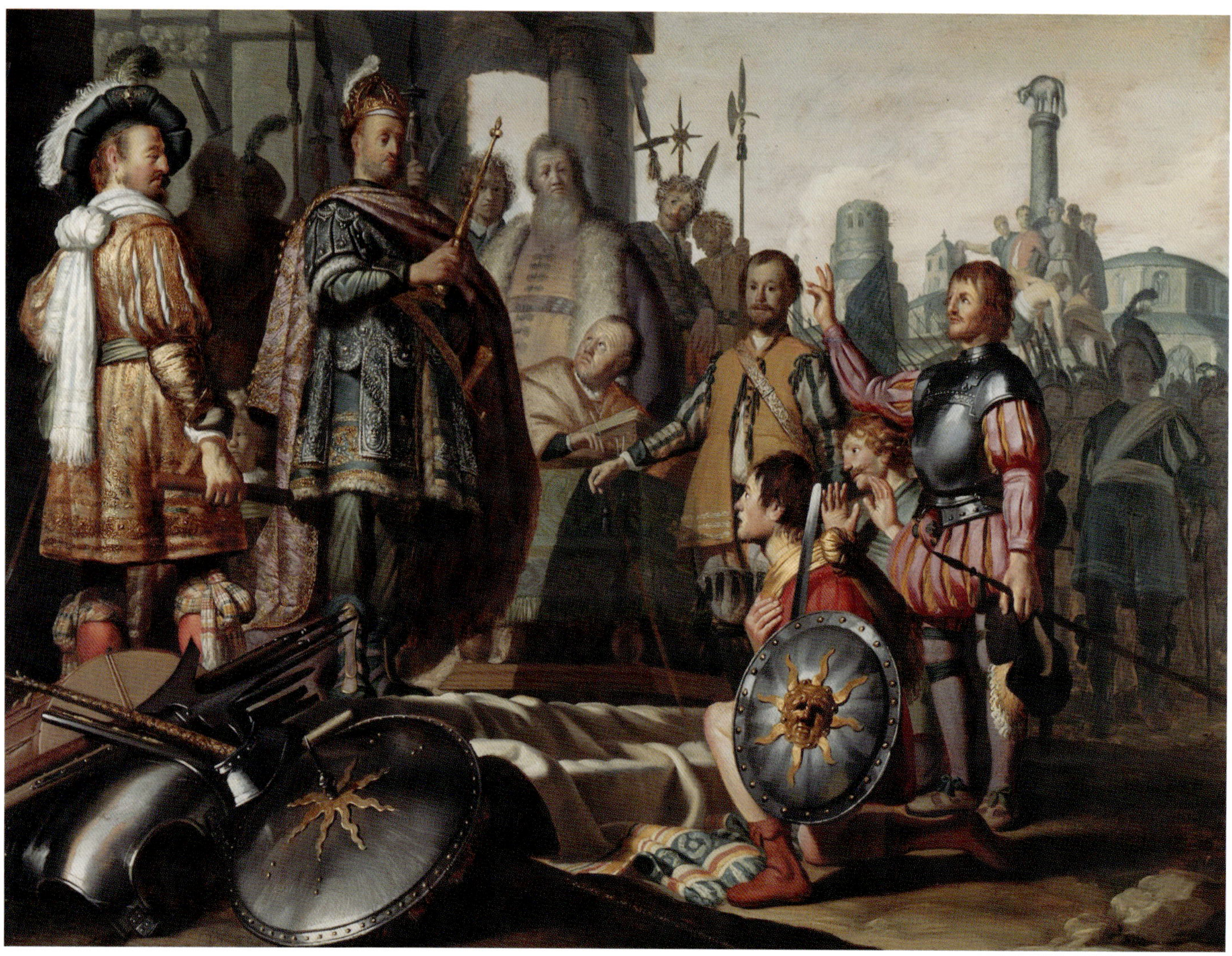

## BEGINNING AS AN ARTIST

Rembrandt opened an independent workshop in Leiden in 1624 or 1625. He may have shared the studio space with his friend and fellow painter Jan Lievens (1607–74), from this time until about 1631. Either way, the two artists spent much time together and the influence of Jan Lievens on Rembrandt's early work is significant. Although a year younger than Rembrandt, Lievens had been a child prodigy and was already working as an artist by the time Rembrandt decided to do so. He too had been an apprentice with Lastman, although at a much younger age, so the two artists had much in common. They were both young, ambitious and highly talented. There was no doubt some friendly rivalry between them, but they were friends with the same passion who bounced off each other, supported each other and encouraged each other to develop their skill and reach a higher level. They experimented with techniques, learned from each other and sometimes painted the same subjects, including Biblical themes such as *Samson and Delilah* and *Christ on the Cross*. It has also been suggested that the two may have painted on each other's paintings during these early years, and certain artworks have been misattributed in the past to each artist.

*History Painting, (The Leiden History Piece) 1626. There is still no consensus as to the subject matter of this painting. The design of the composition is taken from Lastman's* Coriolanus and Roman Matrons, 1622 (Trinity College, Dublin) *which in turn was much influenced influenced by a painting by Giulio Romano's after a fresco in the Vatican by Raphael.*

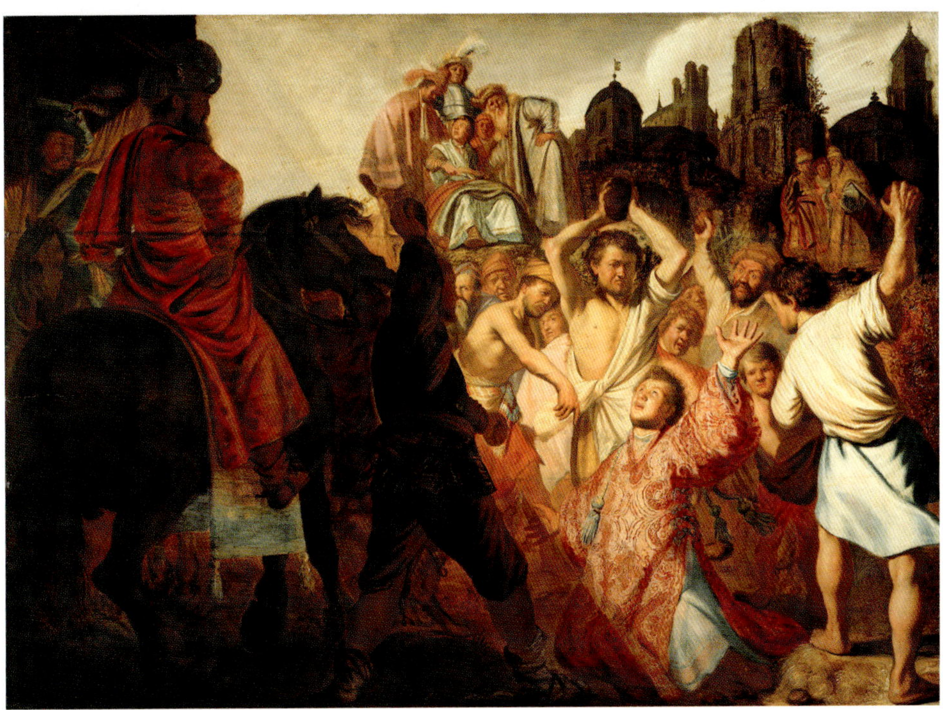

The Stoning of St Stephen, *1625 St Stephen was the first Christian martyr who was stoned to death by his tormentors. He is wearing the clothes of a deacon and looks up to the bright light of heaven.*

Coriolanus and the Roman Matrons, *Pieter Lastman, 1622. Rembrandt learned how to compose complex history paintings by extensively studying paintings such as this one by his teacher, Lastman. Painted in bright, clear colours, Lastman had been much influenced by his time Italy.*

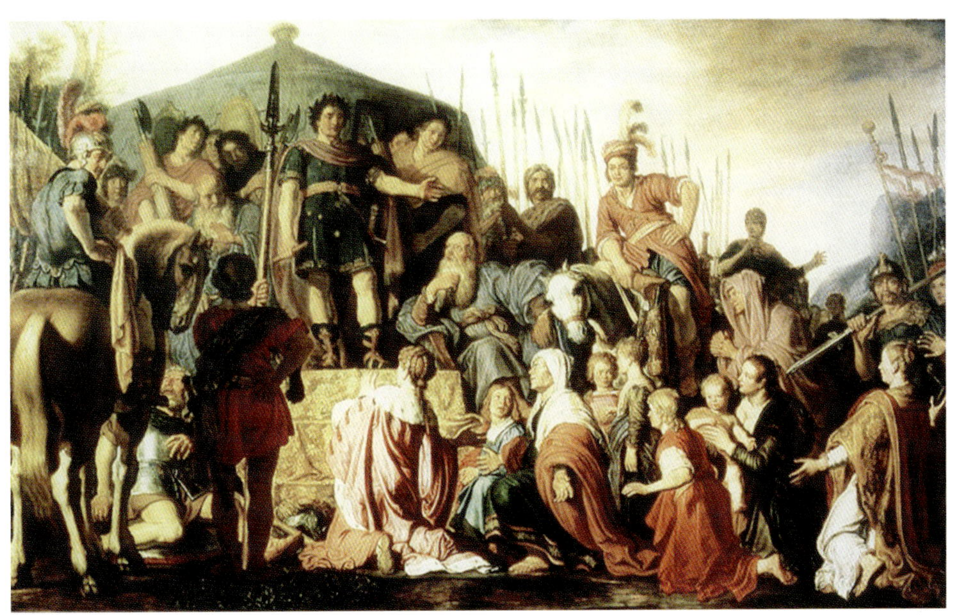

Rembrandt's first paintings were largely small-scale history paintings, such as his earliest signed painting, *The Stoning of St Stephen*, dated 1625 (Musée des Beaux-Arts, Lyon), painted when he was 19. This painting was re-identified as an important early Rembrandt work in 1962. It is painted on panel, as was most of his early work. The image is dominated by the diagonal line of shadow that throws almost half the painting into shade. The following year, 1626, he painted *History Painting* (Stedelijk Museum De Lakenhal, Leiden), so called because scholars have not been able to agree on the subject matter of the work. Although the client who commissioned this work has not been definitively identified, he is probably depicted in the painting as the figure near the centre looking out at the viewer. Rembrandt also included himself in the painting. In the arch in the background is a minor figure with facial features and curly hair, clearly recognizable as Rembrandt himself. This was something that Rembrandt continued to do throughout his career, and he appears in several other history pieces. This is a highly ambitious painting for a young artist and includes 10 central figures as well as further subsidiary figures. Rembrandt had learned from his master Lastman and was indebted to him, but even at this early stage he is not painting exactly in his master's style, as was usual practice, but is instead showing his own approach to the composition of his work.

Also dated to 1626 are the paintings titled *Musical Company* (Rijksmuseum, Amsterdam) and *Tobit and Anna with the kid* (Rijksmuseum, Amsterdam), which has often been described as Rembrandt's first masterpiece. It depicts a scene from the Book of Tobit. Tobit, a wealthy, religious Jew, lost all his money and became blind. His wife Anna began working to keep them and was given a goat to supplement her payment. Tobit wrongly accused her of stealing it and Anna scolded him for his self-righteousness. Realizing his mistake, he prayed to God to take his life. Later in the story their son finds a cure for his blindness and their fortunes are reversed. This was an unusual subject, but it had been executed in an etching by Jan van de Velde after Willem Buytewech, *c.* 1619, which Rembrandt probably used as a source. Rembrandt was showing more skill with each painting he completed: the figures are well placed in the space and the use of light from the window, as well as the fire, bathes the painting and emphasizes the wrinkly skin of Anna and Tobit. There are some exceptional details such as the wicker basket hung above the door, which is meticulously captured. The model for Anna is believed to be Rembrandt's mother, Neeltgen Willemsdr van Zuytbrouck. She is recognizable in several of Rembrandt's early paintings and one of Lievens, *Old Woman Reading*, *c.* 1624–5 (Rijksmuseum, Amsterdam).

Aernout van Buchell (Buchelius), an important visitor to Leiden, recorded a note in his diary about Rembrandt in 1628: 'The son of a Leiden miller is highly thought of, but prematurely.' Rembrandt was not yet 22, and his art was already making an impact

*Musical Company, 1626. This busy painting shows four extravagantly dressed, exotic figures. Three make music, whilst a fourth, an old woman in a striped scarf, looks on. The model for this woman is believed to be Rembrandt's mother. Jan Lievens also painted the same woman wearing the same headscarf (*Old Woman Reading, *Rijksmuseum, Amsterdam)*

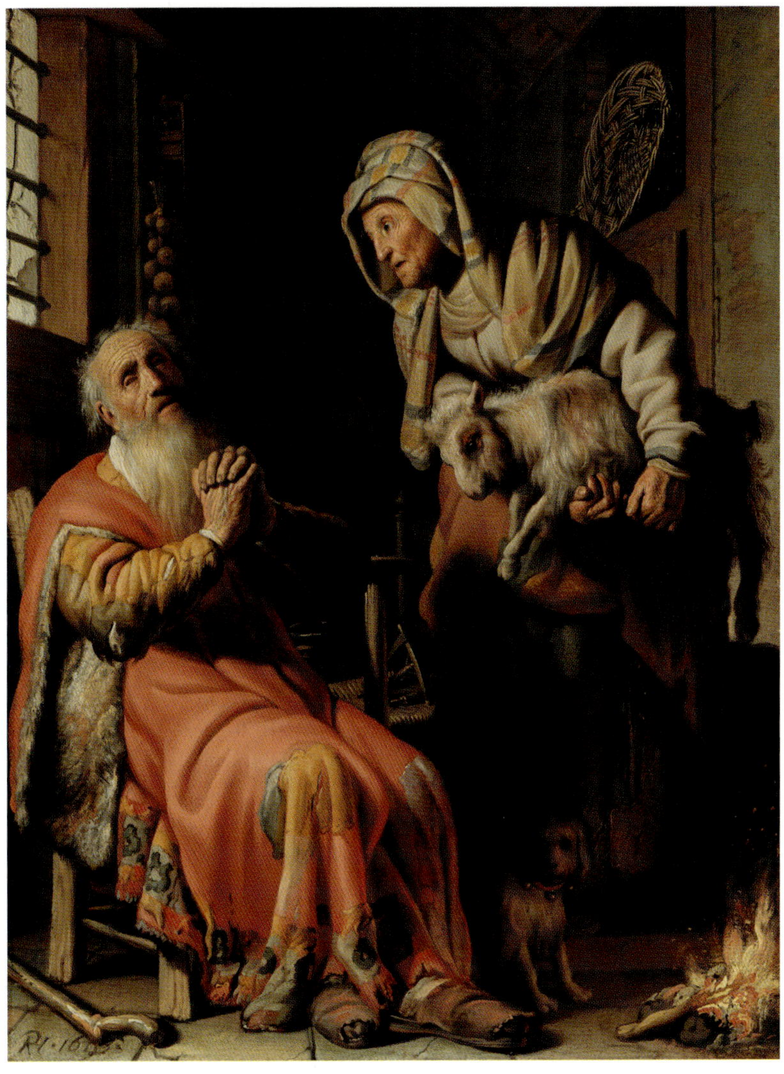

Tobit and Anna with the Kid, 1626. *This is the first ever known painting of this unusual subject, but Rembrandt's master Pieter Lastman had also painted scenes from the Book of Tobit.*

Tobit and Anna, *Jan van de Velde (II), after Willem Pietersz, 1619. Rembrandt's composition was much inspired by this earlier etching. He has also taken and included details such as the string of garlic and thatched roof in his own painting.*

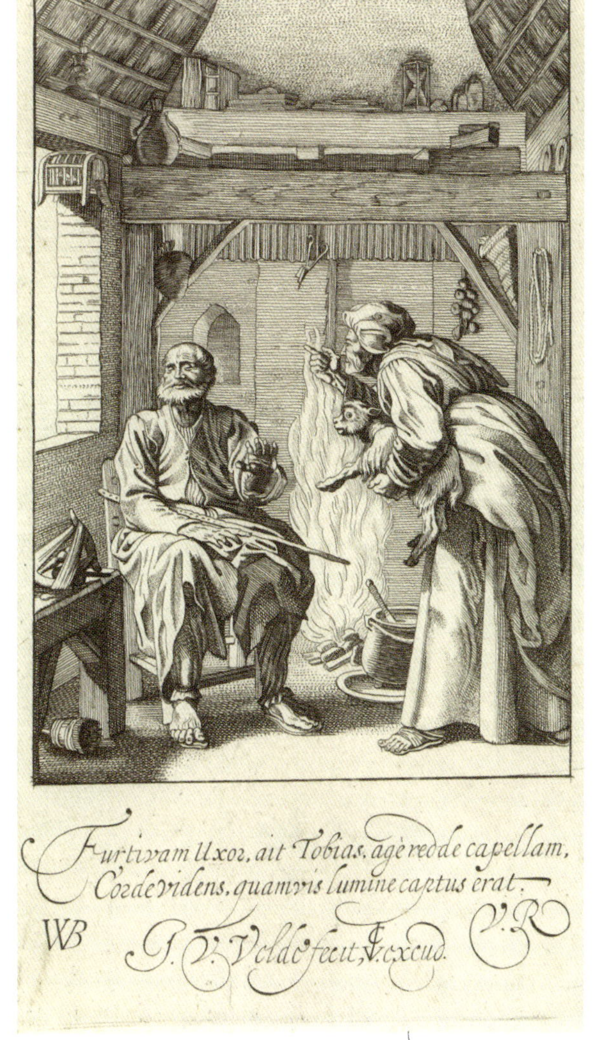


and showing great promise and originality, but as this note suggests, he was still developing as an artist – and his paintings clearly reflected that.

Almost as soon as Rembrandt started painting, he also began to make prints, mainly etchings. He would make prints alongside his paintings throughout his career. These were not copies of his paintings but original artistic expressions. He etched as many different subjects as he painted and drew, if not more, and in the process he revolutionized printmaking (see Chapter 5, page 77).

Today, Rembrandt is perhaps most famous for his numerous self-portraits. Even before he captured his likeness in two early paintings Rembrandt captured himself in print with an etching dating to *c.* 1627/8 on a plate that he reused having abandoned a composition of *The Flight into Egypt*. The portrait is sketch-like, seemingly quickly achieved, with the shoulders suggested only by a couple of lines and the focus on his flowing hair and face.

The two paintings are both titled *Self-Portrait as a Young Man*, one from *c*. 1628 (Rijksmuseum, Amsterdam) and the other dated 1629 (Bayerische Staatsgemäldesammlungen, Munich). In contrast to the print, the *Self-Portrait as a Young Man c.* 1628 (see page 6) shows the artist close up and in a mysterious light; the upper half of his face is largely in shadow, making his features hard to make out. Again, he has shown himself with a tousled head of hair, dynamically painted by scratching back to the underdrawing in some parts. This is a technique that Rembrandt learned from Lievens and used to great effect in his paintings. His glowing cheek portrays his youthful skin and makes a contrast with the shadow that dominates the painting. This painting could be interpreted as a young man aged 22 introducing himself to the world as an intriguing, mysterious artist, full of potential. Indeed, the use of shadow to such an extent would have indicated melancholy. This was the age of a cult of melancholia, when melancholy came to be associated with genius, the state of mind that led writers, philosophers and artists to create their masterpieces. With this self-portrait, Rembrandt is also portraying himself in a role, creating a *tronie*. From the Dutch for 'face', a *tronie* is a portrayal of a person in character, in costume and often with exaggerated facial expressions. Rembrandt's is, therefore, not strictly a self-portrait; rather, in this and other paintings he is using himself as a model to explore expressions, moods, atmospheres and characters. This is also the case for *Self-Portrait with a Plumed Beret*, 1629 (Isabella Stewart Gardner Museum, Boston), where Rembrandt has captured himself in a feathered, bejewelled beret and mustard coloured gown and gold chain. This portrait is larger and allows the artist to capture the costume and give more space around the subject.

There are some fascinating early self-portraits in both print and painting, perhaps none more so than a number of self-portrait etchings that Rembrandt made in 1630 exploring different expressions, *Self-Portrait, Wide-Eyed*; *Self-Portrait with Angry Expression*; *Self-Portrait, Smiling* and *Self-Portrait, Open-Mouthed* (all page 80). To be a great history painter, Rembrandt knew he needed to master the ability to express emotions in his figures, surprise or amazement, laughter, anger and pain in facial features. These are all small prints, but in each Rembrandt has succeeded in successfully expressing these passions by examining his own face. Perhaps he was practising with these prints or perhaps he made them to show potential clients his abilities.

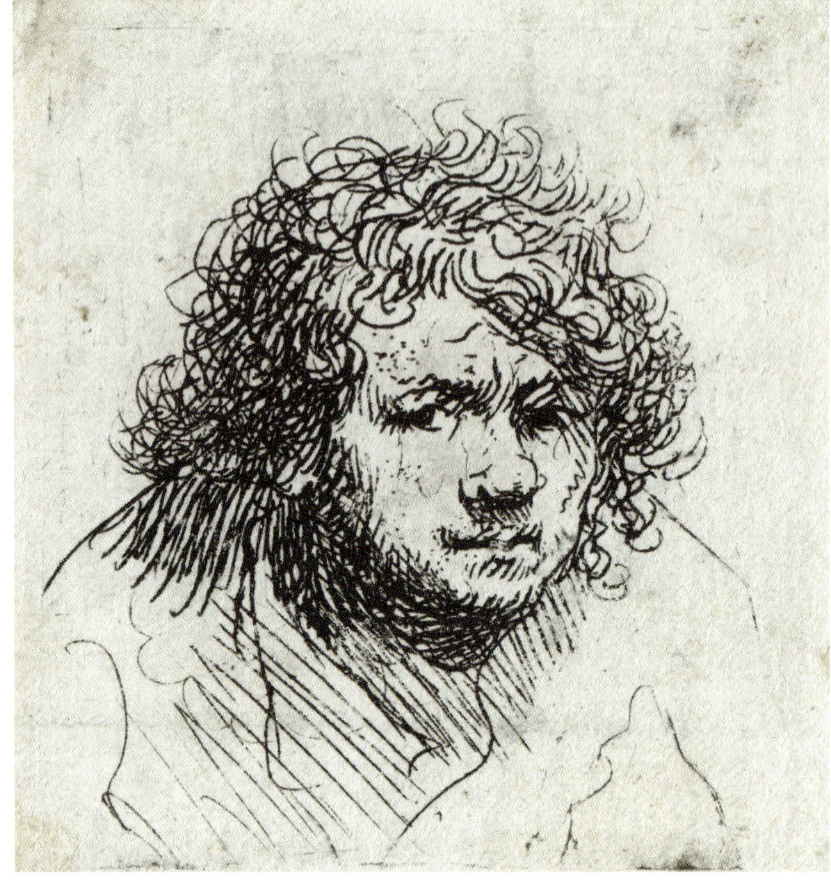

Self-Portrait, c.1627/8. *Rembrandt is 21 or 22 in this early etching. His expression is one of deep concentration which is in contrast to his wild, tousled hair.*

Self Portrait with Plumed Beret, *1629. In this Self-Portrait costume plays an important role, which was a significant element of* tronies. *By dressing in sixteenth-century costume with a magnificent feather plume on his beret Rembrandt is creating a character. He has realistically captured the different textures and used dramatic light and shadow.*

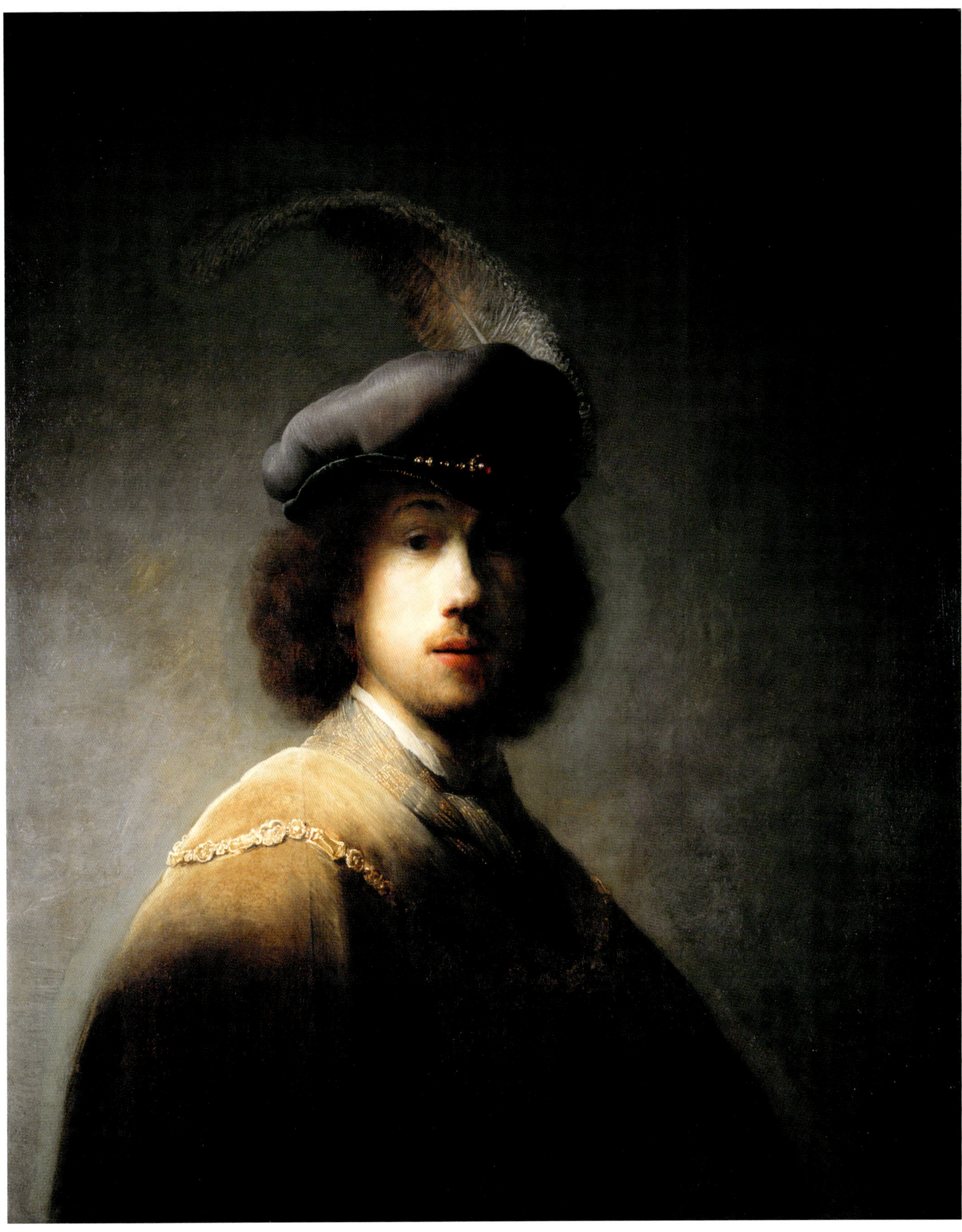

## SELF-PORTRAITS

Rembrandt depicted himself at least 80 times in paintings, etchings and drawings throughout his life. Painting self-portraits was not unusual for artists, but Rembrandt took it to a new level, completing more than any other artist and turning it into a virtual genre in its own right. Through these works we can see not only the effects of the ageing process on Rembrandt's own face, but also the development of his painting style and the progression of his technical ability.

Rembrandt's first self-portraits were as a young man in the 1620s. He took the chance to use himself as a model, often dressing up in historic costumes and painting himself in *tronies*, capturing himself with a particular, exaggerated expression. He mastered the use of light and shadow to capture himself in *chiaroscuro*. He was also learning how to capture his mood as well as his appearance. The self-portraits become more insightful and contemplative as he ages. Even when he had very personal hardships, he presents himself as confident and dignified, still the respected artist. He stares penetratingly and unflinchingly out. His painting style becomes looser and more expressive in his late portraits and he used impasto, thick areas of paint. Rembrandt seems to give us more of himself in the portraits of older age: they are very personal and human, and reveal his vulnerability.

There was a high demand for these self-portraits from patrons in his lifetime, and these works are undoubtedly one of the main reasons why Rembrandt has remained so popular today. Compelling portraits that still speak to viewers, even centuries later, they offer a unique insight into Rembrandt's life: revealing both his character and his psyche, they also allow the viewer to relate directly to the artist.

## PUPILS

In February 1628 Rembrandt accepted his first pupil, Gerrit Dou (1613–1675), who arrived aged 14. By November 1629 he had a second, Isaac Jouderville (1612–1645/8). Dou went on to have a very successful artistic career, specializing in small, highly finished oil paintings of everyday life. He stayed in Leiden and went on to found a Leiden school of painting and was an original member of the Leiden painters' guild. Rembrandt continued to teach throughout his career and his pupils were an important source of income for him.

In the painting *The Painter in his Studio*, c. 1629 (Museum of Fine Arts, Boston), the viewer sees an artist at work, which could indeed be Rembrandt himself at work. Holding numerous paint brushes in his hand, he has stepped back from the easel to get a good look at the work. During his early working years in Leiden, Rembrandt worked almost exclusively on oak panels, which he purchased already manufactured. The panels were primed with glue and then chalk and a thin layer of oil. The composition was then drawn on in thin brown oils, the artist either transferring a composition already worked out on paper or working on the composition at the easel. Now it was time to work up the image in colour, working on the backgrounds first and finishing with the figures. Only when a work was finished did he sign it. At this early stage in his career, he signed his paintings RH (for Rembrandt Harmenszoon) and sometimes RHL (the L for Leiden). After he had moved to Amsterdam, he began to sign with his first name, Rembrant, and from about 1633 he spelt his name Rembrandt. This may have been a means both to emulate and to put himself in the same category as other famous artists he admired and who also used one name, including the Italian masters Titian, Raphael and Michelangelo.

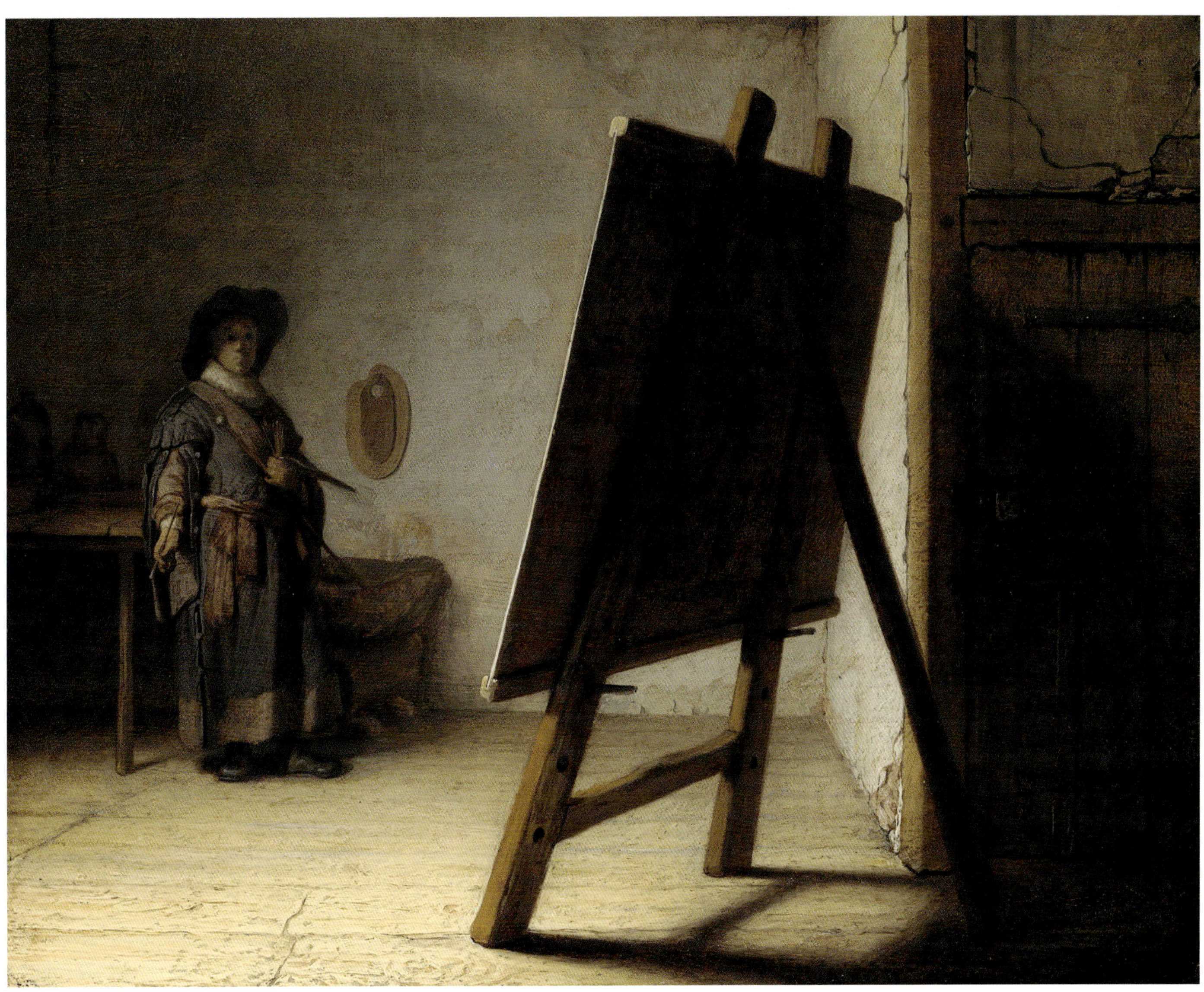

The Painter in his Studio, *c.1629. This sparsely furnished studio contains only functional items, bottles of oil or varnish on the table, two palettes hung on the wall, a tree trunk for preparing pigments and a large easel that dominates the foreground. We see only the reverse of the canvas and not the painting the artist is observing.*

## CONSTANTIJN HUYGENS

To develop his fame and success, Rembrandt needed supporters and influencers backing him as well as patrons, so it was fortunate that he came to the attention of an important visitor to Leiden, Constantijn Huygens (1596–1687), secretary to Frederik Hendrik, Prince of Orange. Huygens was a courtier, but also a poet, composer and art appreciator. He became one of Rembrandt's greatest admirers and dedicated a section of his autobiographical memoir written in 1629/30 to Dutch artists. Discussing both Rembrandt and his Leiden contemporary, Lievens, he described them as 'a noble pair of young men from Leiden … destined to equal the greatest of the superior mortals'. He continued, 'I will not be exceeding the expectations that their astonishing beginnings have aroused even among those [art-lovers] of the most conservative case.'

Making much of Rembrandt's humble beginnings as he saw it, and what he described as his natural gift for art, he commented: 'Rembrandt surpasses Lievens in the faculty of penetrating to the heart of his subject matter and bringing out its essence, and his work comes across more vividly.' He writes specifically about one painting, *Judas Repentant, Returning the Thirty Pieces of Silver*, 1629 (Private Collection). 'It can withstand comparison with anything ever made in Italy, or for that matter with everything beautiful and admirable that has been preserved since the earliest antiquity.' He praised particularly how Rembrandt has captured the figure of Judas, who has tried to return the 30 pieces of silver he received for betraying Christ to the chief priests and elders in the Temple. Their refusal is the moment that he realizes his sin, and he throws the money down. Huygens wrote: 'That single gesture of the desperate Judas – ... of a raging, whining Judas grovelling for mercy he no longer hopes for or dares to show the smallest sign of expecting, his frightful visage, hair torn out of his head, his rent garment, his arms twisted, the hands clenched bloodlessly tight, fallen to his knees in a heedless outburst – that body, wholly contorted in pathetic despair. I place against all the tasteful art of all time past ... Truly, my friend Rembrandt, all honour to you.'

With that vivid description, Huygens honoured the artist, not just for achieving this emotion but in signalling a new direction in Dutch art. He does, however, criticize both Rembrandt and Lievens for not having spent time in Italy to study the artworks by the great masters: Titian, Raphael and Michelangelo. Italy had been a centre for

Judas Repentent, Returning the Thirty Pieces of Silver to the Chief Priests and Elders, 1629. *This dark and powerful painting brilliantly captures human emotion, particularly in the despairing figure of Judas.*

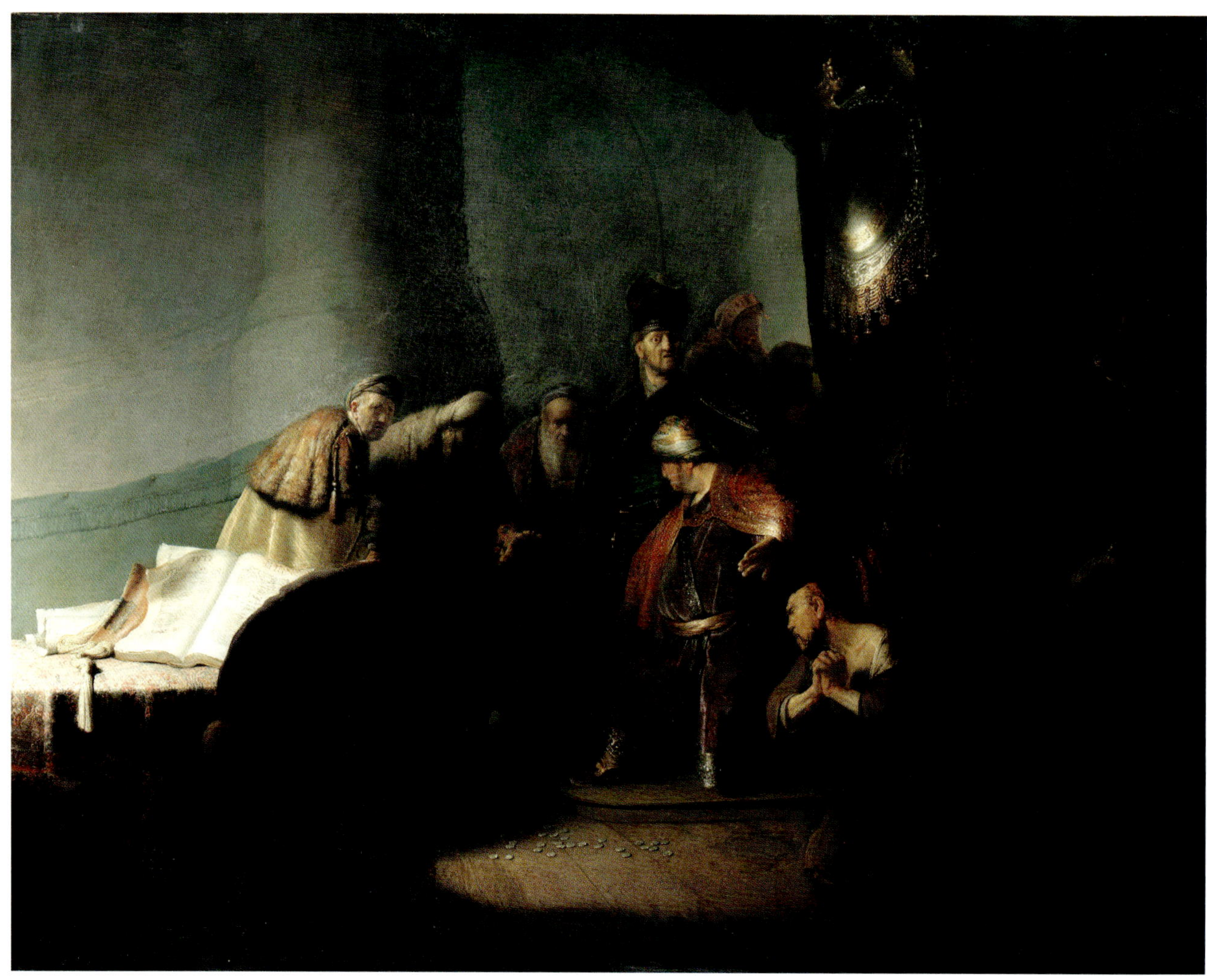

great art for centuries and this was a natural pilgrimage for any artist with great ambitions. Both of Rembrandt's teachers, Swanenburg and Lastman, had visited Italy and been influenced by what they saw there. Rembrandt's explanation to Huygens suggests that the two considered a pilgrimage to be a diversion in the best years of their lives, and unnecessary given that they could find all the art they needed to see in their homeland since so much Italian art was now in private collections. Huygens commended them for such diligence and dedication – and both Lievens and Rembrandt were set on a path. Rembrandt never did travel abroad, despite his later fame and success, while Lievens did, later working in England for several years.

Huygens' association led to commissions from the Court at a young age. He acted as intermediary between Rembrandt and the stadholder's court and encouraged the Prince to buy several paintings. In addition, a family connection (albeit distant) to a court artist, Jacques de Gheyn III, also helped the young artist in this regard. These commissions, from as early as 1628, came with much prestige and the benefit of a higher value for his art. It was a huge step forward in his career. For instance, Huygens bought three paintings for Frederick Hendrik, who gifted them to Robert Kerr, Earl of Ancram, a courtier to Charles I. The three works were at some stage given to the King and they entered the English Royal Collection. One was a self-portrait.

Despite writing that he thought Lievens the better portraitist, Huygens turned to Rembrandt in 1632 to paint the wife of Frederik Hendrik, *Portrait of Amalia van Solms*, 1632 (Musée Jacquemart-André, Paris), which may have been conceived as a pendant to the portrait of Frederik Hendrik by Gerrit van Honthorst. It was also through Huygens that Rembrandt received his most important early commission. He was to paint two paintings from the Passion. *The Raising of the Cross*, c.1633 and *The Descent from the Cross*, c.1634 (Alte Pinakothek, Munich) were clearly well received by Hendrik, as he was then commissioned to paint three more Passion paintings to make a series: *The Ascension, The Entombment, The Resurrection* (Alte Pinakothek, Munich). Rembrandt took his time over these and it took him until the end of the decade to complete this commission. His association with the court continued until 1646, although Rembrandt was never to become a court painter.

By 1631 Rembrandt must have considered himself on the cusp of great things, on an upward trajectory. After six years working as an artist, he had enjoyed a number of successes. He had patrons, both private and from the Court, and had already enrolled students. He was well on the way to creating his own distinct style and was confident in himself. He now looked beyond Leiden to the city offering the opportunities he sought, the most important art market in Europe and his Promised Land, Amsterdam.

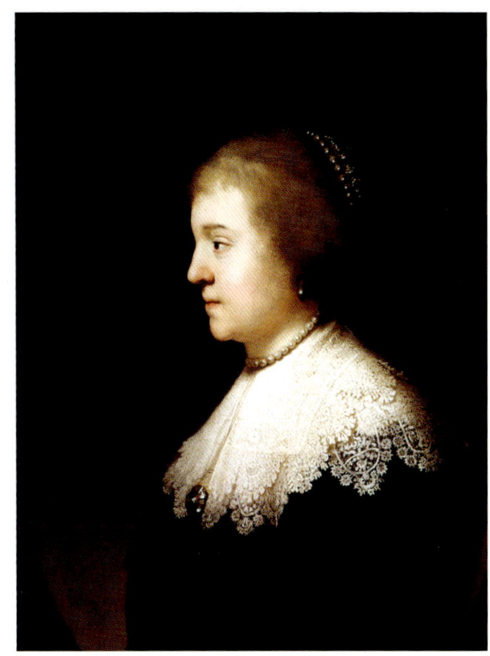

Portrait of Amalia van Solms, *1632. Wife of Frederik Hendrik, Amalia van Soms was Princess consort. She was a political advisor and acted as de facto deputy when Hendik was infirm. As a pendant painting she is shown in profile to the left and would have been hung facing a portrait of her husband.  Rembrandt painted it on a short stay in The Hague.*

Portrait of Constantijn Huygens, *Jan Lievens, c.1628/9.*

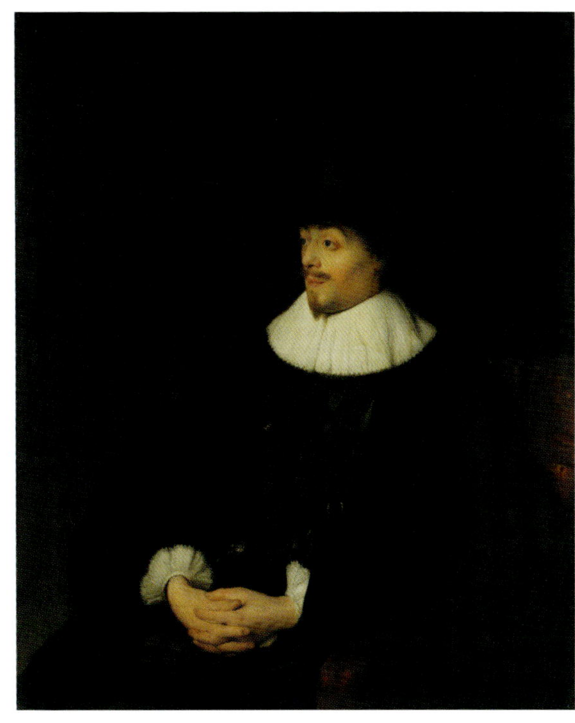

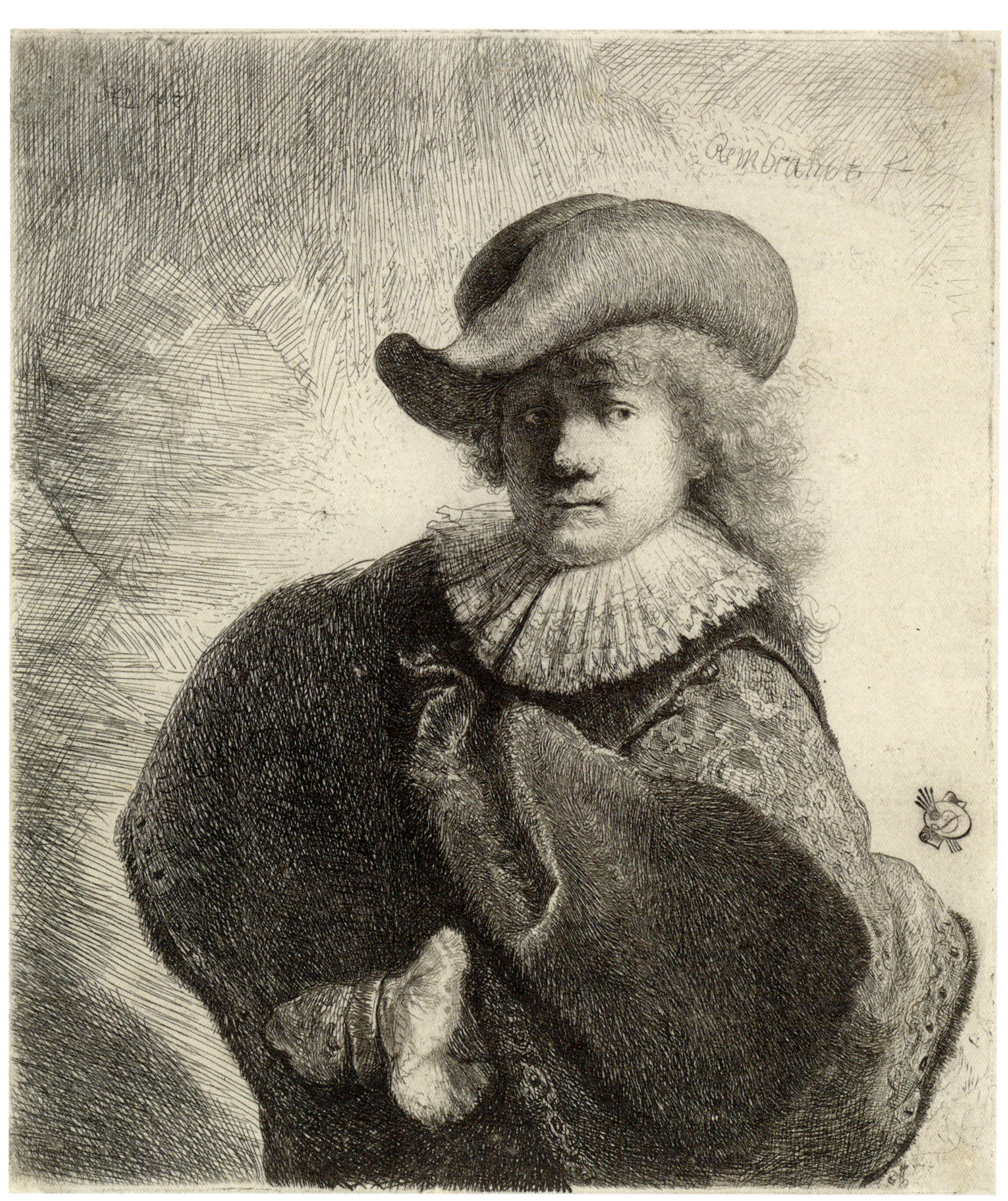

Self-Portrait in
a Soft Hat and
Pattern Cloak,
*1631. The
flamboyantly-
dressed
Rembrandt
stands with his
hand on his hip
and wears an
elaborate collar,
long hair and
a fashionable,
richly textured
cloak and
soft hat.*

# CHAPTER 2

# The Promised Land, Amsterdam, 1631–42

## AMSTERDAM

Amsterdam must have held great appeal to Rembrandt. He had made great progress as an artist in Leiden, but now he may have needed to break free from the close relationship that he had there with his friend and fellow artist Lievens. Lievens was making good sales to the local dignitaries there – rather more than Rembrandt was, in fact – so it is likely that Rembrandt felt the need to spread his wings. What's more, Leiden, having once been a boom town, was now in a decline, with less wealth and opportunity. Amsterdam, on the other hand, was full of potential, and Rembrandt was hungry for success.

Amsterdam was the place to be in the seventeenth century. The population was expanding greatly, growing from around 60,000 in 1600 to 135,000 by 1640. The majority of these new inhabitants had been born elsewhere, in the south and north Netherlands, France and Germany. It was also the preferred city for wealthy Antwerpers, who came to invest their money after the loss of their economic supremacy due first to the sacking of the city and then to a year-long siege by Spanish forces. Having thrown off Spanish influence, Amsterdam became a European leader in the shipment of goods. Full of merchants and craftsmen, the city was flourishing, in no small part due to the founding of the Dutch East India Company in 1602 and the Dutch West India Company in 1621, which opened up trade with the world and bought prosperity and commercial success to the city.

Amsterdam was also a city with a good tradition of supporting artists and was now one of the most important art markets in Europe. In addition, Rembrandt had the advantage of already having a good contact in Amsterdam, Hendrick Uylenburgh (1587–c. 1661). Uylenburgh was exceedingly well connected: as well as being an art dealer he ran a large workshop painting portraits, producing copies of paintings and carrying out restoration works. It is probable that Hendrick Uylenburgh met Rembrandt as early as 1628, when he was in Leiden, and he may even have started representing him as a dealer at this stage.

However, Amsterdam wasn't the only option available: Rembrandt could have also considered making The Hague his home, especially if he wanted to pursue commissions from the court. By 1631 he had already received orders for paintings from Frederik Hendrik, the sovereign Prince of Orange and stadtholder of Holland, and from one of the court painters, Jacques de Gheyn, who was a distant relative. Perhaps it was Rembrandt's time in Amsterdam as a student with Lastman and the excitement of a thriving, growing city that proved more of an appeal. It was a good choice and Rembrandt hit the ground running. In his first year there he received more commissions than he ever had in Leiden. This was indeed his Promised Land.

## HENDRICK UYLENBURGH

Hendrick Uylenburgh's family came from Frisia (Friesland), a coastal region in the north of Holland. They were Mennonites, a minority Anglican Anabaptist religious order. Being persecuted in their homeland, his family had emigrated to Cracow, Poland, in the sixteenth century and it is possible that Uylenburgh was born there. His father was a cabinetmaker to the king of Poland, and his brother Rombout, painter to the king. Uylenburgh also trained as a painter and had acted for the Polish court. He returned to the Dutch Republic in 1620, when the atmosphere in Holland was more tolerant, and moved to Amsterdam in 1625, where there was a growing Mennonite community. There, at what is now 2 Jodenbreestraat, Uylenburgh began to grow his business with a studio and shop. The location was very close to Lastman's studio, so Rembrandt may have first met him as a student. In June 1631 Rembrandt and Uylenburgh entered into a business relationship when Rembrandt lent Uylenburgh 1,000 guilder. Instead of setting up on his own, Rembrandt made the wise decision to set up with Uylenburgh, who gave him access not only to his facilities but also to his extensive network in Amsterdam.

In 1631, just as he moved to Amsterdam, Rembrandt produced the impressive etching *Self-Portrait in a Soft Hat and Patterned Cloak* (page 22). In it, he presents himself to his new audience and potential clients as an young, aspiring artist yet one already successful enough to afford expensive, fashionable clothes. In short, he was one of them, the Amsterdam bourgeoisie. The print shows the influence of the painter Peter Paul Rubens (and the composition pays homage to Rubens' *Self-Portrait*, 1623 – opposite). Rubens was the most successful living Flemish artist and Rembrandt was increasingly modelling his career on him.

## PORTRAIT PAINTING

Rembrandt's rise to becoming a successful portrait painter in Amsterdam was meteoric. He went from having never completed a commissioned portrait to being the most sought-after portrait painter in a matter of months. From 1631 to 1635, in Uylenburgh's workshop, Rembrandt produced a large number of portraits, almost immediately becoming the go-to portrait painter and rapidly succeeding in dominating the market. He charged between 50 guilders for a single head, 100 guilders for a bust portrait and 500 guilders and more if the sitter wanted a full-length painting or group portraits.

His first clients came to him through Uylenburgh and many were from the Mennonite community, such as *Nicholaes Ruts*, 1631 (The Frick Collection, New York), and

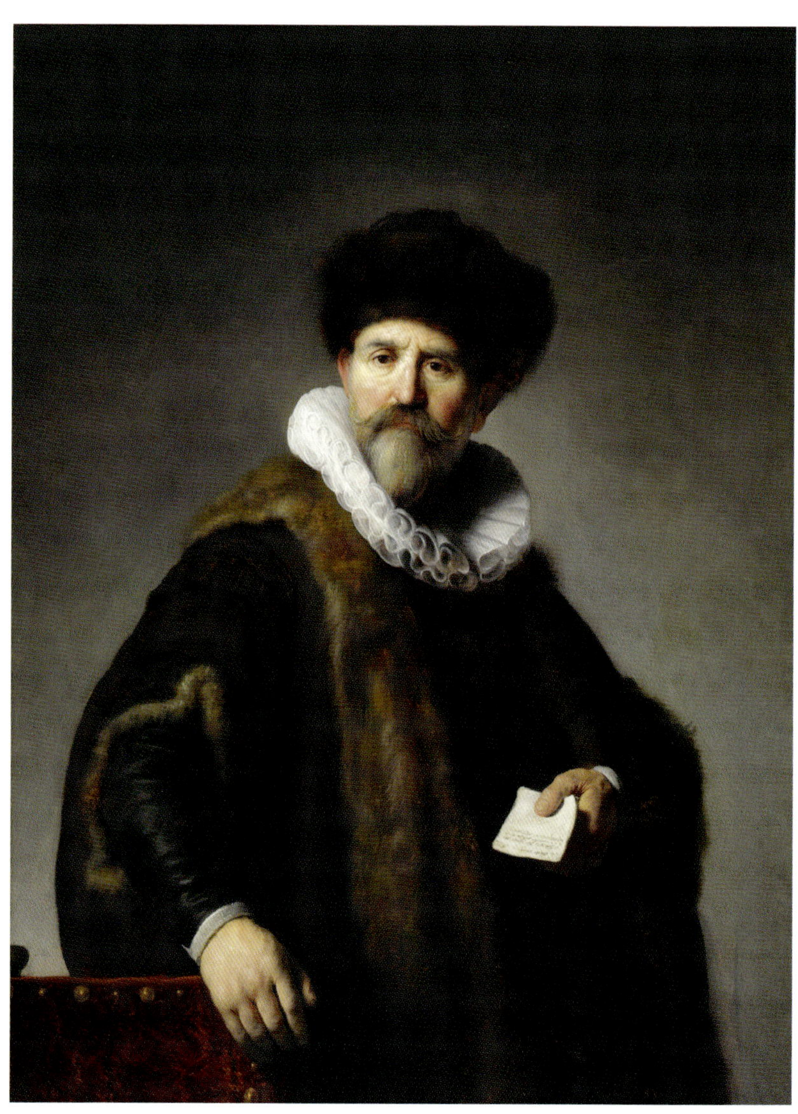

Portrait of Nicholaes Ruts, 1631. *This portrait shows Rembrandt's early skills at combining a dramatic contrast of light and shadow with skilful painting of different textures.*

# PETER PAUL RUBENS (1577–1640)

Rubens was the greatest and most influential of the Flemish Baroque painters. Born in Siegen in Germany, the son of an Antwerp lawyer and alderman, he moved to Antwerp when he was 10. By the age of 13 he was working as a court page to a countess, but changed direction shortly afterwards to train as an artist. In 1600 he travelled to Italy to study the Renaissance artists and worked in Mantua, Genoa and Rome. Rubens returned to Antwerp in 1608 when he received the news that his mother was dying. Although he did not make it back before her death, once home, he decided to stay.

He was soon appointed a court painter to Archduke Albert and Archduchess Isabella, joint sovereigns of the Spanish Netherlands and set up a large studio in a grand house in a fashionable area of Antwerp. Rubens was based in the south Netherland, ruled by the Spanish empire, and King Philip of Spain became one of his most patrons, commissioning more than 80 works. In his lifetime he was known as 'the prince of painters and the painter of princes'. His works entered royal collections around Europe.

He also responded to a demand for large-scale altarpieces for Catholic churches and some of Rubens' finest paintings are in this form, including *The Raising of the Cross* and the *Descent from the Cross*, in Antwerp Cathedral. Some of his most famous works such as *The Massacre of the Innocents*, (Art Gallery of Ontario) and the *Horrors of War*, (Palazzo Pitti, Florence) are history paintings – of classical mythology, allegories and religious subjects, but Rubens also painted many portraits and even landscapes towards the end of his life. The term 'Rubenesque' refers to the voluptuousness of many of his figures.

Rubens remained in favour with the court and, as well as being a very successful painter, he worked as a high-ranking diplomat, travelling around Europe, including to France and England, with a reputation that was noted throughout Europe. Rubens married twice; his first wife, Isabella Brandt (1591–1626) probably died of the plague and he married his second wife Helena Fourment (1614–73) with whom he had five children, four years later in 1630. Both of his wives were the subject of his paintings.

Given Rubens' renown as an artist, it is not surprising that Rembrandt looked to him both for inspiration and to measure his own success, particularly early in his career. Rembrandt's own large history paintings reveal Rubens' influence, particularly in the depictions of figures, and he also studied Ruben's compositions. Rembrandt became the leading artist of the northern Netherlands and Rubens of the southern Netherlands and their art compared in quality, but they came from very different backgrounds and had very different careers.

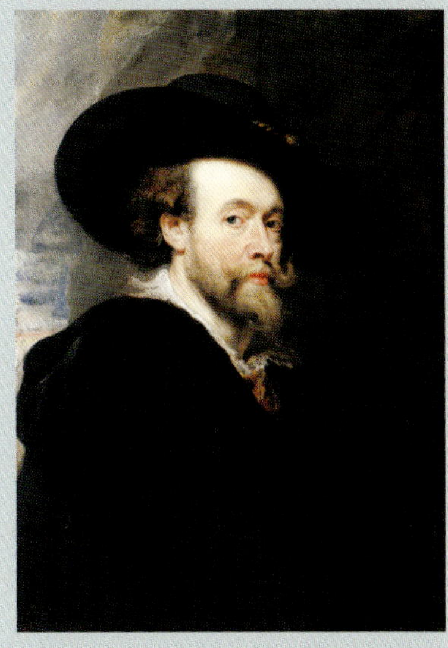

Self-Portrait, *Peter Paul Rubens, 1623.*

Prometheus Bound, *Peter Paul Rubens, c.1612. One of the Titans, Prometheus angered the god Zeus and was sentenced to have his liver torn out repeatedly by an eagle.*

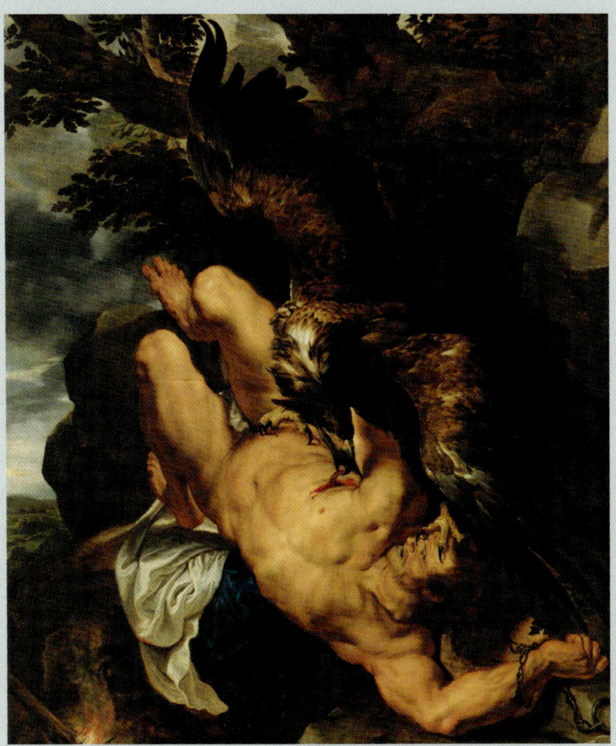

*Marten Looten*, 1632 (County Museum of Art, Los Angeles). For both he painted three-quarter length portraits with simple, undefined backgrounds. The sitters stand with their shoulders turned, facing forward, each holding an important piece of paper in their right hand. Ruts was born in Cologne to a Mennonite immigrant. He settled in Amsterdam before 1617 and was a trader with the Russian market, a connection alluded to by the inclusion of a Russian sable fur over his shoulders. This painting dated 1631, may well have been Rembrandt's first commission. Lootens, in comparison, is painted in simple, black and white clothes, much more in line with Mennonite sobriety. He too had come to Amsterdam having earlier fled from the southern Netherlands, and was a partner in a trading company. Rembrandt painted over 50 such portraits between 1631 and 1635, more than any other portrait artist in Amsterdam. His clients were mainly wealthy traders and merchants and their families.

So what made Rembrandt so successful as a portrait artist? There were certainly other painters working in this genre in Amsterdam, and artists such as Frans Hals (1582–1666) in Haarlem and Van Dyck (1599–1641) in Antwerp. The composition of his own single portraits was not ground-breaking, and in fact followed a long international tradition in portraiture, but how Rembrandt executed the works and captured likenesses was certainly innovative, and they obviously appealed greatly to his Amsterdam clients. The sitters in his portraits seem so lifelike and he seems to look into their soul, reflecting their character. His paintings were also more dynamic than other artists', suggesting movement. Using light and shade, he wonderfully captures the different surfaces in the paintings. He paints skin so well, so realistically: he includes wrinkles and lines and does not flatter. He also manage to capture the textures of clothes with the upmost detail: the lace of the collars and the softness of the fur both look so lifelike. He frequently leaves the background void of detail, thus concentrating the viewer on the sitter's face.

At this time couples were usually painted separately in companion paintings, two separate paintings that hung together, and which were usually linked with gestures or glances. Rembrandt broke the mould with several, innovative double portraits, including the painting *The Shipbuilder and his Wife*, 1633 of Jan Rijcksen (1560/2–1637) and Griet Jans (*c.* 1560 – after 1653) (Royal Collection). The couple interact and are captured in a moment in time, and indeed the painting offers us a narrative. Now in old age, the master

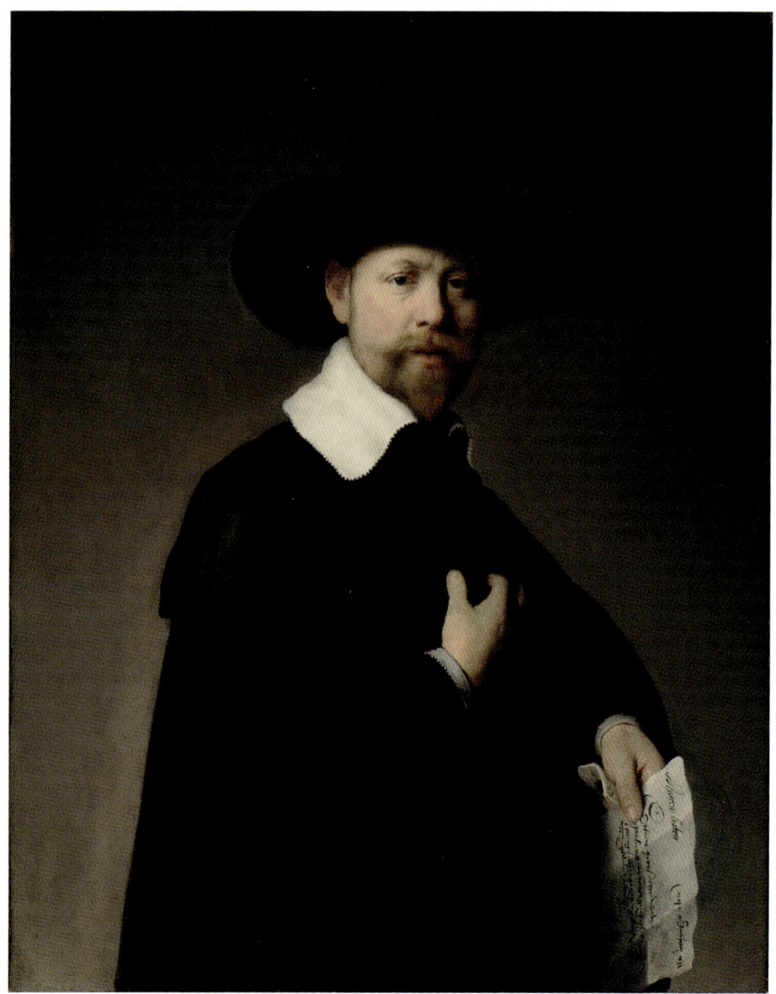

Portrait of Marten Looten, *1632.*
*Looten is captured as if he has just been disturbed whilst reading a letter. The neutral background contributes to creating a strong, sculptural effect.*

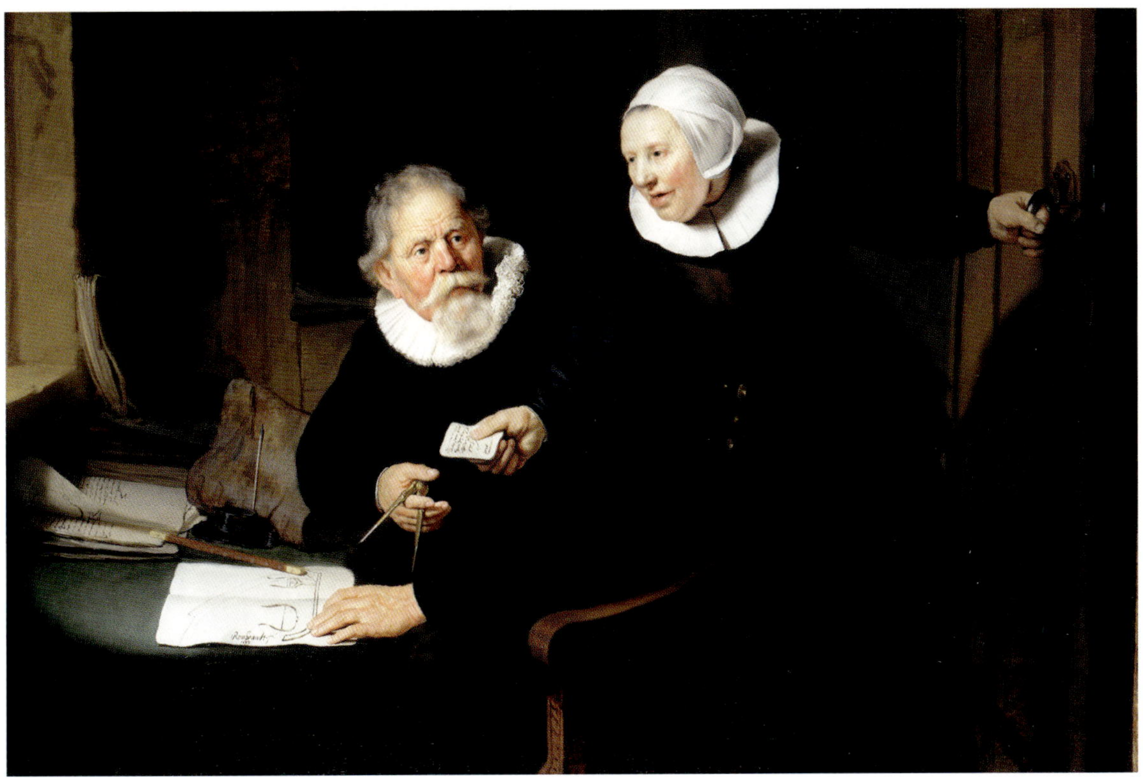

The Shipbuilder and his Wife, *1633.*
*Jan Rijcksen is shown seated at a table, a compass in hand making ship drawings. His wife Griet Jans has entered the room with a letter addressed to him. The drawing on the table bears Rembrandt's signature and date.*

Portrait of Aechje Claesdr (Portrait of an 83-Year-Old Woman), *1634. Rembrandt's depictions of older people are often very honest but also have great appeal.*

shipbuilder of the Dutch East India Company is sat at his desk, and his wife has burst into the room to hand him a piece of paper. Her hand is still on the door handle. There is great movement in the painting, which is naturalistically lit from the window on the left.

Rembrandt also received commissions outside Amsterdam and in Rotterdam on 22 July 1634, was commissioned by Dirck Jansz Pesser (1587–1651), to do portrait busts of Pesser himself (Los Angeles County Museum of Art), his wife Haesje Jacobsdr van Cleyburg (Rijksmuseum, Amsterdam) and mother Aechje Claesdr. *Portrait of an 83-Year-Old Woman,* 1634 (National Gallery, London) was once thought to be Rembrandt's grandmother, but is now identified as Aechje Claesdr, the widow of Jan Pesser, a Rotterdam brewer. Rembrandt was exceptionally good at the depiction of older people and paints her aged skin convincingly. Wiith a powerful use of light and shade, he creates a lifelike portrayal with the illusion of three-dimensionality.

The same year Rembrandt was commissioned to paint a pair of marriage pendants, his most expensive and opulent portraits. Unlike many of the religious Mennonite and Remonstrant followers who were painted in simple, sombre clothes, *Marten Soolmans* (1613–1641) and *Oopjen Coppit* (1611–1689) (Rijksmuseum, Amsterdam and Louvre, Paris), were Calvinists, and were painted in lavish, fashionable clothes. The couple had recently married in Amsterdam, in June 1633. The groom was the

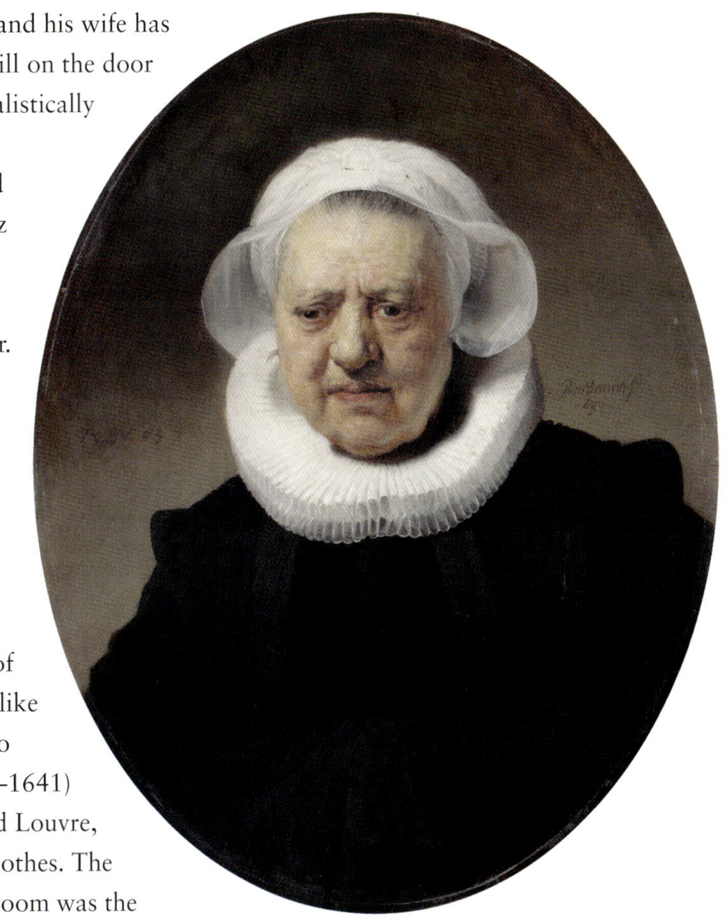

# THE ANATOMY LECTURE OF DR. NICHOLAS TULP

In 1632, Rembrandt was commissioned to paint a group portrait, *The Anatomy Lecture of Dr. Nicholas Tulp*, now recognized as one of his early masterpieces. Rembrandt painted this group of seven surgeons around the physician Dr. Tulp for the board room of the Guild of Surgeons. This was the fourth time the Guild had commissioned a painting of anatomical demonstrations. To receive a commission from a guild, for a group portrait, was a great privilege, perhaps the highest form of patronage for a portraitist – and Rembrandt had achieved it within a year of arriving in Amsterdam.

The annual public autopsies were important occasions and a vital way for surgeons to gain a greater understanding of human anatomy. They were carried out under the supervision of the praelector, here Dr. Tulp, and this was his second public autopsy since becoming reader of the Guild of Surgeons. Rembrandt captures a sense of drama in his painting, as though portraying a single moment. Rembrandt treated the subject not so much like a group portrait, but more like a history painting, and he may well have taken inspiration from history paintings such as Rubens' *The Tribute Money*, 1612–14 (Fine Arts Museum, San Francisco). Rembrandt is telling a story: the figures crowd around the cadaver, forming a triangle that leads the viewer's eye around the painting, while Dr. Tulp demonstrates the arm tendons. There is a sense of concentration and fascination in group. The cadaver is lit brightly, the sallow skin painted brilliantly in contrast to the crisp, white collars worn by the doctors. The dramatic scene seems to encapsulate the atmosphere of excitement of a new era of science. The commission coincided with the opening of a new university in Amsterdam to rival that of Leiden. The doctors in the painting are all named on the piece of paper held by the man at the back of the painting. The cadaver for demonstrations was always the body of an executed criminal, in this case, Adriaen het Kint.

The Anatomy Lecture of Dr Nicholas Tulp, *1632. Several of Rembrandt's most famous works are group portraits. Each of the doctors in this painting would have paid a commission to have their portrait included.*

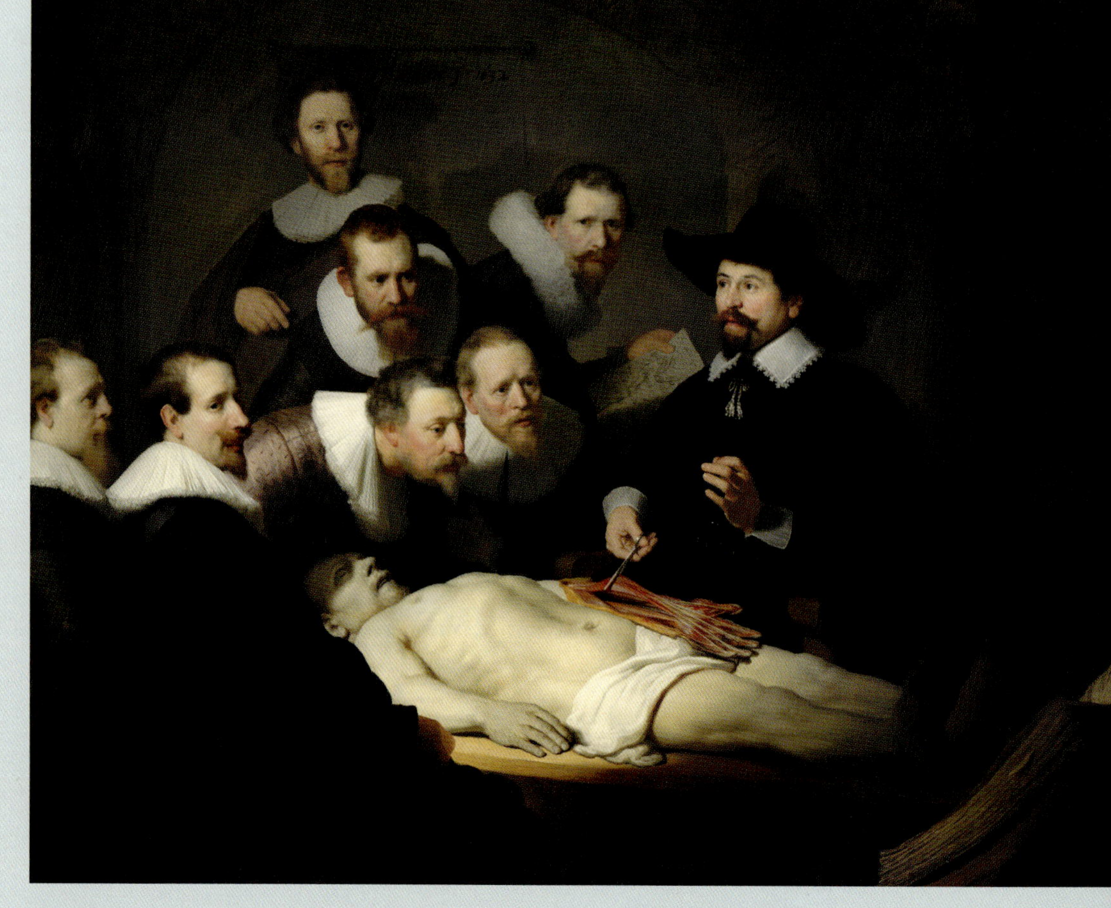

son of Protestant refugees from Antwerp, who had made a fortune as the proprietor of a sugar refinery. His wife Oopjen was from an old, elite Amsterdam family. The couple are shown in full-length, standing portraits, a format usually reserved for royalty rather than commoners. These were two very rich, young and vibrant Amsterdamers, and the painting reflects their status and celebrates their wealth. The way in which Rembrandt has captured the detail of their clothes is extraordinary. Oopjen has the most detailed lace on her collar, and is adorned with gold and pearls, while Marten wears an ostentatious outfit with eye-catching rosettes on his shoes. Rembrandt has added movement: as Marten steps to his left, holding out a glove in his hand, Oopjen steps down towards him. The paintings could have cost 1,000 guilders or more, a huge sum of money. The couple also bought the painting *Holy Family*, 1634 (Alte Pinakothek, Munich), and Marten's brother-in-law, Martin van den Broeck, became an important patron. The only full-length standing portraits that Rembrandt is known to have been commissioned to paint, in 2016 they were purchased jointly by the Rijksmuseum and the Louvre for €160 million, having rarely been seen in public.

Marten Soolmans, *1634 and* Oopjen Coppit, *1634. These most lavish full-length portraits were commissioned as marriage pendants.*

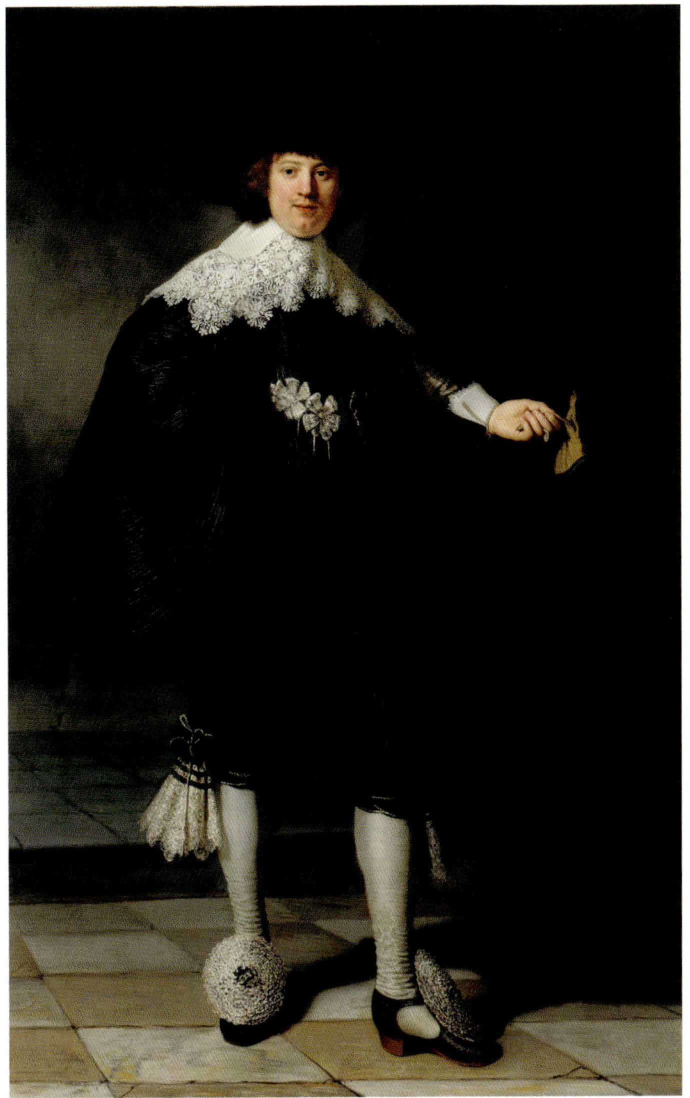

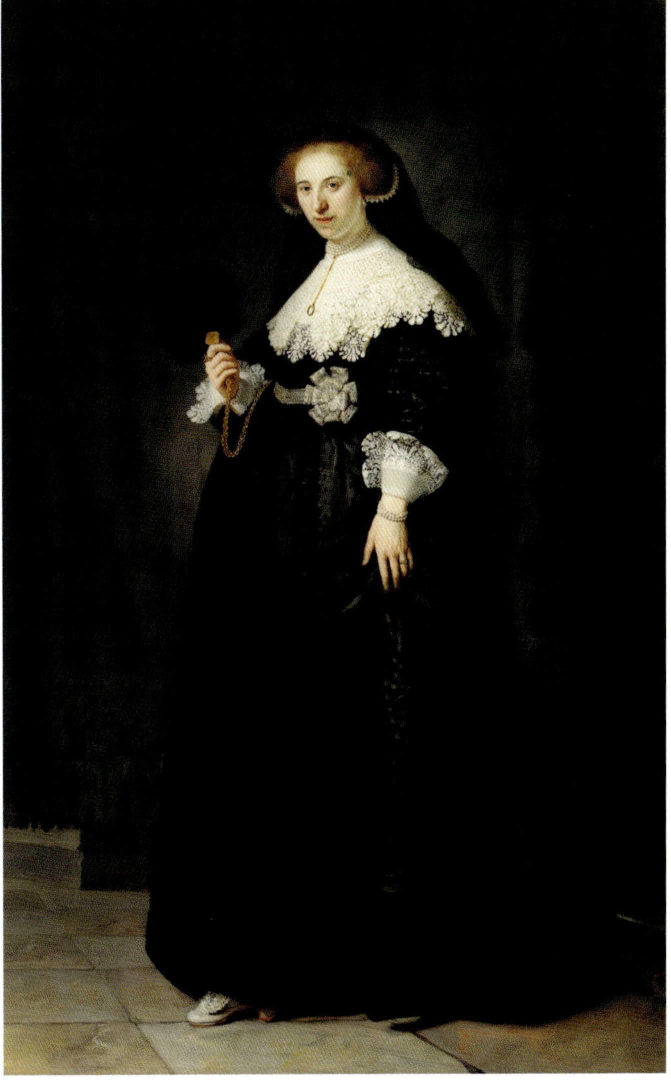

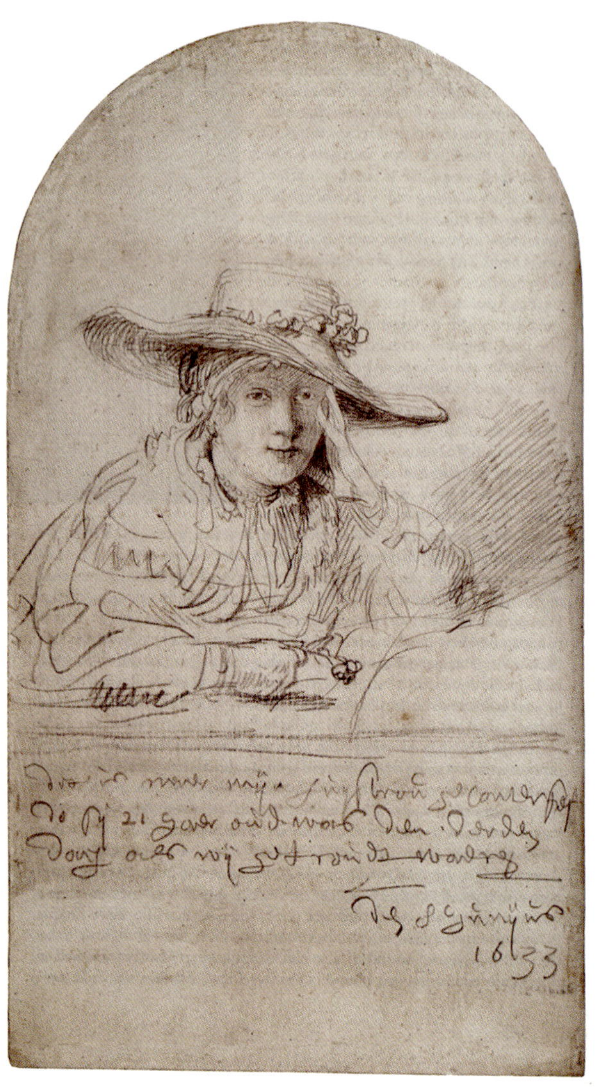

Portrait of Saskia Uylenburgh, *1633.*
*This is a very personal work: an*
*engagement memento. Saskia holds*
*a flower, perhaps a rose with which*
*Rembrandt may be alluding to themes*
*such as marriage, love and life.*

## SASKIA VAN UYLENBURGH

Rembrandt had Hendrick Uylenburgh to thank for introducing him to his wife-to-be, Saskia Uylenburgh (1612–42). Saskia was Hendrick's cousin, although she was not one of his Mennonite relatives but from a branch that belonged to the Protestant Reformed faith. It is believed they met soon after Rembrandt moved to Amsterdam when she was there visiting. Saskia was born in Leeuwarden, a municipality in Friesland. She was one of eight children and by far the youngest. Her father was Rombertus van Uylenburgh (1554–1624), who had already served a distinguished public career by the time of her birth and was one of the most important men in Friesland. After studying law at the University of Heidelberg, he had become a lawyer in Leeuwarden, where he married Sjoukje Ozinga (or Siuckien Ulckedr Aessinga). At the age of just 30, he became pensionary of the Court of Friesland and burgomaster of Leeuwarden. Due to his expertise in the Friesland judicial system, he became an advisor to William I, Prince of Orange (also called William the Silent, 1533–84), who led the Dutch revolt against the Spanish Hapsburgs. Indeed, Uylenburgh lunched with the Prince on the day that he was assassinated. By the time of Saskia's birth, Rombertus had retired from public life and the family were living off the proceeds from two farms that they owned.

Sadly, Saskia's mother died when she was six was and her father died when she was twelve. Saskia initially stayed in the family home, looked after by her eldest sister. In 1628 she became the ward of her brother-in-law Gerrit van Loo, when she moved to live with her other sister Hiskia.

Rembrandt may have only felt able to propose marriage once he had established himself as one of the leading artists in Amsterdam and was generating a good income. He was certainly marrying into an erudite, connected family. Saskia's brothers were all scholarly, two following their father to become lawyers, as were three of her brothers-in-law. Rembrandt and Saskia got engaged at the home of Hiskia and Gerrit in Friesland on 8 June 1633. An engagement was a binding union at the time, which meant that the couple could live as husband and wife. Rembrandt recorded the day in a very personal, small drawing of his new fiancée, a keepsake, on which he wrote, 'This is drawn after my wife, when she was 21 years old, the third day of our betrothal, the 8th of June 1633'. The drawing, *Portrait of Saskia Uylenburgh*, 1633 (Staatliche Museen, Berlin) was completed in silverpoint, a drawing technique that uses a silver stylus to draw on specially prepared paper. Saskia is shown wearing a wide brimmed straw hat, informally leaning on her elbow and holding a flower. She smiles tenderly as she is drawn. Saskia and Rembrandt got married a year later in early July 1634, in St. Annaparochie, Friesland.

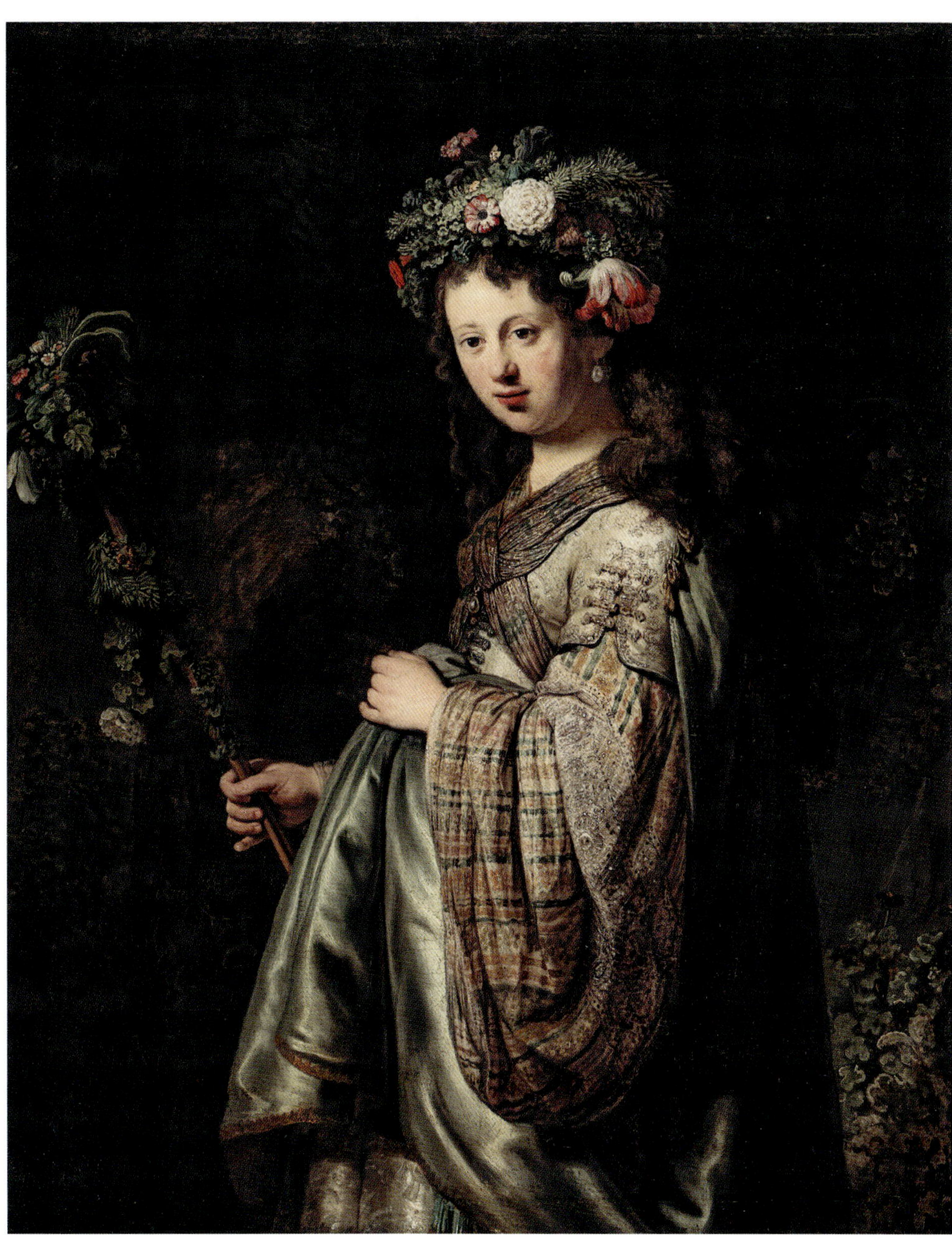

Saskia as Flora, *1634, This life-size, three-quarter length painting shows Saskia in character as the goddess Flora. She is wearing elaborate clothes, a lavish floral headdress and holding a staff also decorated with flowers. She stands in a dark grotto but is herself bathed in a warm light.*

On returning to Amsterdam they initially lived with her cousin Hendrick Uylenburgh before moving in the course of 1635 to a rented property on the Nieuwe Doelsenstratt, facing the river Amstel. Saskia was drawn and painted many more times by Rembrandt during their marriage, sometimes as herself and at other times in character.

In the year of their marriage, 1634, Rembrandt painted *Saskia as Flora*, the Roman goddess of spring and fertility (State Hermitage Museum, St. Petersburg). He was clearly devoted to his new wife. In 1634 Rembrandt also became an Amsterdam citizen and began measures to set up on his own and cut his ties with Hendrick Uylenbugh. He became a member of the Amsterdam St Luke's Guild for painters, engravers, sculptors and other visual art trades. He also painted her in the striking portrait *Saskia in a Red Hat*, 1633–42, which remained with Rembrandt until the 1650s and which he completed after her death. Saskia is shown as an historical figure, dressed in a theatrical costume. She wears a distinctive, flamboyant hat and Rembrandt has succeeded in capturing the details, including the bracelets around her wrist and her pearl earring, which contrast to the soft texture of the fur over her shoulder.

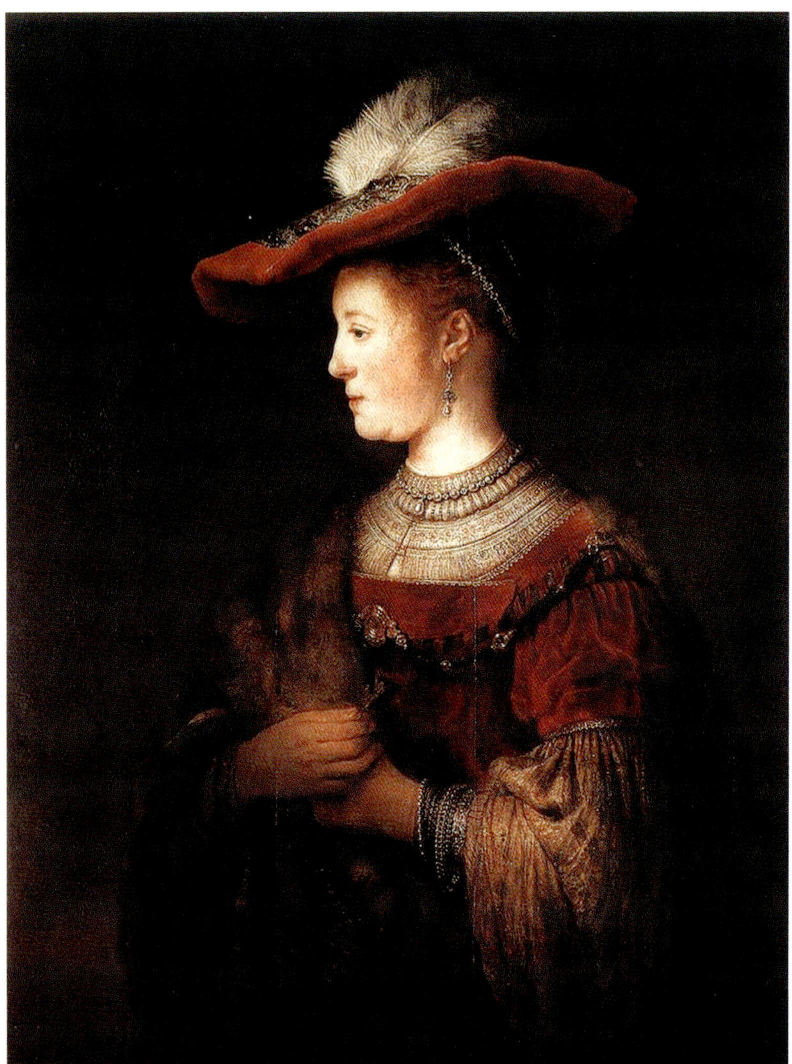

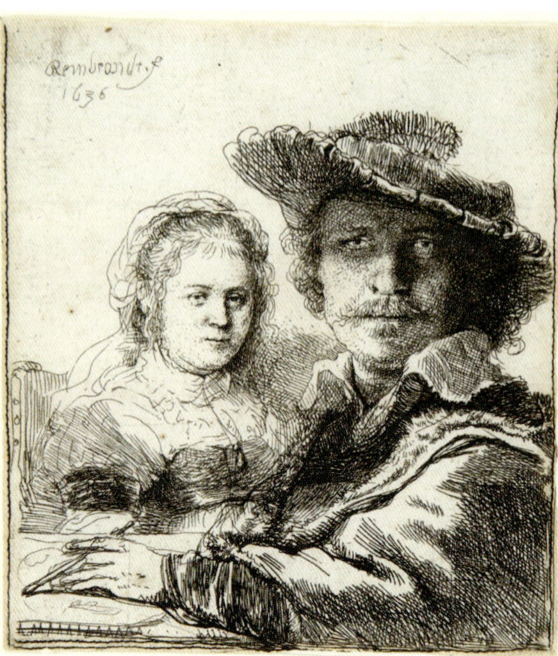

Self-Portrait with Saskia, *1636. Rembrandt and his wife are seated at a table and Rembrandt appears to be drawing. His image dominates the foreground being both larger and darker in comparison to lightly etched image of Saskia.*

Saskia in a Red Hat, *1633-42. Saskia is seen in profile in this striking half-length painting. The light falls directly on her face and her skin glows. Begun in about 1633 Rembrandt went back to it after Saskia's death and only sold it when he was in financial trouble.*

Not long after they married, the newly-weds must have been excited to learn that they were expecting their first child. Saskia gave birth to a boy in December 1635, who they named Rumbertus after her father. He was baptized in the Oude Kerk on 15 December, but their joy was short-lived as Rumbertus died after two months. The year 1635 had seen the plague sweep across Amsterdam and over 10 percent of the population perished. Infant mortality was a cruel part of seventeenth-century life for many people and, unfortunately, this would not be the only time that Saskia and Rembrandt would have to bury a child.

In 1636 Rembrandt made the etching *Self-Portrait with Saskia*, a double portrait. As was usual for Rembrandt he did not choose to do a simple likeness portrait but captured both himself and Saskia in imagined roles. They both wear historic outfits, Rembrandt a sixteenth-century plumed beret and fur-trimmed coat, and Saskia may have a veil pinned in her hair. This is the only etching that Rembrandt made of the couple together and it has the feel of a marriage portrait. On the other hand, the work may be an illustration of the popular Dutch saying 'Love brings forth art'.

It seems that Rembrandt also painted companion paintings of himself and his wife and painted double portraits. Several archival papers make reference to these works, but they have not been conclusively identified. The oil painting *Rembrandt and Saskia in the Scene of the Prodigal Son*, c. 1635, (Staatliche Kunstsammlungen, Dresden) could be one such work. If it is them, it is unclear to what extent the two were simply modelling for the characters or if Rembrandt intended this work to be viewed as portraits of them. The painting is set in a tavern. In the foreground, the male figure turns to face the viewer and raises a glass; in

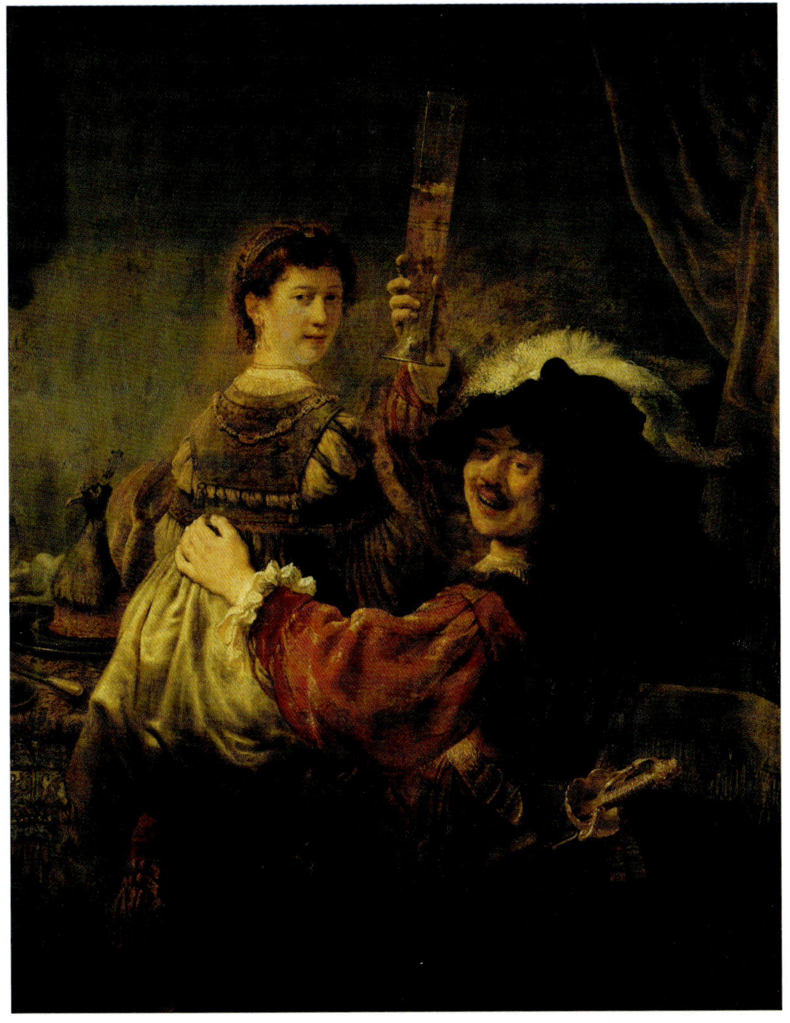

the background, the young woman turns to look over her shoulder at the viewer. It is a very dynamic work, full of movement.

Some of Rembrandt's most insightful works, which can only lead the viewer to conclude just how beloved Saskia was to Rembrandt, are not the finished paintings but the drawings that he made of his wife at home. These intimate works show Saskia in a domestic setting, in bed or unaware she is being observed. In one red chalk drawing she is sitting up in bed, her head at an angle and looking towards Rembrandt, who has paid particular attention to her hands firmly gripped together. One of the most poignant drawings, completed in brown ink is titled *Bedroom with Saskia in Bed, c.1638* (Rijksmuseum, Amsterdam). Saskia is propped up in her bed, glancing out, and on the floor in front of the bed lies a support to assist with nursing a baby. The drawing can therefore be dated to around the birth of their second child, a girl they named after Rembrandt's mother, Cornelia. She was christened on 22 July 1638 but lived for only three weeks and was buried on 13 August 1638. Whether it was drawn just before she gave birth or just after, it is very moving drawing of what must have been another terrible time for the couple.

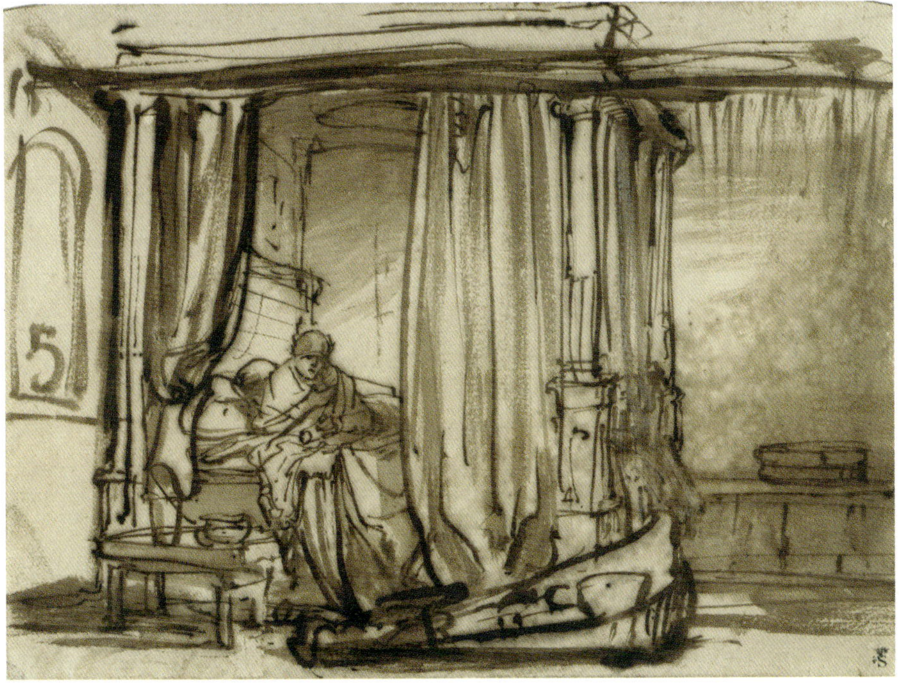

**Top:** Rembrandt and Saskia in the Scene of the Prodigal Son, *c.1635. Both figures wear extravagant costumes in this dynamic double portrait. Saskia, in the role of the courtesan, sits on Rembrandt's lap as he raises a glass. It is believed to portray the Prodigal Son, a popular theme for paintings.*

**Below:** Bedroom with Saskia in Bed, *c.1635/1638. One of a number of drawings Rembrandt drew of Saskia at home, this drawing is typical is showing Saskia in a private moment, in bed.*

# REMBRANDT'S DRAWINGS

Rembrandt was a prolific and innovative draughtsman. He produced thousands of drawings during his lifetime. Although many of them have been destroyed or misattributed over the years, there are still more than 1100 surviving and identified drawings. These works are very varied. They range from small sketches to fully worked sheets and are in different styles and made using different techniques and materials. Rembrandt's preferred medium was ink, which he used with reed pens, quills and brushes, but he also used black and red chalk and even silverpoint. Unlike his paintings and prints his drawings were not made to sell, but were made mainly as part of Rembrandt's ongoing study and work as an artist. They are almost all unsigned and undated.

The subject of his drawings range from biblical and historical subjects, to figures, portraits, self-portraits, animals, landscapes, observations of his surroundings and his family and copies of works by other artists. They should be considered as working drawings and Rembrandt sorted them, filed them by subject and stored them for easy reference. They would also have been studied and copied by his many pupils, who had to master the art of drawing before moving on to copying oil paintings.

Only a small proportion of these drawings can be described as preparatory drawings that relate directly to specific, finished oil paintings or prints. Unlike Italian Renaissance artists this was not such a custom in the seventeenth century Netherlands. However, on some sheets such as *Studies of the Magdalen and Virgin Mourning*, c.1635–36 (Rijksmuseum, Amsterdam) Rembrandt has drawn the figures

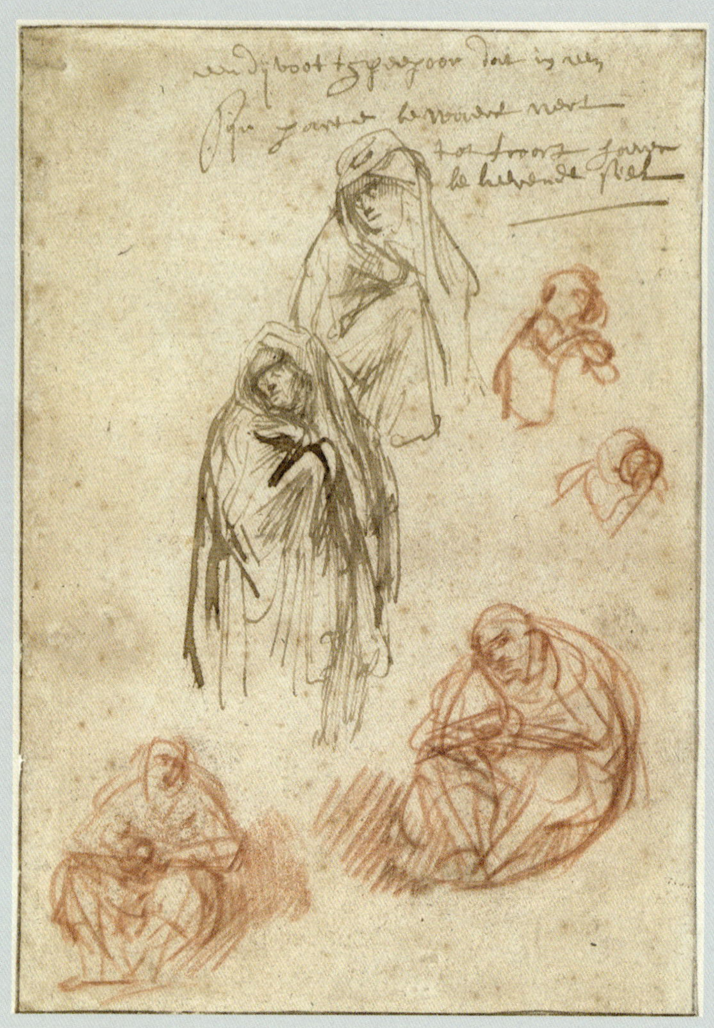

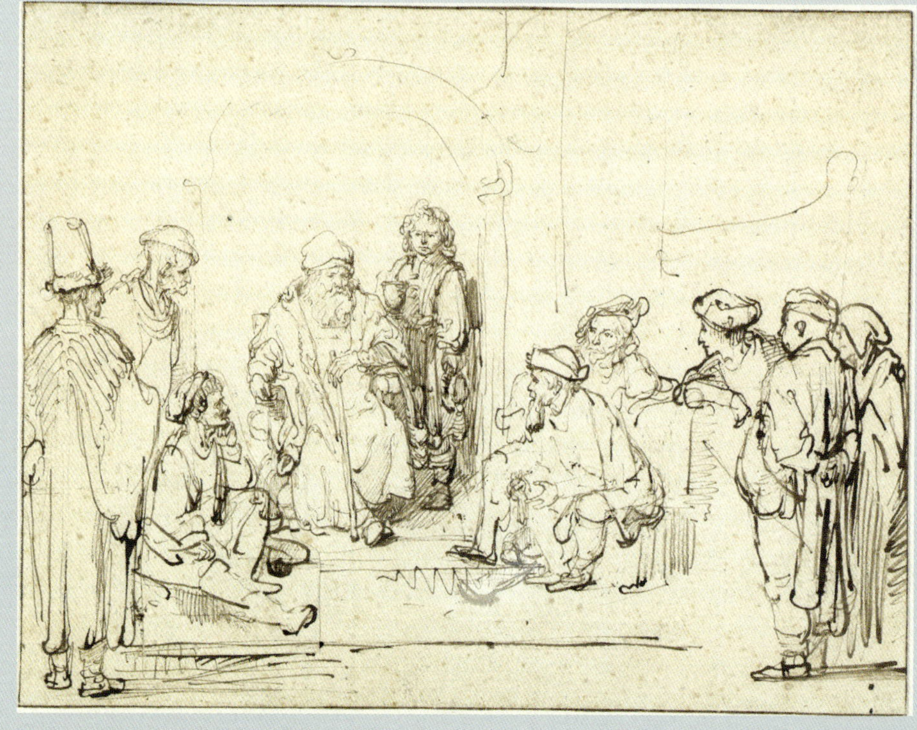

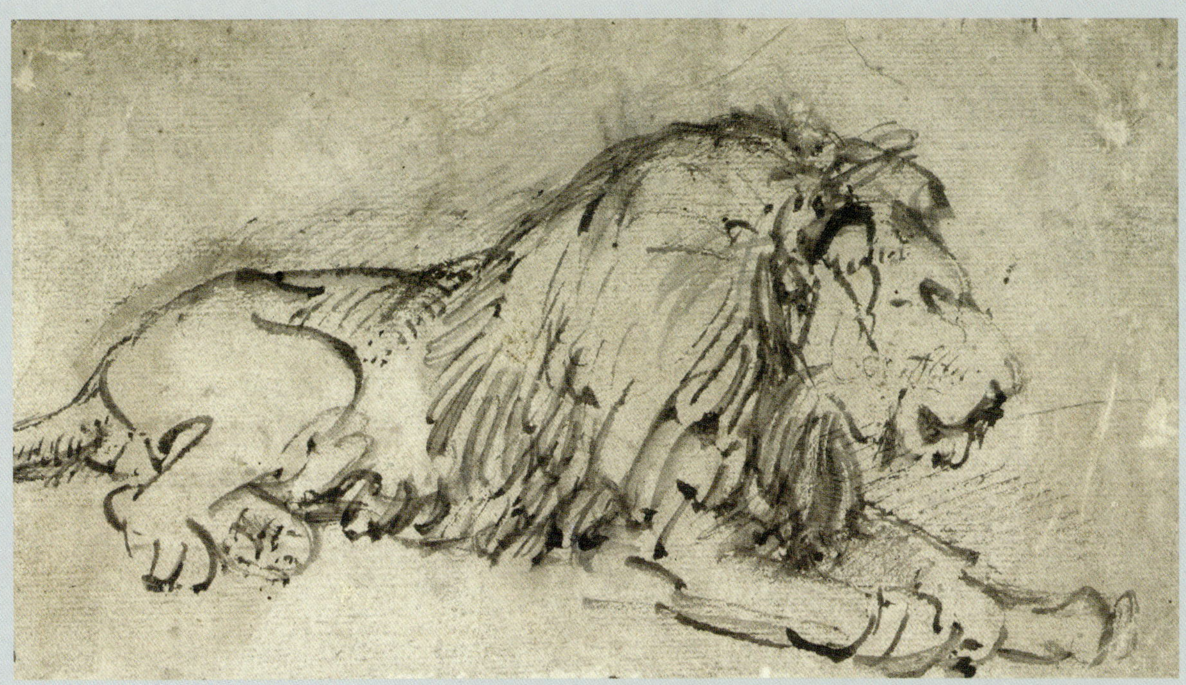

several times as he works out how to express the emotion in his representation of these figures as they witnesses the entombment of Christ for the painting *The Entombment of Christ*, 1639 (see page 30). Rembrandt's drawings can be very expressive and show the artist keenly observing the world around him, some are domestic (see page 33), whilst others show observations of Amsterdam life, such as *The Pancake Woman*, c.1635 (Rijksmuseum, Amsterdam).

A significant proportion of the surviving drawings by Rembrandt are landscapes. Many of these drawings show an economy of line and not only an interest in the Dutch topography but also in how to depict weather and atmosphere. Some were probably completed '*en plein air*' whilst Rembrandt was on one of his many walks around the Amsterdam countryside. The majority, however, are imaginary scenes inspired by his walks.

These drawings are a significant part of Rembrandt's work. They show a freedom of expression and are important in our understanding of how he worked and what he observed.

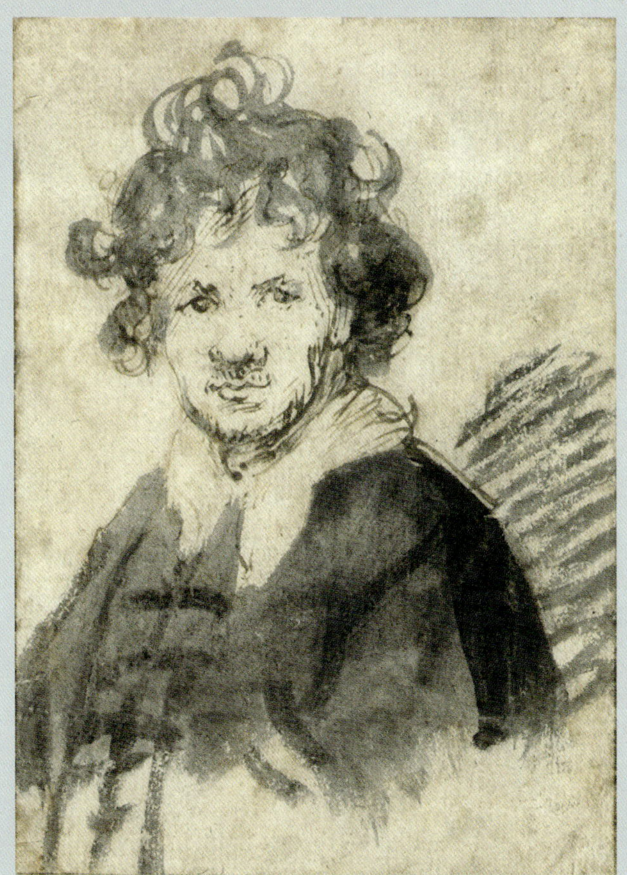

*Opposite top:* Studies of the Magdalen and the Virgin Mourning, *c.1635–36.*
*Opposite below:* Jacob and his Sons, *c. 1641.*
*Top:* Reclining Lion, *c.1660.*
*Below*: Self-Portrait, *c.1628–29.*

## SELF-PORTRAITS AND TRONIES

Despite being kept very busy with endless requests for portraits from the wealthy of
Amsterdam and beyond, Rembrandt continued with his passion for recording his
own likeness. From the early 1630s, headwear becomes a recurring element in his
self-portraits and he is often depicted wearing berets. In 1634 he painted *Self-Portrait
Wearing a Helmet* (Staatliche Museen, Kassel) where he is dressed as a soldier with
a gleaming helmet on his head that the light brilliantly reflects off. Rembrandt is not
looking directly at the viewer, but over their shoulder into space. He has paid particular
attention to his facial features, perhaps because he was doing so many portraits at this
time. He has an uneasy look and his eyebrows are furrowed in a frown.

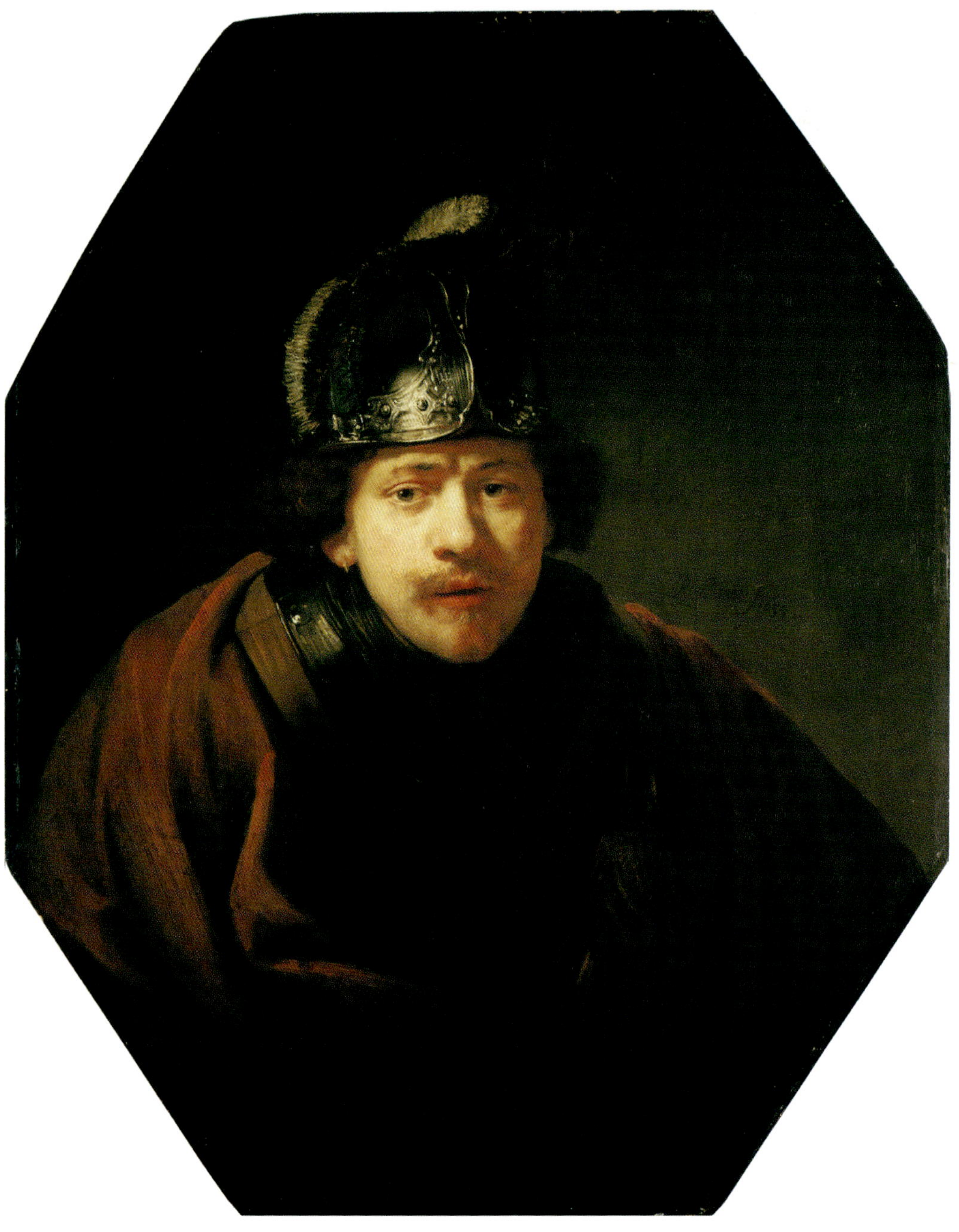

Self-Portrait Wearing a Helmet,
1634. *Rembrandt frequently
painted tronies capturing himself
and others in fanciful costumes.
This portrait has an intensity as he
leans forward looking intently into
the distance.*

In fact, this painting is not strictly a self-portrait but a *tronie*. This was a genre that initially allowed Rembrandt to hone and showcase his skills and combine his success as a portrait painter with his desires as a history painter. Rembrandt had started to paint *tronies* while in Leiden and he continued to paint them with much success. One of the best examples from this period is *Bust of a Man in Oriental Dress*, 1635 (Rijksmuseum, Amsterdam). The sitter is dressed in an elaborately knotted turban with a gold band around it. Rembrandt had a fascination with the exotic, as did many others in the Dutch Republic, and these types of paintings were very popular. They were known as *Oriental tronies*. The light in this painting falls on the turban and the right side of the face, putting the left side in shadow.

## HISTORY PAINTINGS

Rembrandt still held serious ambitions as a history painter. This was the most highly regarded art form, however good his portraits were and despite how much money he made from them. So it was a genre he continued to pursue alongside his portrait painting. At this time, most artists in the Dutch Republic at this time chose to specialize and find their niche in the market, but Rembrandt refused to be confined to a single specialism.

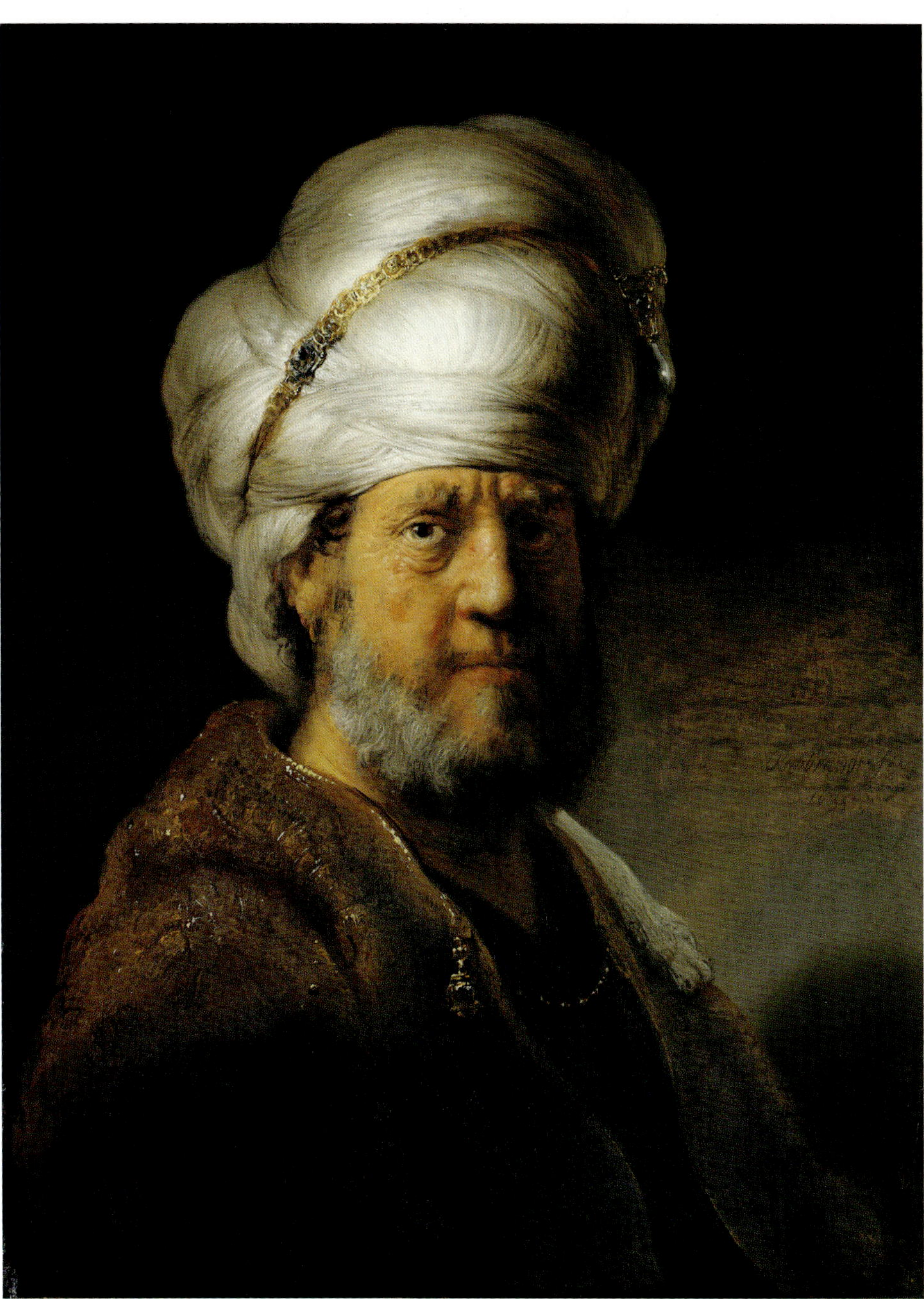

Bust of a Man in Oriental Dress, *1635. The sitter has a serious, determined look of authority on his face. The popularity of these paintings of sitters in oriental costume was no doubt due in some part to the expanding trade between the Dutch Republic and the Middle East.*

The most important commission of Rembrandt's early career came via Constantijn Huygens for the *Passion Series* of paintings for the Stadholder Frederik Hendrik. Rembrandt worked on this commission for a decade. Both Hendrik and Huygens were great admirers of the work of Rubens and Hendrik owned six paintings by him, but Rubens lived in the Spanish controlled south, so acquiring and commissioning works from him was almost impossible. Hendrik and Huygens looked for other artists to commission works from who they thought could rival or equal Rubens, and chose

Rembrandt. Hendrik already owned a painting of the *Descent from the Cross* by Rubens, but commissioned Rembrandt with the same subject.

The first two paintings that were commissioned from Rembrandt were *The Raising of the Cross* and the *Descent from the Cross*, both dated to around 1633. These were well received and the stadholder commissioned three more in the same series, *The Ascension of Christ*, *The Entombment* and *The Resurrection* (Alte Pinakothek, Munich). *The Ascension* was completed in 1636 but *The Resurrection* and *The Entombment* were not finished until 1639. All the works are the same size, but they differ considerably in style and influence and they were produced over several years, so they perhaps don't hang as well together stylistically as a series might.

The composition of the first two paintings show the influence of Rubens on Rembrandt at this time. However, Rubens was working on a much grander scale when he painted the same subjects as altarpieces for St Walburga, Antwerp and Antwerp Cathedral in 1610–12. By contrast, Rembrandt's works are less than a metre high.

Rembrandt painted himself into *The Raising of the Cross*, as one of the figures assisting. He has, therefore, included himself as a witness to the crucifixion of Christ. The figure of Christ is lit brightly as he looks to the sky. The *Descent from the Cross* shows a realistic, lifeless Christ, his head slumping to the side. The action all happens in the brightly lit centre of the painting, that is in contrast to the darkness around.

**Left:** The Raising of the Cross, *1633.*
**Right:** The Descent from the Cross, *1633.*

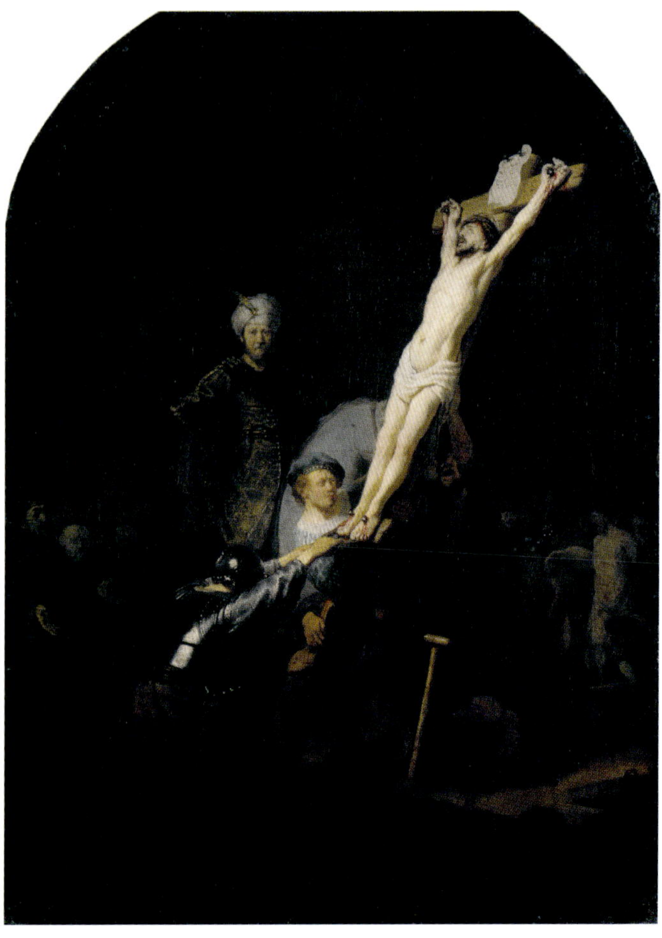

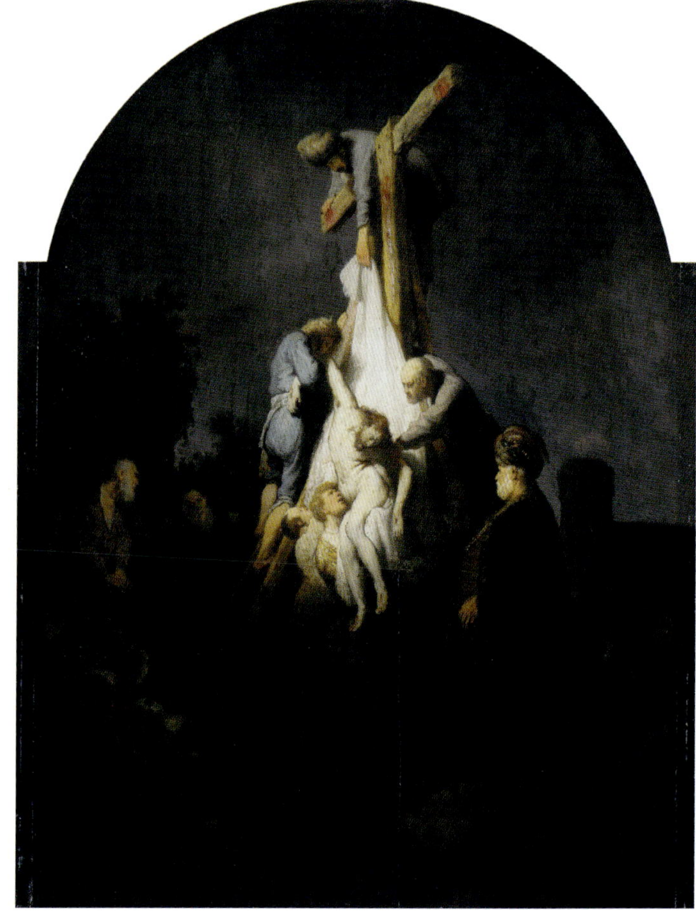

Rembrandt wrote seven letters to Huygens about these paintings, which are his only known surviving letters. They offer a glimpse into the artist and his dealings. In 1636 he wrote to say that he was 'diligently engaged in completing as quickly as possible the three Passion pictures which His Excellency himself commissioned me to do' and that he had completed *The Ascension*. Rembrandt ships the painting and writes again to suggest Hendrik pay a higher price than originally agreed, 'I have certainly deserved 1200 guilders for it, but I shall be satisfied with what His Excellency pays me.' He wrote again in January 1639 to say that he had completed the remaining two paintings. He states, 'the greatest and most natural emotion has been expressed, which is also the main reason why they have taken so long to execute.' *The Entombment* is certainly full of emotion as the body of Christ is captured at the moment of being lifted into the tomb. Rembrandt also requested payment and again suggested that the works were of such quality that he should pay 'no less than a thousand guilders each', but Hendrik and Huygens stuck to the original agreement of 600 guilders each. Rembrandt was seeking prompt payment as he had just bought a grand house and no doubt needed that money for the deposit (see page 44).

**Left:** The Ascension of Christ, *1636.*
**Right:** The Entombment of Christ, *1639.*
*The five paintings Rembrandt painted in the Passion series for the Stadholder Frederik Hendrik were a major commission that spanned many years. The painting* The Resurrection of Christ *was also delivered in 1639.*

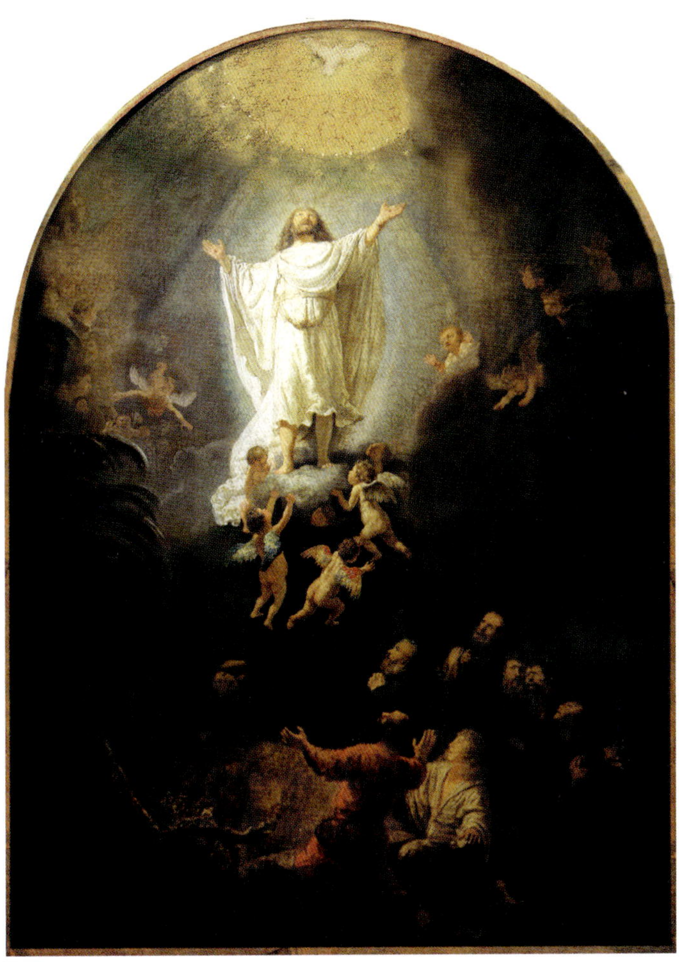

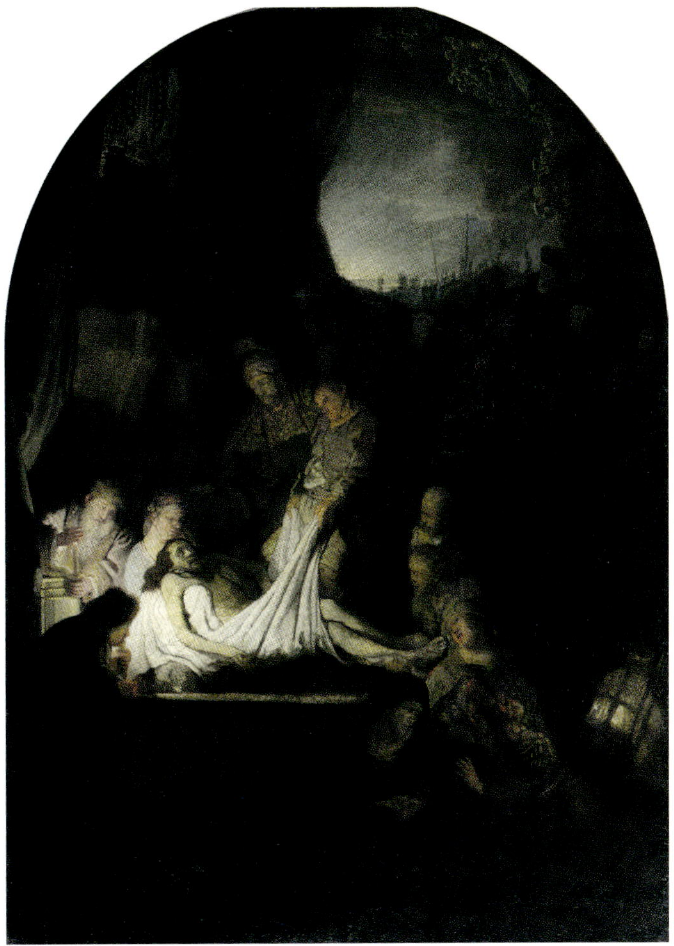

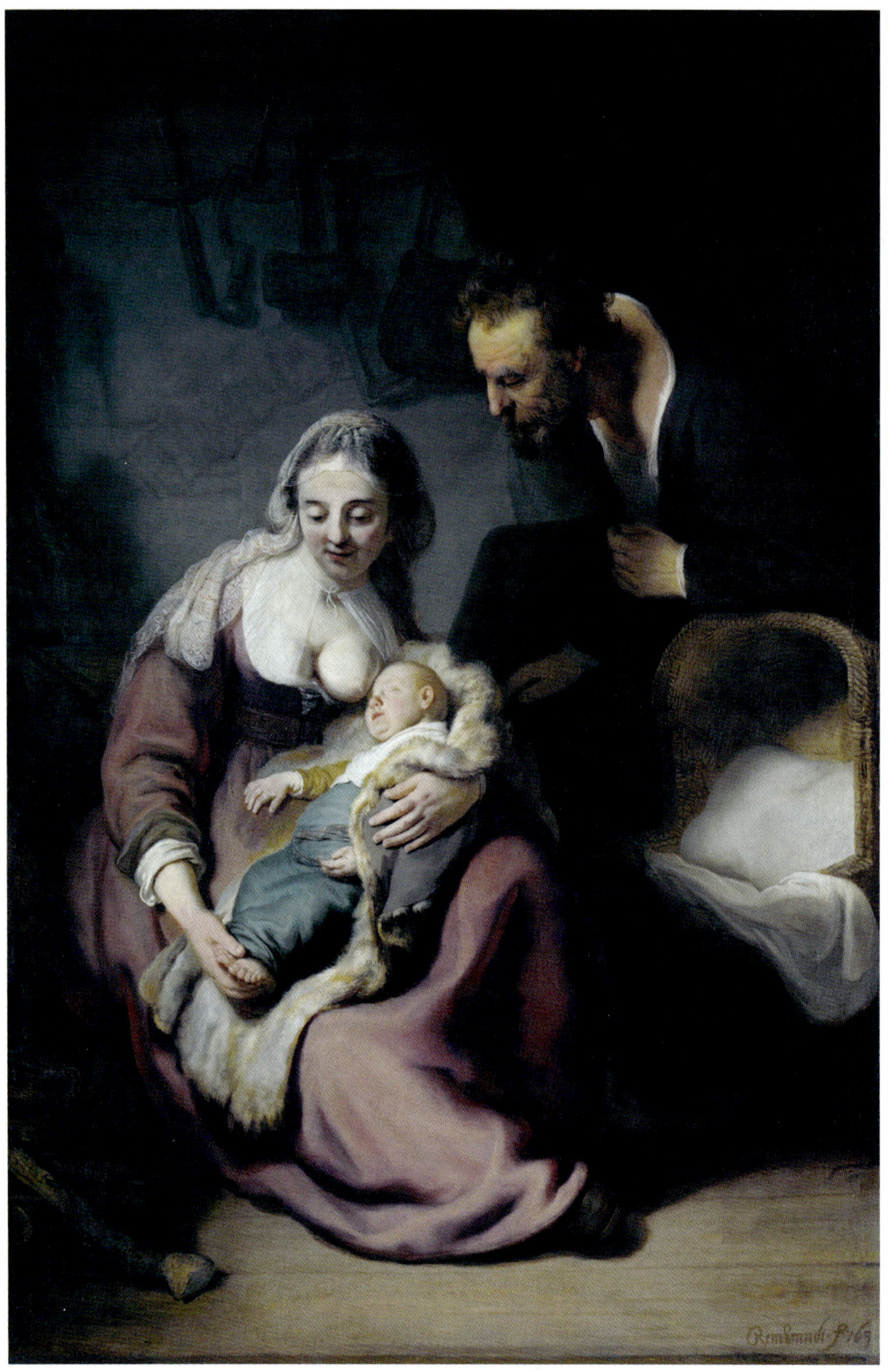

The Holy Family, c.1634. *This is one of only a few history paintings that Rembrandt completed in his first years in Amsterdam, at a time when he was concentrating on portrait painting.*

Outside of this commission Rembrandt continued to create dramatic history scenes. As Rembrandt developed as an artist and his ambitions grew, so too did the size of paintings. *The Holy Family*, c. 1634 (Alte Pinakothek, Munich) is Rembrandt's first history painting with life-size figures. He had moved away from the small, panel paintings that he painted in Leiden to much larger canvases. It is highly likely that this painting was the one painted for Marten and Oopjen (see page 29), whose portraits were life-size too. Mary cradles the baby Jesus, who is wrapped in a fur-lined blanket, and tenderly holds his feet as Joseph looks on.

*Belshazzar's Feast*, c.1635–8 (National Gallery, London) may have been a commission or simply painted as a means for Rembrandt to showcase his skill as a history painter. It is a highly dramatic painting. Belshazzar, King of Babylon, is dressed in a gold cloak and turban. He has commanded that the vessels of gold and silver stolen by his father from the temple in Jerusalem be used at this feast. This was sacrilege. As the guests use them, there is a thunderclap and writing appears on the wall behind, a message of doom, that they will die and the kingdom will perish. In deciding the moment to depict, Rembrandt has as usual chosen the turning point, the most dramatic moment as the guests react to Belshazzar. This allows him to capture an array of facial expressions on the guests' faces. The words on the wall, written in Hebrew script shine out, bathing the painting in a theatrical light that echoes the storyline.

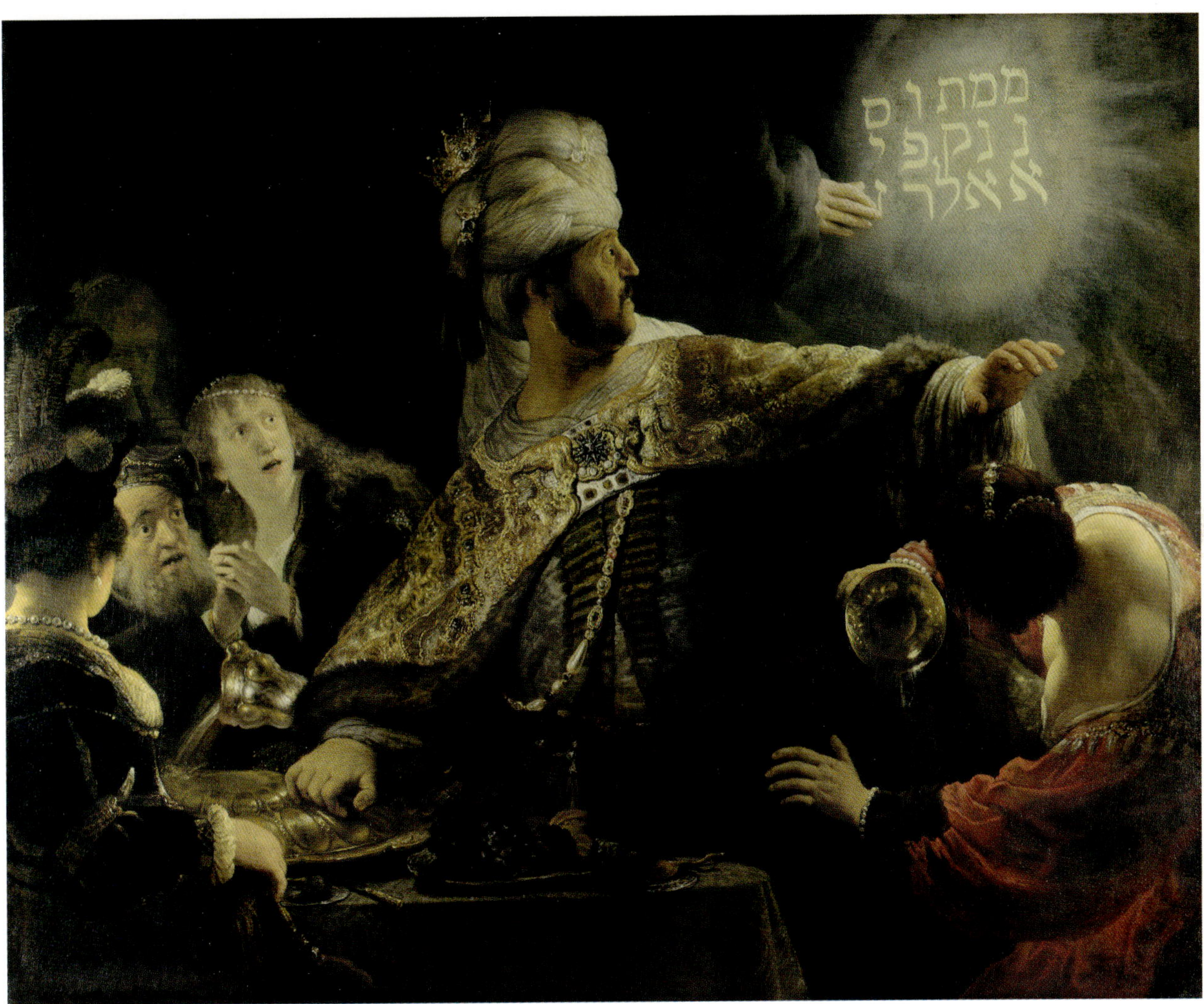

Belshazzar's Feast, c.1635. Churches in Amsterdam at this time were plainly decorated as it was a Calvinist city so religious paintings like this would have been for domestic settings. Rembrandt probably consulted his neighbour, the Jewish scholar Menasseh ben Israel, for his interpretation of this scene.

Rembrandt took the drama of history painting one step further in *The Blinding of Samson*, 1636 (Städel Museum, Frankfurt). This gory painting is on a huge canvas, 3 m (9 ft) high and 4 m (13 ft) wide. It is one of three paintings of the story of Samson painted by Rembrandt painted in the 1630s, the others being *Samson Threatening His Father-in-Law*, 1635 (Gemäldegalerie, Berlin) and *Samson Posing the Riddle to the Wedding Guests*, 1638 (Gemäldegalerie Alte Meister, Dresden). He had also painted Samson at the start of his career in Leiden, *Samson and Delilah*, 1628 (Gemäldegalerie, Berlin). In *The Blinding of Samson*, Rembrandt decided to paint the moment when Samson, his hair cut by Delilah, has lost his strength and is captured, and his right eye then gouged out. It was the first time that an artist depicted this violent moment – as usual, Rembrandt was not afraid of making bold choices. This gruesome scene shows Samson writhing in pain: the toes on his raised foot curl up and his face contorts. Delilah is in the background holding his hair and he is surrounded by the soldiers. The pose is inspired by Ruben's *Prometheus Bound* of 1612. The drama of the scene is added to by the dramatic use of light. Rembrandt is thought to have had trouble selling this painting and he offered it as a gift to Constantijn Huygens in 1639 in recognition of his support.

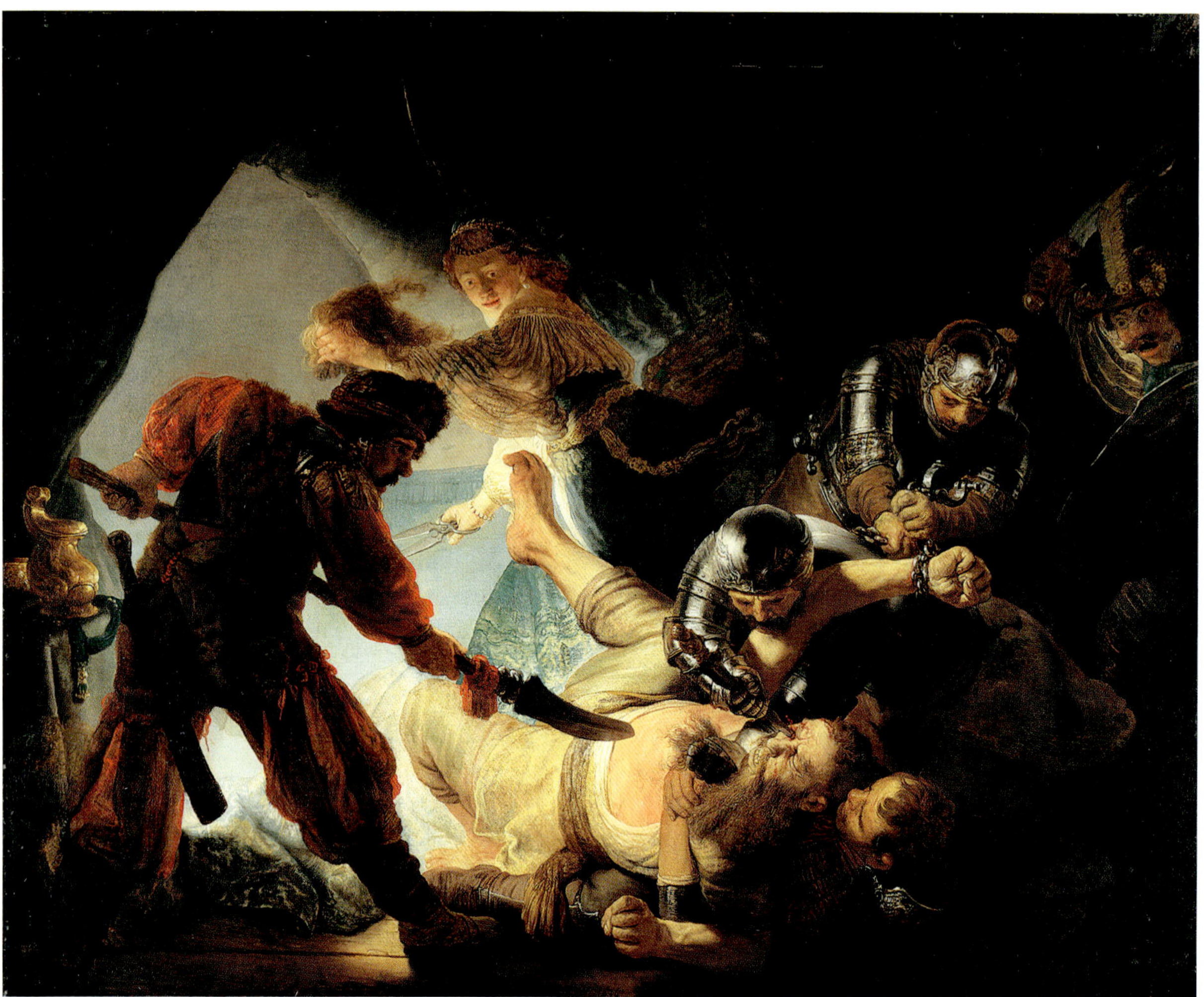

## THE LATE 1630S

The second half of the 1630s saw Rembrandt complete fewer portrait commissions, although he did not give it up completely. He painted portraits of Aletta Adriaensdr (1589–1656), the second wife of Elias Trip (1570–1636), and their daughter Maria Trip (1619–83). Trip had made his fortune as an iron merchant. Maria Trip's portrait is bigger and more elaborate than her mother's. She wears fashionable clothes, captured in minute detail, and it is probable that this was painted to present her to potential suitors.

The end of the 1630s saw Rembrandt venture into new subject areas, including seascapes, still-life painting and landscapes. His only known seascape is also a history painting, *Christ in the Storm of the Sea of Galilee*, 1633 (stolen in 1990 from the Isabella Stewart Gardner Museum, Boston). It shows the story of Jesus calming the storm in the sea of Galilee. The small figures look frail and vulnerable against the natural power and might of the stormy sea. In about 1639 Rembrandt painted the still-life painting, *Still Life with Dead Peacocks* (Rijksmuseum, Amsterdam), in which he has brilliantly created an optical illusion with the head of the dead peacock – it seems to protrude into our space.

The late 1630s also saw Rembrandt begin to paint a few landscape paintings. He had, of course, painted landscapes as backgrounds to other paintings, but these were pure landscapes

*The Blinding of Samson, 1636. This dramatic painting is one of the most impressive of several history paintings that Rembrandt painted in the second half of the 1630s having set up his own studio. He is thought to have had difficulty selling it and offered it as a gift to Stadholder Frederik Hendrik.*

Christ in the Storm on the Sea of Galilee (St Peter's boat), *1633. Painting on canvas allowed*
*Rembrandt to paint on a much larger scale.*

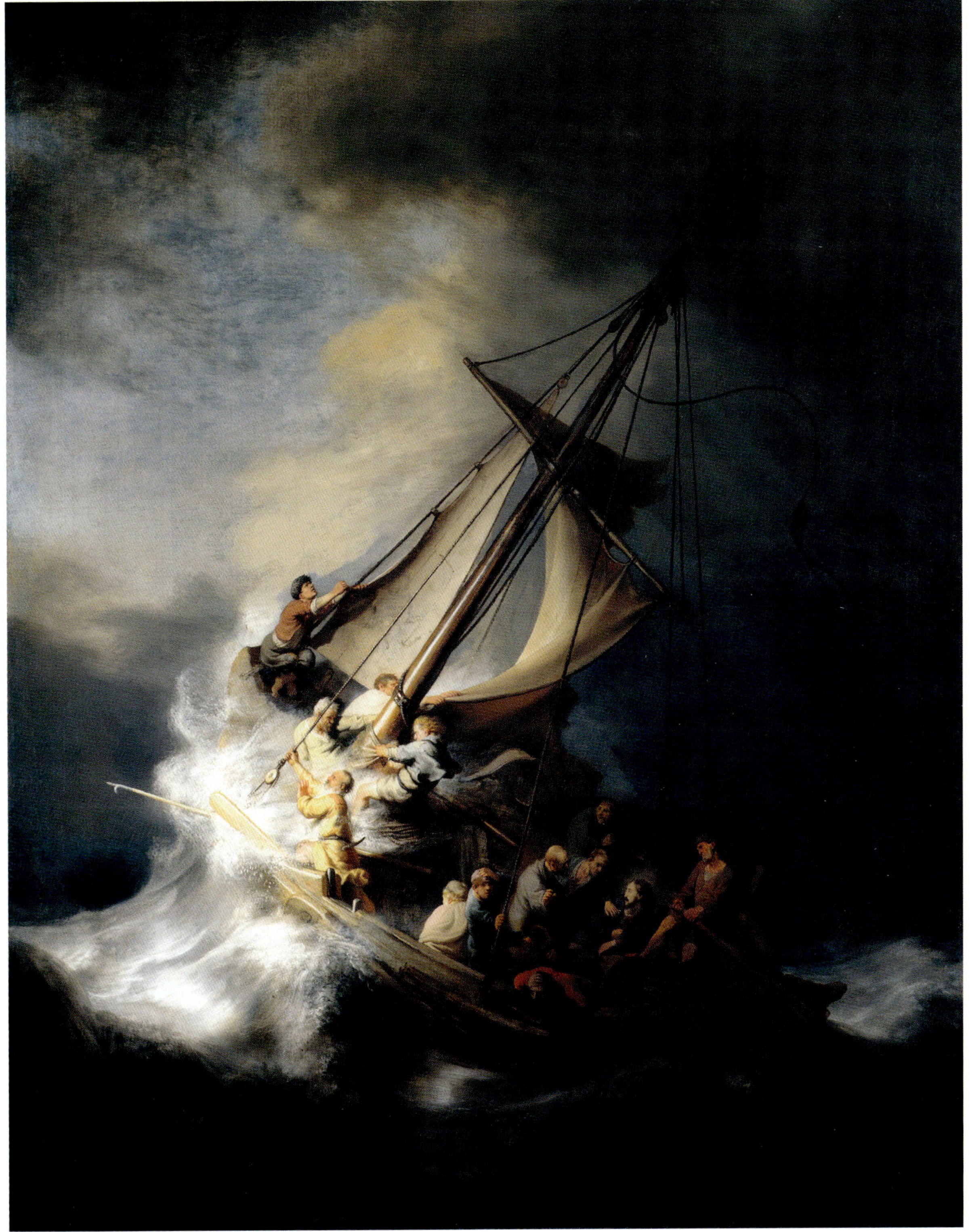

without additional stories, paintings such as *Landscape with a Stone Bridge, c.*1638 (Rijksmuseum, Amsterdam*)* and *Mountain Landscape with a Thunderstorm, c.*1640 (Herzog Anton Ulrich-Museum, Braunschweig). They do not have precise locations but have the essence of the Dutch landscape. Rembrandt frequently drew the landscape in and around Amsterdam and etched far more landscapes than he painted, some of which certainly are identifiable locations.

## A GRAND NEW HOME

By the end of the 1630s Rembrandt could justifiably consider himself to be the leading artist in Amsterdam and was earning good money. On 5 January 1639 he signed the title deeds on a grand house on Sint-Anthonisbreestraat, the same street where Uylenburgh had his studio and where he lived as an apprentice with Lastman. It was a large, beautiful but expensive house and he paid 13,000 guilders for it – more than £2 million in today's money. He set up a payment plan to acquire it, much like a modern-day mortgage: a down payment with the balance to be paid over the next five to six years. The house was set over five floors and Rembrandt had enough space to accommodate his family, receive his guests and patrons, house his apprentices, display his paintings and prints, and also to display his growing art and curiosity collection. It also had good light for his studio, on the second floor. Today, this house is the Rembrandt House Museum and is set up to reflect how it was used in his lifetime.

On 29 July 1640 Rembrandt and Saskia baptized their third child, another girl that they again named Cornelia.

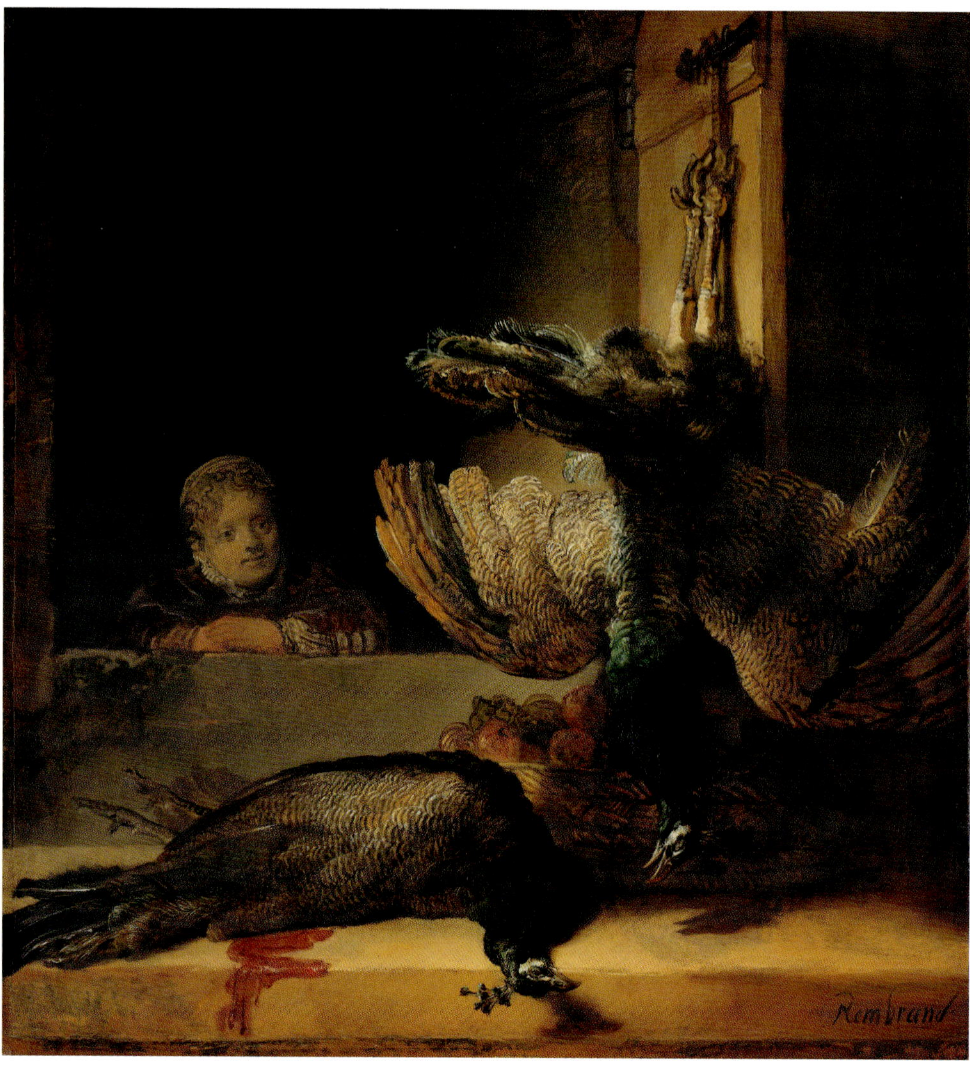

*Still-life with Dead Peacocks, c. 1639. This painting is not strictly a still-life as it includes a girl looking through the arched window. Rembrandt has brilliantly captured the plumage of the birds.*

Tragedy struck once again and their baby lived for only a week and was buried on 12 August. A month later Rembrandt's mother also died aged 72 and was buried in Leiden on 14 September 1640.

Rembrandt continued to draw Saskia at home, sketching her in bed or asleep, and in 1641 he painted *Saskia with Red Flower* (Gemäldergalerie, Dresden), a painting full of emotion. Saskia and Rembrandt had now buried three children, and this is a moving, tender painting. His wife holds out a red flower, the emblem of fidelity, while her other hand is at her chest, holding her chemise. This is a very different Flora, a much more serene depiction, than the Flora painted 10 years earlier as they were just setting out on their lives together.

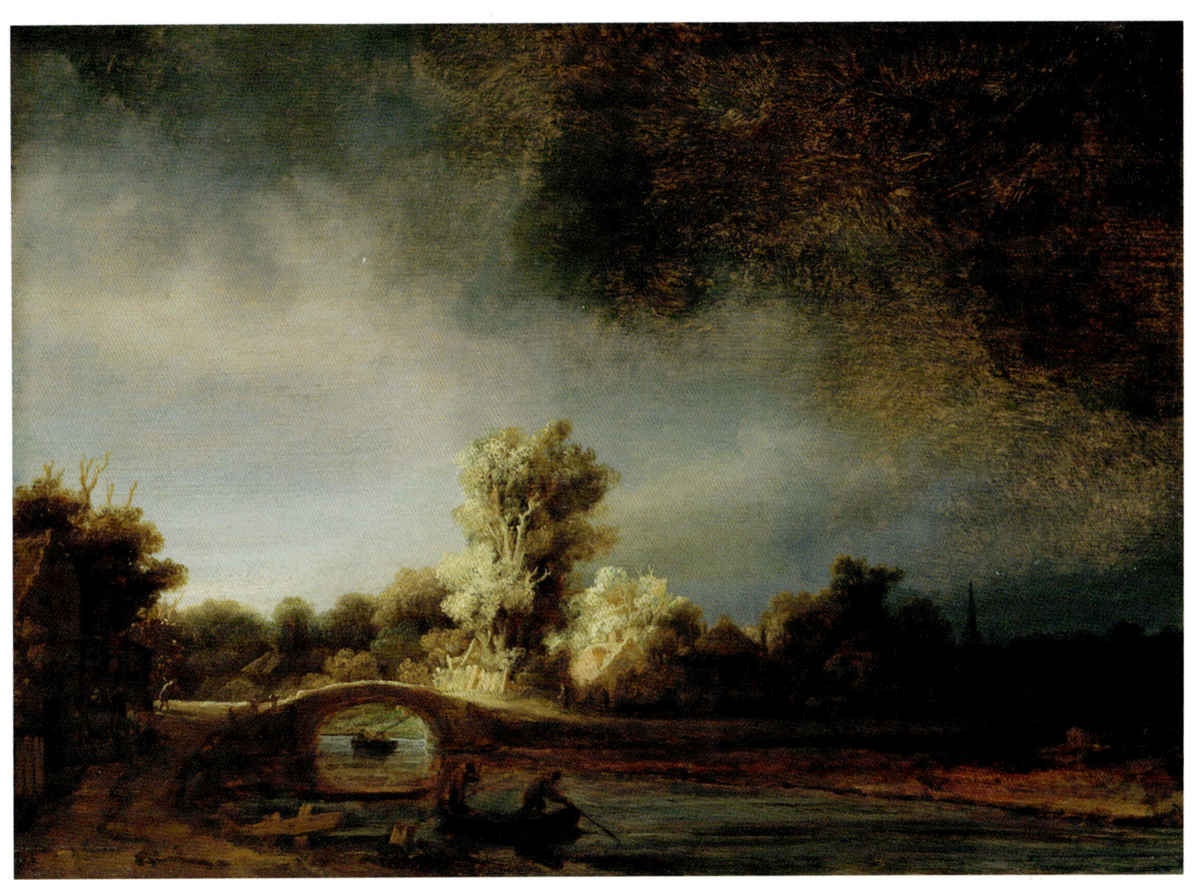

Landscape with
a Stone Bridge,
*1638.*

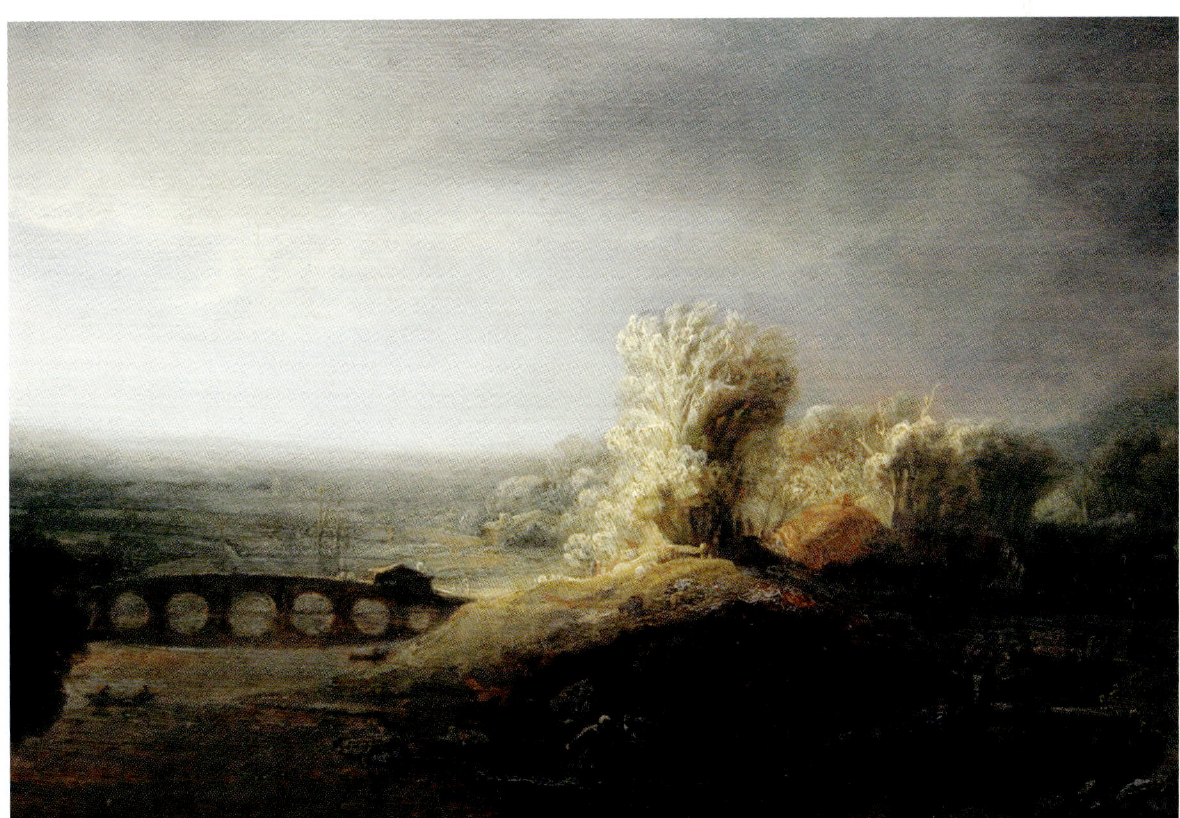

Landscape with
a Long, Arched
Bridge, *1638.*
*Rembrandt
only painted a
handful of pure
landscapes.
Some of the
paintings look
unmistakably
like the Dutch
landscape,
but were
imagined scenes.
Rembrandt took
inspiration from
the landscape
in and around
Amsterdam.
He drew and
etched far more
landscapes than
he painted.*

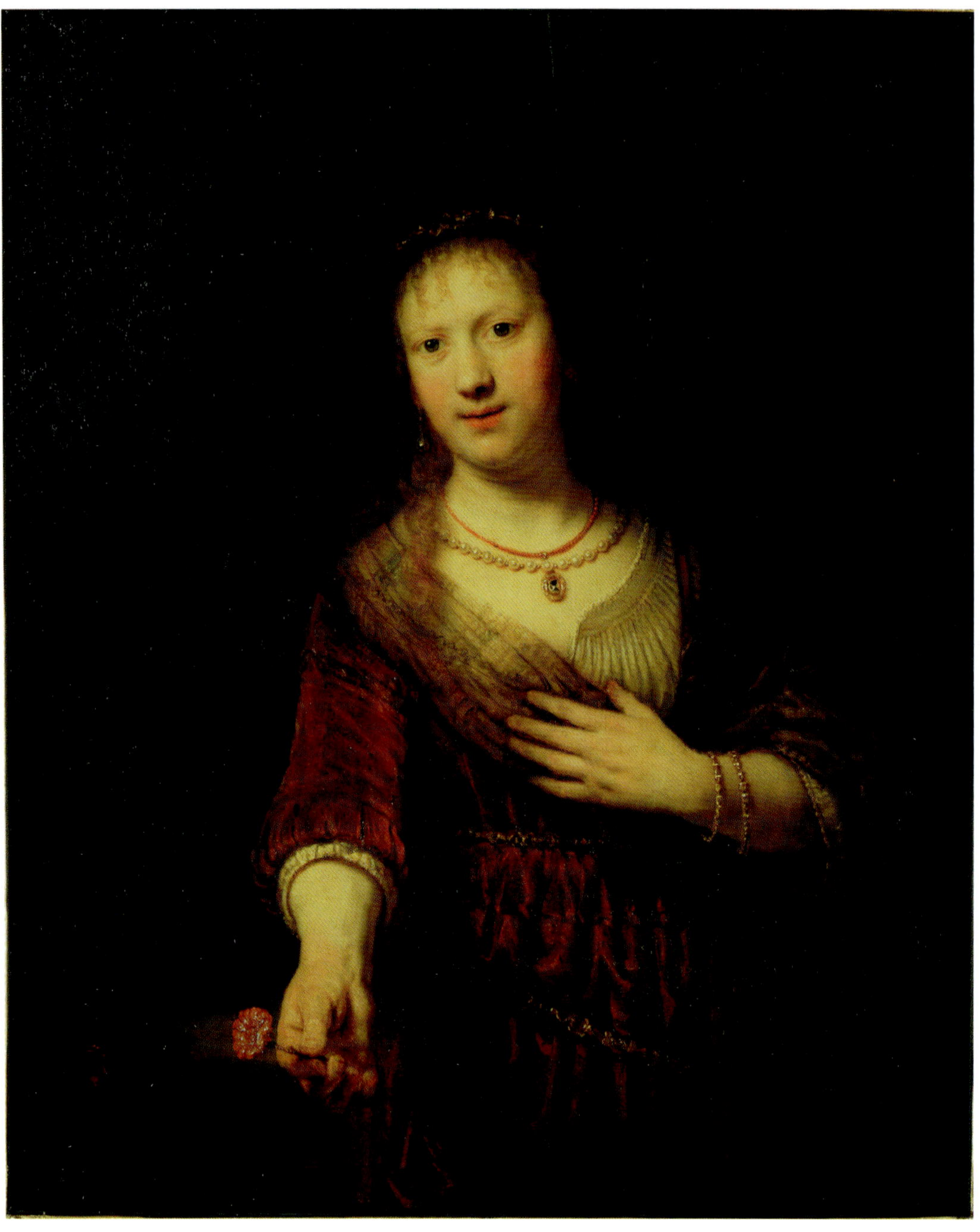

Saskia with Red Flower, *1641.*
*The plain, dark background*
*focuses all the attention*
*on Saskia as she steps into*
*the light in this absorbing,*
*intimate portrait. Her smile,*
*pose and gestures suggest she*
*is engaging with Rembrandt as*
*he paints her.*

A lot had happened in the intervening years and it is possible she was expecting her fourth child at the time of painting.

On 22 September 1641, Rembrandt and Saskia's son Titus was christened in the Zuiderkerk. He was named after his Aunt Titia, who had been godparent to all three of their previous children but who had died herself on 5 June that year. His godparents were Titia's husband, Francois Coopal, Gerrit van Loo and Saskia's cousin, Aeltje Uylenburgh. Titus was their only child to survive infancy. At last Saskia and Rembrandt had the child that they had tried so hard for. The joy was not, however, unbridled because Saskia was not well.

Rembrandt was now at the height of his career. In 1639 he created a different self-portrait in etching that reflected this, titled *Self-Portrait Leaning on a Stone Sill*, 1639. Sitting behind a stone wall, Rembrandt turns his body towards us; his hair is long, his beret at an angle. The pose and composition are derived from two Italian masterpieces that Rembrandt saw in Amsterdam: Titian's *Portrait of a Man with a Quilted Sleeve*, *c*.1512 (National Gallery, London) and Raphael's *Portrait of Baldassare Castiglione*, before 1516 (Louvre, Paris), which was being sold at auction and which Rembrandt had sketched. By taking these two paintings as inspiration, Rembrandt was aligning himself with these great masters, perhaps justifiably so: he was now the most famous and sought-after artist in Amsterdam. His move there 10 years earlier had proved to be a good choice. He had produced a great number of paintings, he had numerous paying apprentices, a grand house and patrons lining up – and he had his wife Saskia and a son Titus.

Now he received a new commission – for a monumental painting. It would be the most ambitious painting that Rembrandt ever executed, one that made him a household name, and one of the most famous artists of all times. *The Night Watch* is now widely appreciated as Rembrandt's masterpiece (*see* page 48).

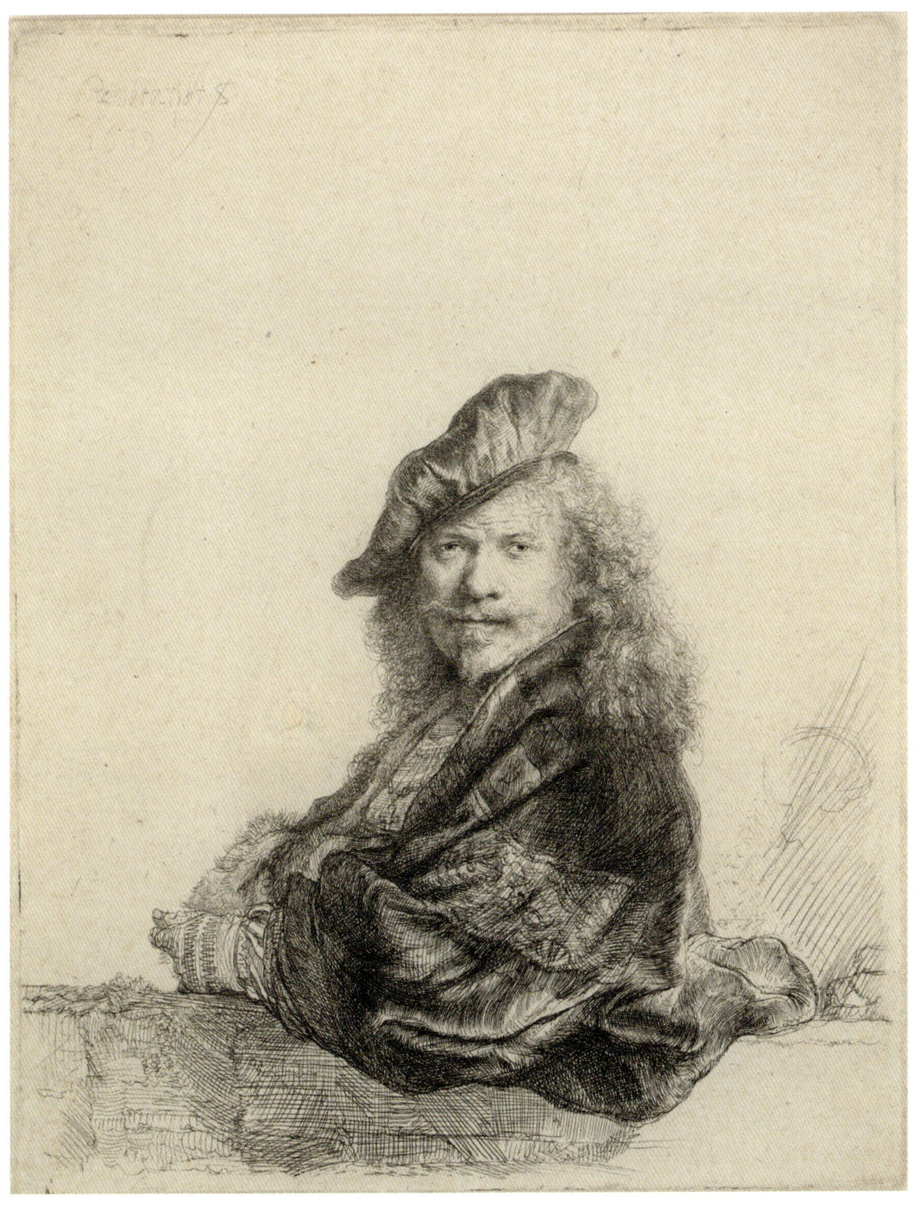

Self-portrait Leaning on a Stone Sill, *1639. Rembrandt looks assured and confident as he stares directly out with his beret at an angle. He gives himself space, leaving the background totally plain apart from the date and signature in the top, left corner. A year later Rembrandt used this same pose for a painted self-portrait.*

# REMBRANDT'S MAGNUM OPUS:
## *THE NIGHT WATCH*

Referred to as *The Night Watch* for the first time in 1797, this painting is also known as *Civic Guardsmen of District II under the Command of Captain Frans Banninck Cocq.* It was commissioned by the company to be hung in the great hall in the recently built Kloveniersdoelen, a civic guard headquarters. The civic guards were the guardians of the city, who had at one time kept it safe from invasion by Spanish forces. The painting is immense, over 4 m (13 ft) wide and 4 m (13 ft) high, and the figures in it are life-size. It was originally even bigger: it was cut down on three sides in 1715 when it was moved to a new location in the city hall. This trimming, particularly of the left-hand side, has affected the composition and balance of the painting. The original composition is known from a seventeenth-century copy by Gerrit Lundens (1622 – after 1683).

It was not uncommon in the seventeenth century to commission large-scale group portraits, and indeed this was one of six civic guard pieces commissioned to hang in the headquarters. Usually these paintings showed the figures in a line of likenesses with minimal interaction with each other, as in seen in Nicolaes Eliaszoon Pickenoy's contemporary painting of District IV (page 50), or Frans Hals' militia paintings. Rembrandt, however, decided to do away with this tradition and approached the commission in a totally novel way. In doing so he created what is widely regarded as his greatest work, an icon of the Dutch baroque period. Approaching the commission as a history painting, he shows the guardsmen in motion as they gather and Banninck gives the order to march out on parade. The painting also looks back to a time of pride when the guards did protect the city; at the time the painting was commissioned, the companies' duties had become more or less ceremonial.

The painting is full of action and movement in what at first looks like a chaotic scene. Rembrandt was commissioned to paint portraits of 16 members of the company but added extra figures into the scene in order to suggest a large group of people. Dressed in black, the Captain gives his order to his Lieutenant and the guardsmen prepare. The company were musketeers, and we see several men loading, aiming or cleaning their muskets, while others raise banners or talk. One guard bangs the drum, while a dog at his feet barks and children run. Each figure has a different pose or gesture and there are numerous different facial expressions. The painting also has numerous diagonal lines throughout, created by the banners and swords and gestures and helping to suggest space and movement, which creates a dynamic composition.

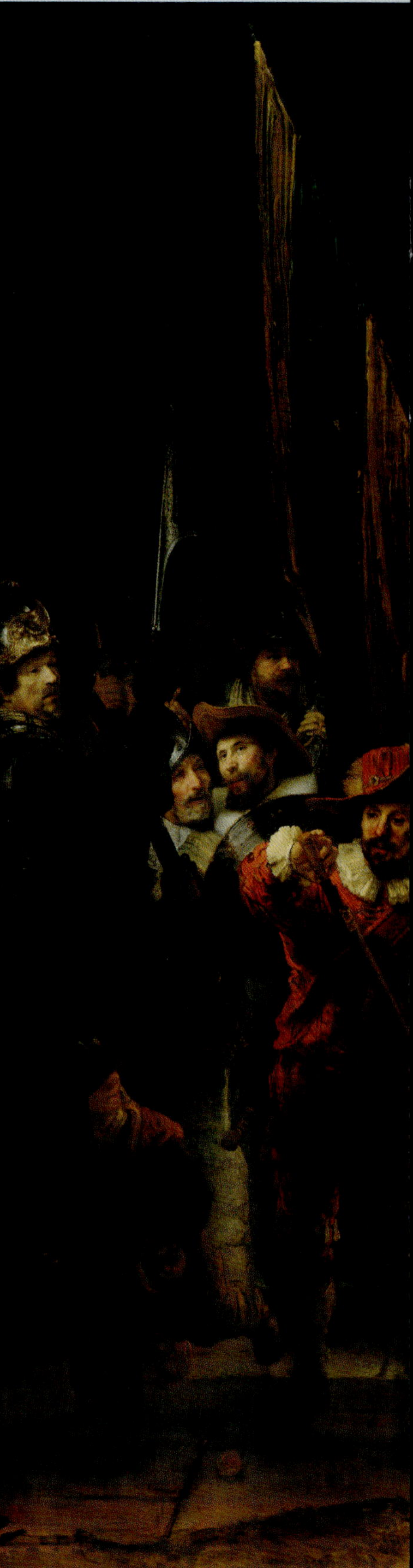

The Nightwatch (Civic Guardsmen of District II under the Command of Captain Frans Banninck Cocq.), *1642.*

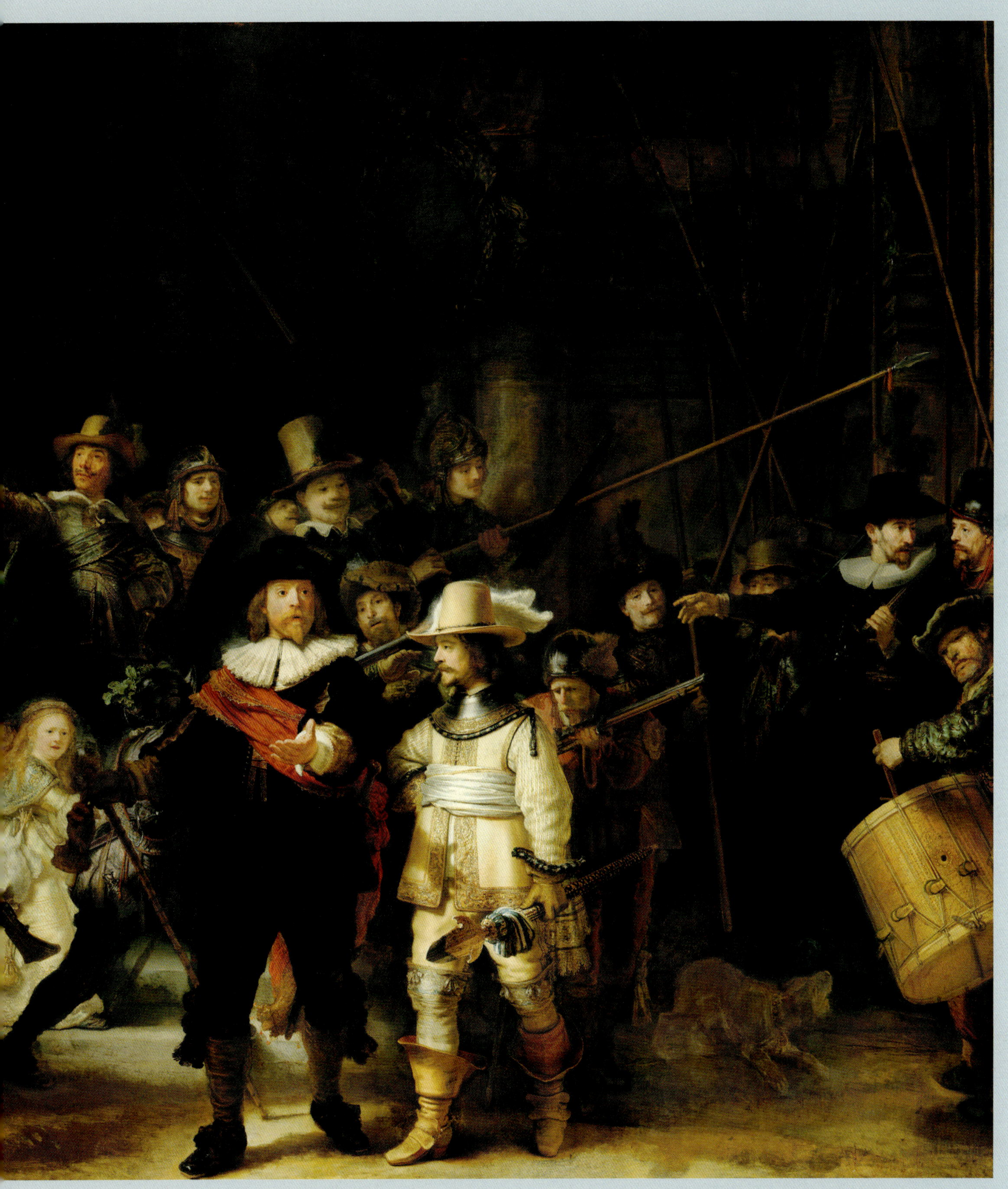

The scene features a strong use of light and shadow – *chiaroscuro*, showing the influence of the sixteenth-century Italian painter Caravaggio. The Captain has his arm outstretched, casting a strong shadow on Ruytenburch. There is a great contrast of light and shade used to picks out the important, central figures, such as the girl dressed in yellow, who is probably the company mascot and holds symbolic objects, including a dead chicken. The painting is very dark in large areas, which led to the assumption that it was a night scene and hence the title *The Night Watch* – in fact, this is daytime.

The painting still holds many mysteries and is full of symbolism: the Xs on Ruytenburch's jacket are the symbol of Amsterdam; oak leaves on a helmet are a symbol of heroism; and there is a particular use of yellow, a colour associated with victory. The girl, whether intentionally or not, bears a strong resemblance to Rembrandt's wife Saskia, who was gravely ill while Rembrandt was creating this work. Rembrandt also included himself in the painting, as he had done in previous paintings; here he is hidden in the back behind two of the guards, his eye and distinctive beret just visible.

The painting took perhaps two years to complete and was so huge that a shed had to be built in the courtyard of Rembrandt's house to accommodate it while he was painting.

Officers and Other Civic Guardsment of the IV District of Amsterdam, under the Command of Captain Jan Claesz van Vlooswijck and Lieutenand Gerrit, *Nicolaes Pickenoy, 1642.*

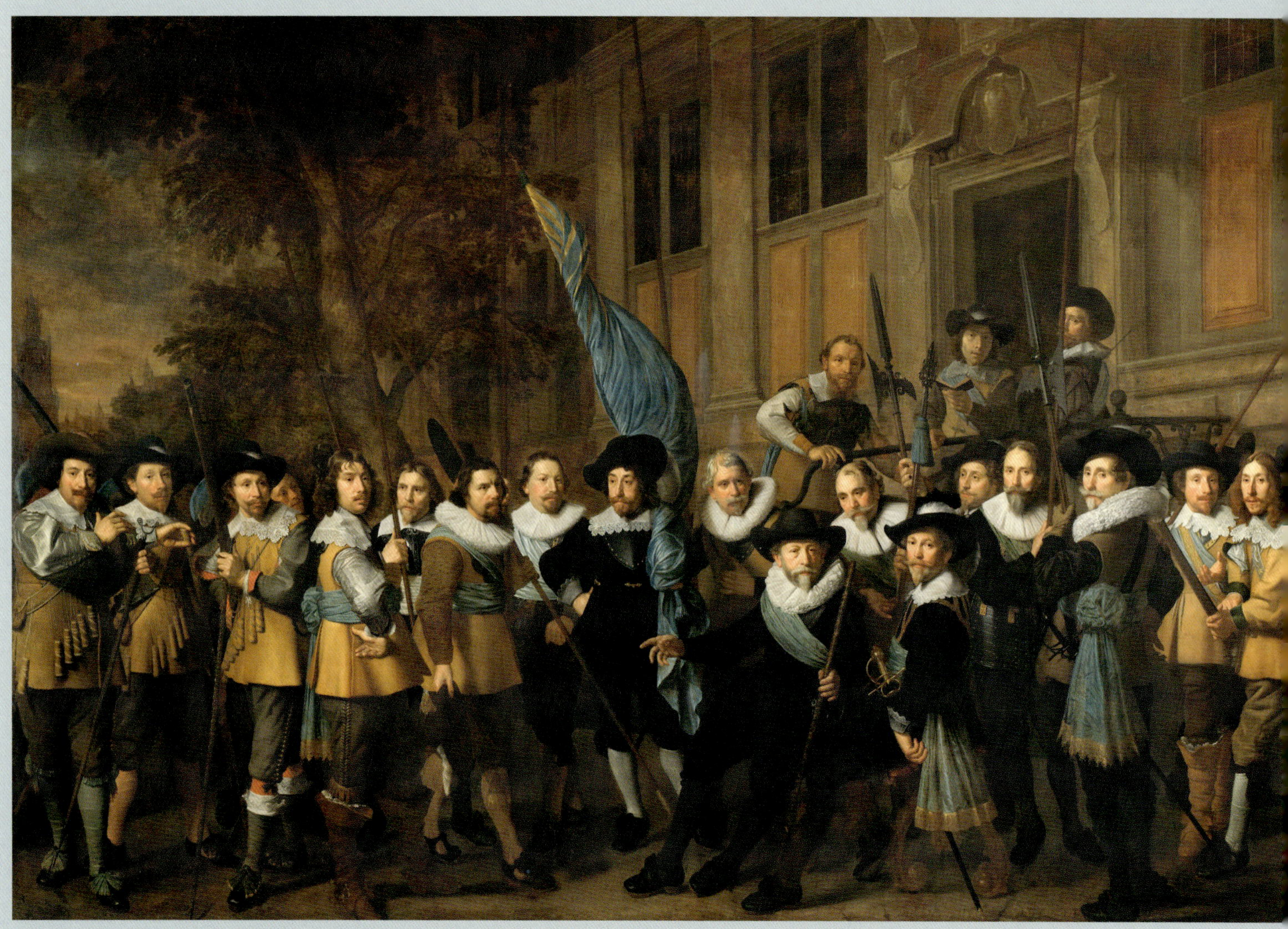

The company paid between 1,600 and 4,000 guilders. Eighteen members each paid at least 100 guilders for their own portrait to be included. What Rembrandt did with this commission was revolutionary: no other artist had approached a militia group portrait in such a way. He combined an innovative dynamic composition with a brilliant use of light and shade on an enormous scale. The result is a truly powerful and captivating painting. The figures look like real people, like you can walk into the painting – and that is perhaps why the painting has an enduring appeal. The painting received much praise and admiration in Rembrandt's lifetime. However, it certainly did not receive universal approval, some criticizing him for paying too much attention to the overall design and not enough attention to the individual portraits, and others suggesting that the composition was jumbled and confused. Despite this mixed early reception, the painting has certainly stood the test of time, and is now regarded as one of the great masterpieces of the world.

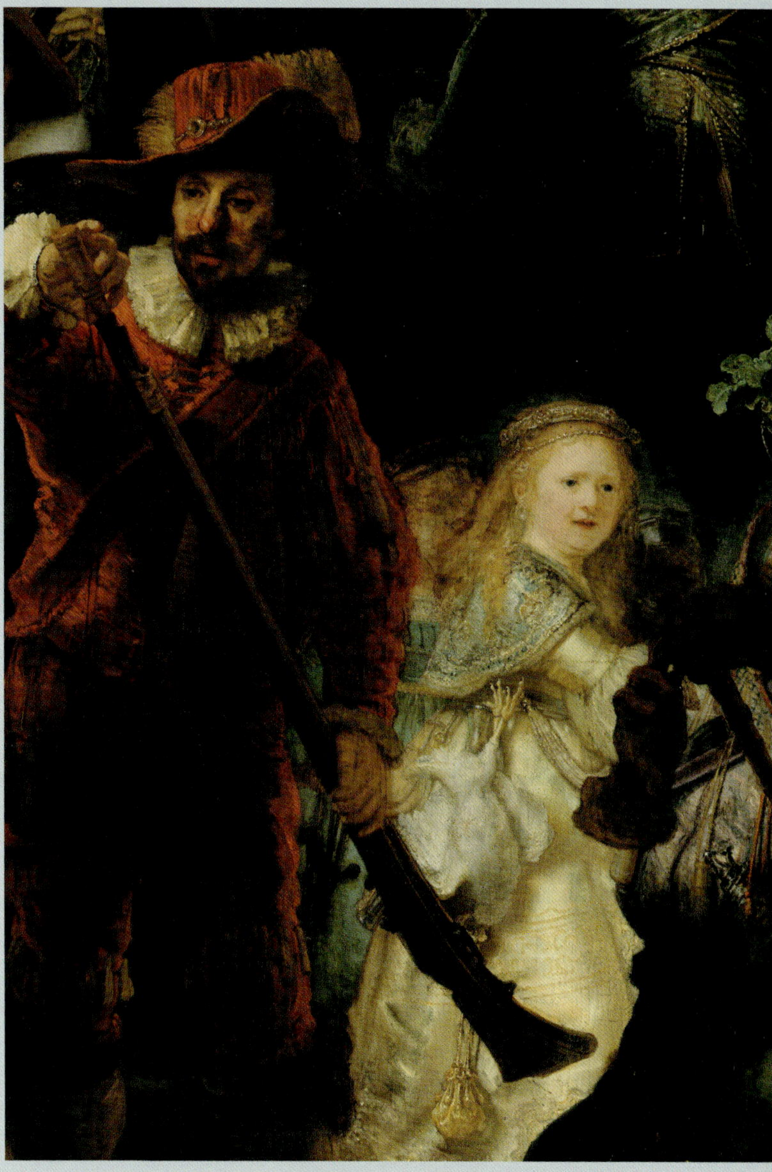

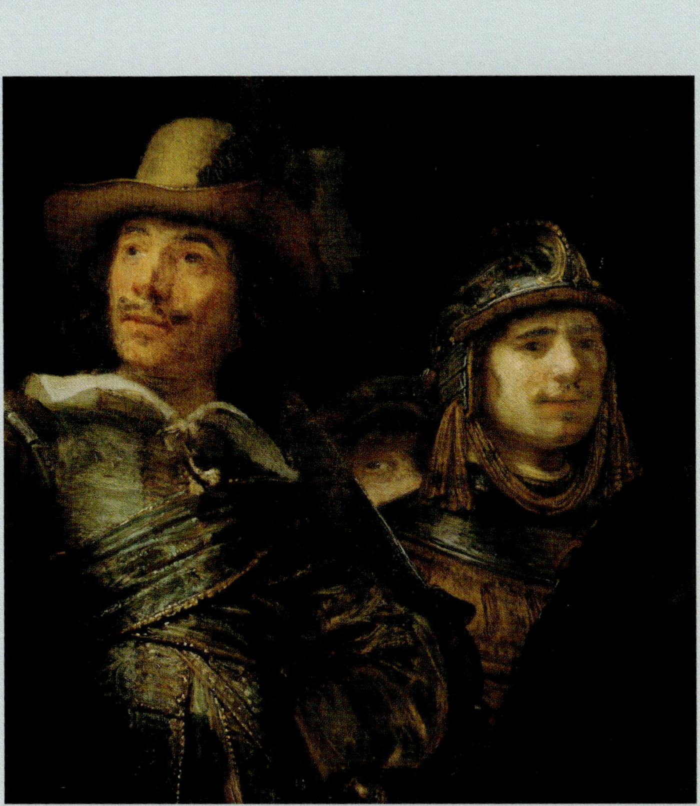

*Above:* Detail showing the girl with symbols.
*Left:* Detail showing Rembrandt's self-portrait hidden at the back of the crowd

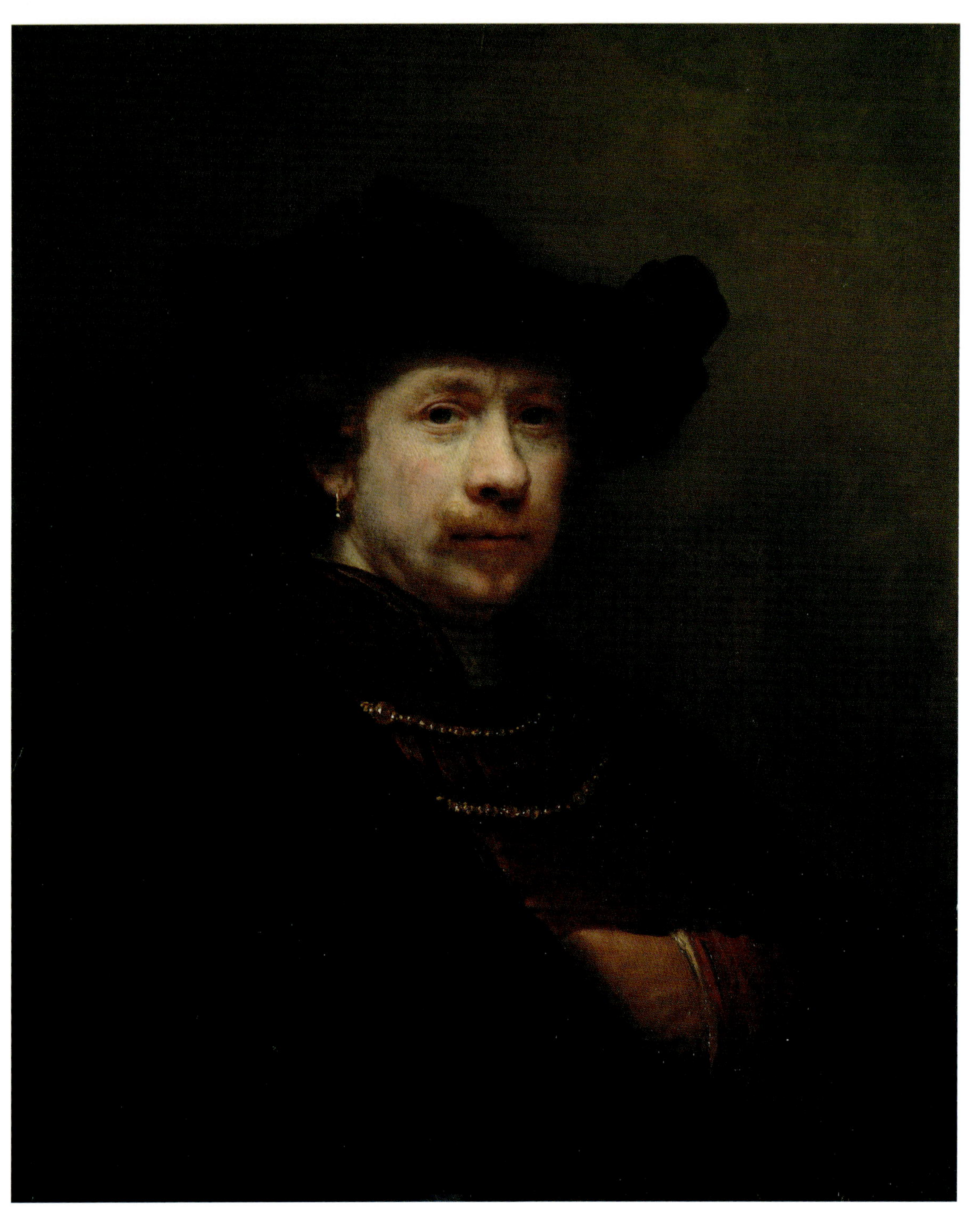

Self-Portrait in a Flat Cap, *1642. Rembrandt exudes confidence and success. He painted many self portraits at different stages of his life. This one is painted over another earlier portrait, which was either unfinished or which he scraped down before painting over.*

# CHAPTER 3

# Success, Tragedy and Change, 1642-56

Rembrandt should have been thrilled with the monumental success of *The Night Watch*. It was his greatest achievement as an artist to date, and an Italian critic, Filippo Baldinucci (1625–97), wrote that it 'brought him such fame as was scarcely ever achieved by any other painter in those parts'. However, just as he was finishing his most important commission, Rembrandt suffered a huge loss. His beloved wife Saskia died on 14 June 1642. She was not yet 30 and their son Titus was only eight months old. It is unclear whether she died from complications from the birth or whether she had contracted tuberculosis.

Saskia's will had been written to protect her inheritance for her son, which was not unusual for this time, but it put restrictions on Rembrandt in terms of remarrying and these would prove detrimental for him in years to come. Her legacy was calculated to be around 20,000 guilders, and Titus would inherit her estate when he came of age at 25 or on Rembrandt's death. If, however, Rembrandt remarried, Titus was entitled to his inheritance at that point. Moreover, if Titus died, Saskia's side of the family were entitled to the estate. In the years that followed, Saskia's family became increasingly concerned about the inheritance, so much so that in 1647 they requested Rembrandt account for it.

Rembrandt must have made a significant amount of money as a successful artist with a large studio and many paying students, but he was also spending a lot. In addition to the large payments on the house, he was an avid collector and was regularly buying art and curiosities from auctions. To put together a rich and varied collection, he was willing to bid high and spend huge sums on artists he appreciated. He is first recorded as buying at an auction in 1635, but it is probable he was collecting well before this. He collected paintings, and many prints, including works by old masters such as Albrecht Dürer (1471–1528) and Lucas van Leyden (1494–1533), a master printmaker from his hometown. In 1642 he paid 179 guilders for a small engraving *Owl Glass* by Lucas van Leyden and one of his pupils is quoted as saying he 'saw his teacher Mr Rembrandt bid 1,400 guilders at a public auction for 14 fine impressions of prints by this artist'.

In addition to art he also collected costumes, weapons, busts, curiosities and natural history specimens. His collection of 'graphic arts, curios, antiques, medals and marine inhabitants' was valued at 11,000 guilders in 1640 and his collection of paintings at 6,400. This collection therefore formed a significant amount of the estate at the time of Saskia's death. Rembrandt probably thought of the collection as a good investment. Certainly, he and his pupils and friends used it as reference for their artworks. A good example of this is the etching of *The Shell*, 1650, a study of a marbled cone, a *conus marmoreus*, which was most likely in Rembrandt's own collection. He did buy shells and in March 1637 he is recorded as paying 11 guilders, an auction record, for a conch shell.

The death of his wife is believed to have had a profound effect on Rembrandt. In the decade following this and the completion of *The Night Watch*, his artistic production plummeted and his interests changed. He stepped off the treadmill of portrait commissions that had dominated his output up to this point, and appears to have been painting more for his own interest and less on commission. This was a radical alteration of his working practice and he produced far fewer works, but the reasons for it are unclear. Some historians have speculated that this was a period of personal crisis for Rembrandt and that he experienced some kind of breakdown following the death of his wife. This is certainly possible, but he may also have been suffering the artist's equivalent of writer's block. Alternatively, having achieved fame and recognition, perhaps he was now questioning the direction he was taking and searching for the kind of artist he wanted to be and the subjects he wanted to paint. His exploration of etchings continued unabated in this period, however, and he produced some of his most successful and complex prints at this point in his career.

In 1642 he painted a *Self-Portrait* (Royal Collection) on a reused panel. He was at the height of his career and the portrait reflects this status: he wears a velvet beret, with an earring and two chains. The painting of his face is particularly well modelled. He was now about 36 and his face was starting to show signs of ageing. In stark contrast to this painting and the *Self-Portrait* print of 1639 (*see* page 47) is the print *Self-Portrait Etching at a Window*: etched six years later in 1648, it captures Rembrandt drawing on an etching plate. It is a much humbler image: gone are the rich fabrics and jewels in favour of plain clothes and a narrow-rimmed hat; this is an artist at work, at his trade. Rembrandt used tone and darkness to create an almost photographic effect. At this date, he was able to achieve effects that no other artist could. It was during this period that Rembrandt made one of his most famous prints, *Christ Healing the Sick*, 1648 – also known as *The Hundred Guilder Print* (*see*

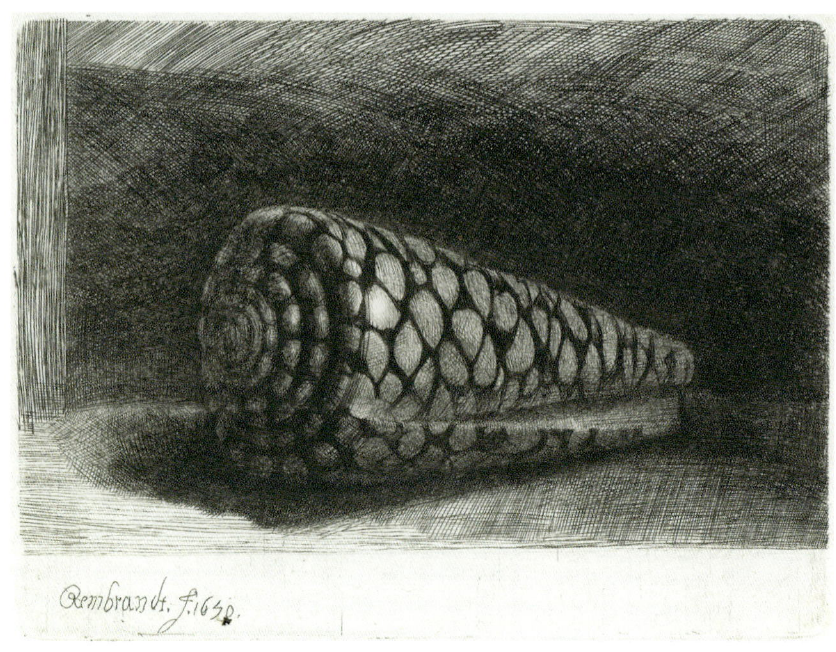

*Above:* The Shell, *1650.*
*Below:* Self-Portrait Etching at a Window, *1648. Rembrandt works at a small table, using a needle to draw his reflection on an etching plate. The elaborate clothes and hats of earlier portraits are replaced by simpler garb.*

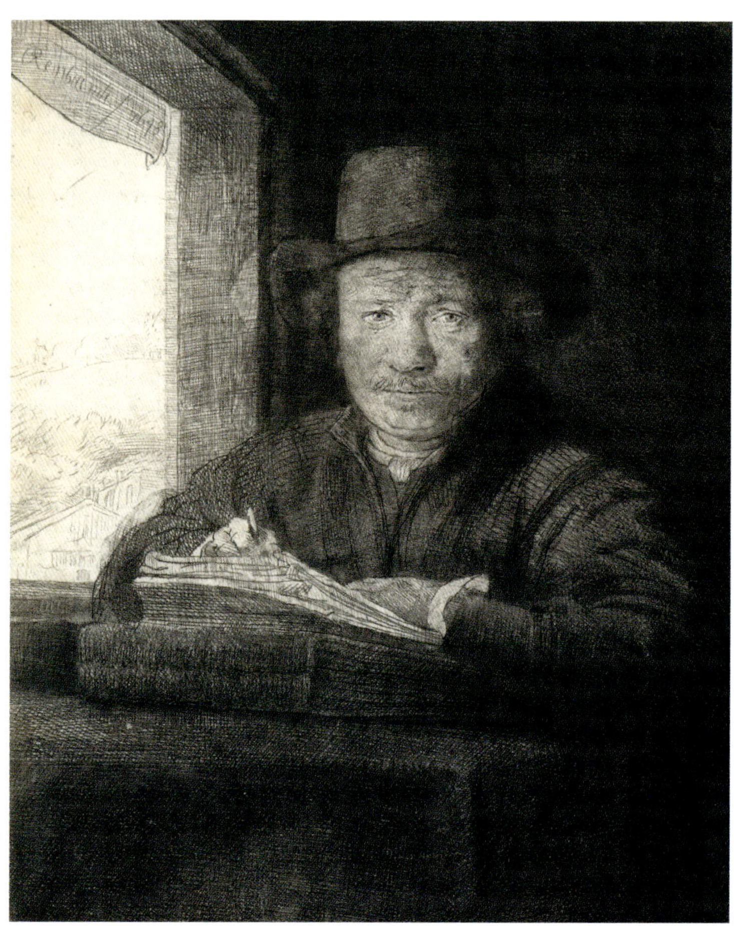

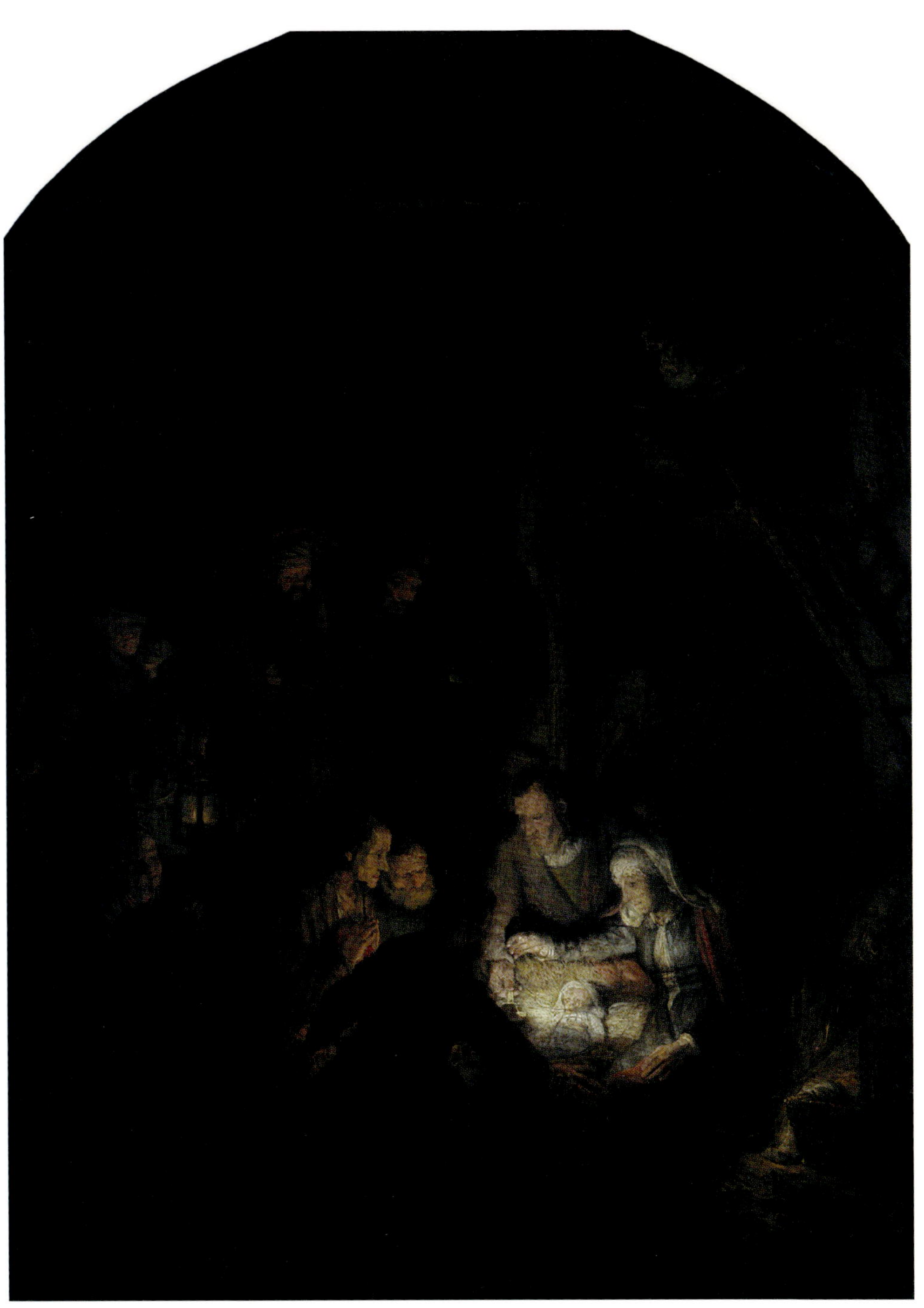

The Adoration of the Shepherds, *1646.*
*The baby Christ seems to radiate light*
*in the darkness of the stable as the*
*shepherds gather around to gaze*
*at him.*

page 76) due to the high price paid for it. The print uses light in a very painterly way, some areas bathed in light while other areas are very dark indeed. The complex composition and the masterly handling of light and dark has led to this work being compared with *The Night Watch* and it has been hailed as one of Rembrandt's best etchings.

The few commissions documented in this period are for history paintings and one of the most important orders that Rembrandt received was from Frederik Hendrik. Seven years after the last delivery of two paintings to him, *The Entombment* and *The Resurrection of Christ*, Rembrandt received a commission for two more paintings: *The Adoration of the Shepherds* (Alte Pinakothek, Munich) and *The Circumcision of Christ*. The commission after such a gap may have had something to do with his brother-in-law, Anthonis Coopal, who was leading a daring plan to capture Antwerp for Frederik Hendrik. He was ultimately unsuccessful in taking Antwerp, but his actions put the family, including Rembrandt, very much in favour. *The Circumcision* was lost and is now known by a copy only. For these paintings, which Rembrandt delivered in 1647, he received 2,400 guilders, more than double the amount he had received for the *Passion Series*. The paintings were the same size and in the same frames as the *Passion Series* and although not part of the series the paintings all hung together. Perhaps Rembrandt would have received more such commissions had Frederik Hendrik not died on 14 March 1647.

These are two of a series of biblical subjects that Rembrandt executed in the 1640s, including several images of the holy family, *The Holy Family with Angels*, 1645 (State Hermitage Museum, St. Petersburg) and *The Holy Family with Painted Frame and Curtain*, 1646 (Gemäldegalerie, Kassel).

His interest in recording landscapes increased significantly during this period. Rembrandt took long walks in the areas around Amsterdam, often sketching the scenery around him. He drew distant views of the city, thatched cottages and trees. He was particularly interested in making landscape etchings. These vary from what look like quick, spontaneous, sketch-like, unfinished works to fully worked, large prints that he printed in several states. During this decade he produced some of his most acclaimed prints, including *The Three Trees* (*see* page 84), his largest and most detailed landscape etching. Despite the family owning a mill, it is surprising that Rembrandt produced only one print of *A Windmill*, 1641.

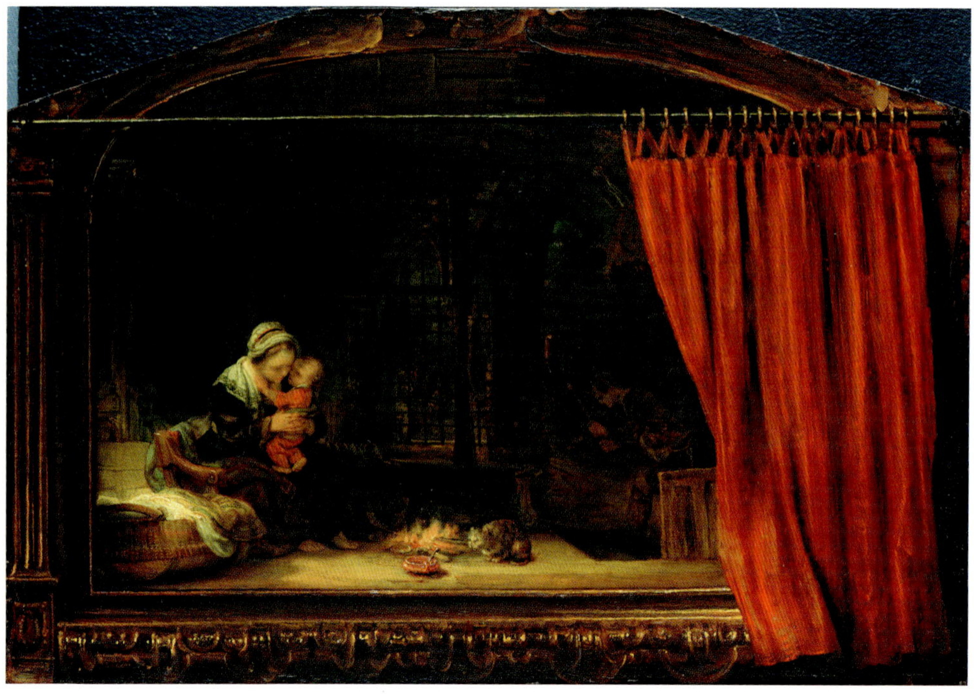

The Holy Family With Painted Frame and Curtain, 1646. *This is a painting of a painting, a curious, but not uncommon illusion found in Dutch art at this time. The painted* trompe-l'oeil *curtain is drawn back to reveal a domestic, genre family scene within a detailed painted frame. A mother holds her child, a cat sits by the small fire and a man chops wood. However, it is in fact a depiction of the Holy family interpreted as a contemporary, everyday scene.*

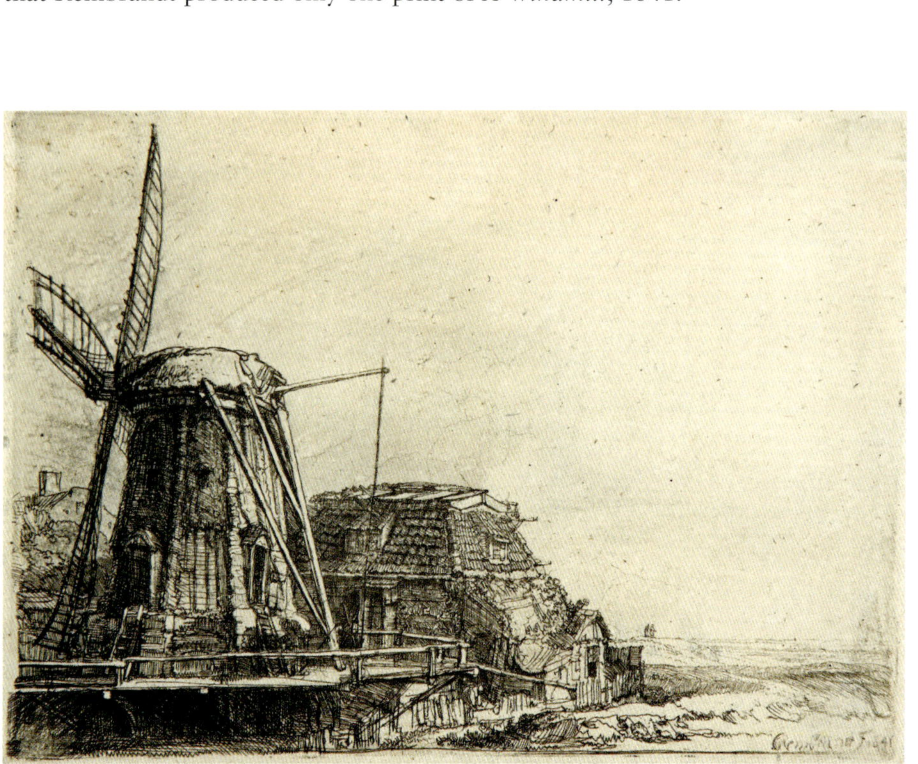

A Windmill, 1641. *For some time, this was thought to depict Rembrandt's family mill in Leiden, but it was later identified as a mill in Amsterdam. Nicknamed the 'The Little Stink Mill', it was used by the guild of leather-makers to soften leather with cod liver oil. He has captured the scene in great detail.*

## THE DUTCH GOLDEN AGE

During the 17th century the Netherlands achieved immense prosperity, coming to the forefront of world trade, as well as science and art, a period now known as the Dutch Golden Age.

In 1568, William I of Orange led the Netherlands in a revolt against King Philip II of Spain, which initiated the Eighty Years' War. The Spanish forces dominated at first but in 1588 the northern, Protestant areas who had successfully fought for and maintained their freedom from Catholic Spain, formed the Republic of the Seven Provinces. However, Spain did not recognize their independence until 60 years later, in 1648.

The new Dutch Republic benefited from substantial numbers of immigrants to its cities, not least the many merchants and traders who fled Antwerp for Amsterdam after it was conquered by Spanish forces in 1585. As a result, Amsterdam was transformed from a small port into the world's leading maritime city to become the centre of world trade. The formation of the East India Company in 1602, the largest commercial enterprise in the world, overseeing more than half of all ocean trade at the time, led to the Dutch Republic dominating both trade and banking. Other cities around Holland also prospered and although Amsterdam was the economic centre, it was The Hague that was the diplomatic and political centre where Stadtholders from the House of Orange sat.

The official religion in the Dutch Republic was Calvinism; the Reformed Church, which was strictly Protestant, valuing hard work and a strong sense of morality. However there remained great tolerance of other religions including other forms of Protestantism, such as Anabaptists, Lutherans and Mennonites, some of whom had been persecuted elsewhere in Europe, as well as Catholics and Jews.

With economic supremacy came a vibrant cultural scene and today the Dutch Golden Age is mainly known as a period of outstanding artistic achievement. Although the painting of religious subjects declined as the Republic broke from Catholic tradition, and Protestant churches forbade religious paintings, there was a proliferation of artists who thrived, producing mainly secular paintings for domestic settings.

In this time of extraordinary creativity, artists such as Frans Hals (1582–1666), Johannes Vermeer (1632–75), Hendrick Goltzius (1558–1617), Jan Steen (1626–79), as well as Rembrandt, all flourished. A new and distinctive feature of the art of this period was that artists tended to specialize in specific genres of painting, painting either history paintings, portraits, scenes of everyday life, landscapes or still-lifes.

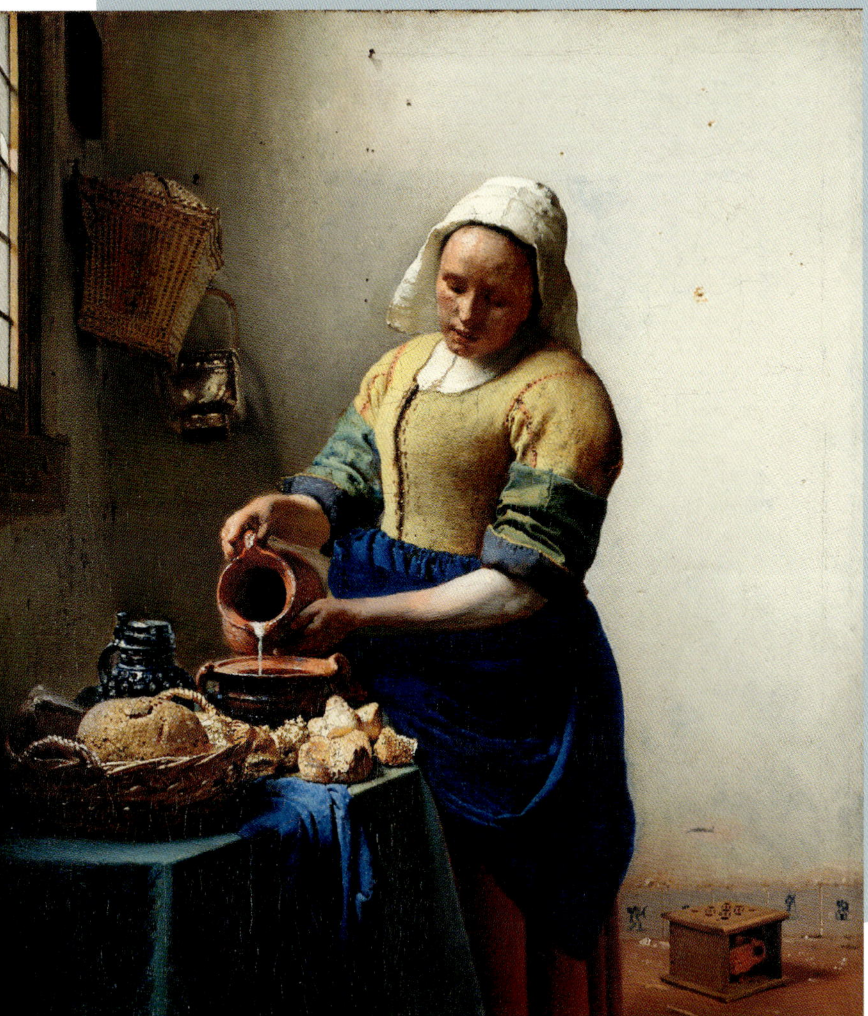

The Milkmaid, *Johannes Vermeer, c.1660. An exquisite painting that captures its subject almost as a still-life, the only movement being the careful pouring of milk into a pot.*

## GEERTJE DIRCKS

Sometime before or just after Saskia's death, Rembrandt hired Geertje Dircks (*c.* 1610–56) as a nanny for Titus. Born in Edam, she was a widow of a ship's trumpeter, who had been living with her brother Pieter, a shipbuilder for the Dutch East India Company before entering Rembrandt's household. At some point, and behind closed doors, Rembrandt and she became lovers.

Links can often be made between Rembrandt's choice of subject for paintings and his own life, and in 1644 he completed the painting *The Woman Taken in Adultery* (National Gallery, London). A weeping woman is brought before Christ in a temple, accused of adultery. The members of the Jewish council plan to trick Christ to speak against Jewish law and say to him, 'Teacher, this woman has been caught in the act of adultery. Now in the law Moses commanded us to stone such some. What do you say about her?' (John 8: 3–7). Rembrandt captures the air of expectation as the crowd await his decision. His reply is one of the most famous quotations of Christianity: 'He that is without sin among you, let him first cast a stone at her.' As was his way, Rembrandt created a most dramatic image: darkness surrounds the woman, who is as brightly lit as the figure of Jesus.

There are no identified portraits of Geertje Dircks, but it is likely that she posed for Rembrandt and she may be the model for the intimate painting *A Woman in Bed, c.1647* (National Galleries Scotland). A woman pulls back the curtain on her bed to see what is happening in the room. The pose is both intimate and very real. The subject is possibly Sarah, wife of Tobias, from the Book of Tobit. She wears a golden headdress and is surrounded by expensive bedding. Rembrandt uses deep shadows and strong light.

*A Woman in a Bed, c.1647. Although the model for this intimate work was perhaps Geertje Dircks, it is probably not a portrait, but a history painting. If it is Sarah, wife of Tobias, Tobias defeated a jealous demon on their wedding night, a creature that had killed her previous seven husbands on the nights of their wedding to her.*

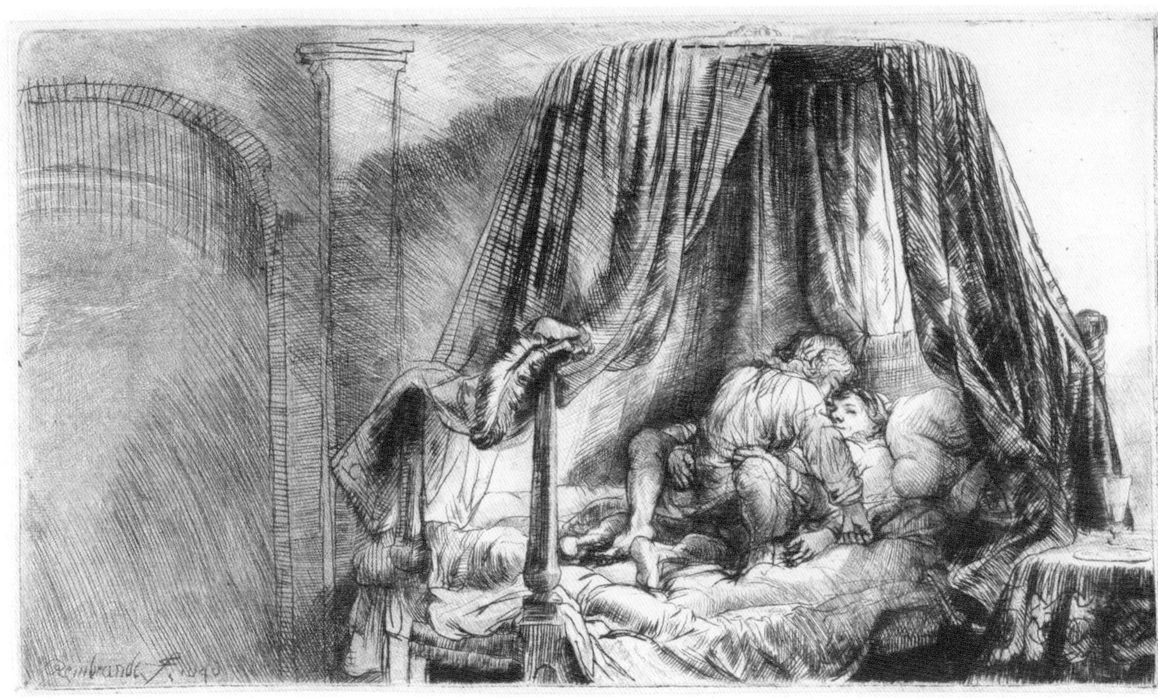

The State Bed
(Het Ledikant),
1646. *This
salacious print
is also known as*
The French-style
Bed.

Rembrandt also produced a number of voyeuristic, erotic images of lovers in the 1640s, including *The Monk in a Cornfield*, *c*. 1646, *The State Bed (Het Ledikant)*, 1646 and even *The Flute Player*, 1642, where a lecherous flute player stares up the skirt of a shepherdess. *The State Bed* shows two lovers in bed, the curtains pulled back to reveal them. The woman has two left arms and it appears that Rembrandt chose not to disguise the alteration. These prints must have shocked some people, but they certainly had a market and an audience.

The relationship between Geertje and Rembrandt carried on for perhaps six years, but came to a very acrimonious, messy end. By the time they separated, another housemaid had joined the household and captured Rembrandt's attention, Hendrickje Stoffels (1626–63).

In January 1648 Geertje made a will in which she left her possessions and in particular her jewellery to Titus. The jewellery had been Saskia's and Rembrandt wanted to ensure that they would come back to the family. She moved out of the house on 15 June 1649 to a small lodging, with an agreement that she could keep the jewels provided she did not sell them, pawn them or change her will, and Rembrandt agreed he would give her 160 guilders and an annual allowance for the rest of her life and help if further funds were needed. She initially agreed to this settlement, but then changed her mind and made a complaint to the Chamber of Matrimonial Affairs

at the city hall. Rembrandt initially refused to attend a hearing and was fined. Geertje had not signed their agreement and now pawned off some of the jewellery to a bargewoman-moneylender in Edam. In the end, both Rembrandt and Geertje appeared before the commissioners. Geertje stated that Rembrandt had made verbal promises to marry her, that he had given her a ring and that they had slept together on numerous occasions. He denied the allegation of a promise of marriage and declined to state whether they had slept together. Even if he had wanted to marry her, Saskia's will prevented this because Rembrandt did not have the funds to pay Saskia's inheritance to his son Titus as was required by the terms of her will. The commissioners believed Geertje to a certain extent, increasing the amount Rembrandt had to pay her to 200 guilders a year.

This, however, was not the end of the story. Geertje assigned her brother Pieter Jansz her legal authority in April 1650, and instead of showing loyalty to his sister, Pieter came to some arrangement with Rembrandt. The two men now collected malicious gossip from neighbours of Geertje who were prepared to swear that she was of unsound mind. In August 1650 Geertje was admitted to the Spinhuis, Gouda, a place of confinement and correction for women judged unstable. The women there included prostitutes, alcoholics, vagabonds and others considered morally fallen, who all lived to a strict routine that included prayers, sermons and endless work spinning wool. She was initially sent there for five years, but Rembrandt tried to extend her detention by eleven years; he failed. Geertje, however, reclaimed legal responsibility for herself and, with the help of a friend, managed to persuade the authorities that she was safe to release on 31 May 1655. No doubt her health had been seriously affected by her time in confinement, for she died not long afterwards.

This whole incident could not have done Rembrandt's reputation any good, as it unfolded in public. He had played a large part in having Geertje committed, which shows an unforgiving, malicious side to his character. The episode also appears to have affected his work, and there are no paintings or etchings dated to the year 1649.

## PORTRAITS

Rembrandt completed very few, if any, painted portrait commissions in the period up to 1652. The reasons for this are unknown and can only be surmised. Presumably it was his choice to step away from portraits, rather than that he received no commissions. Certainly, other artists, including some of his former pupils, such as Govert Flinck (1615–60) and Ferdinand Bol (1616–80), were painting portraits. Rembrandt did, however, complete a number of portrait prints, including one of a fellow artist, the landscape painter *Jan Asselyn* 1647 (see page 83). This included an easel behind the artist in an early state, but Rembrandt later burnished it out. He also etched the physician *Dr Ephraim Buena, Jewish Physician and Writer*, 1647 and made a second etched portrait of Saskia's guardian after his death, *Jan Cornelisz Syvius*, 1646. This second print is much more expressive than his first print dated 1633, and Syvius literally reaches out of the oval surrounding him, casting a shadow with his hand, his bible and his head.

## HENDRICKJE STOFFELS

Hendrickje Stoffels (1626–63) succeeded Geertje as Rembrandt's housemaid and as his mistress. She was born in the east of the country and her father Stoffel Stoffelse was in the army. After he died, her mother remarried and Hendrickje entered into service. Hendrickje was 20 years younger than Rembrandt. She is often cited as the second great love of his life and they stayed together through

*Opposite:* Aristotle with a Bust of Homer, 1653. *Rembrandt has used a dark palette to create this dramatic image. Aristotle pays homage to Homer, his inspiration; he also wears a gold medallion with an image of his own pupil, Alexander the Great, perhaps contemplating his own place in history.*

Portrait of Jan Cornelisz Syvius, Preacher, 1646. *The preacher is shown gesticulating as if mid speech. The text testifies to his eloquent communication skills. The print was commissioned by Sylvius's son after his death.*

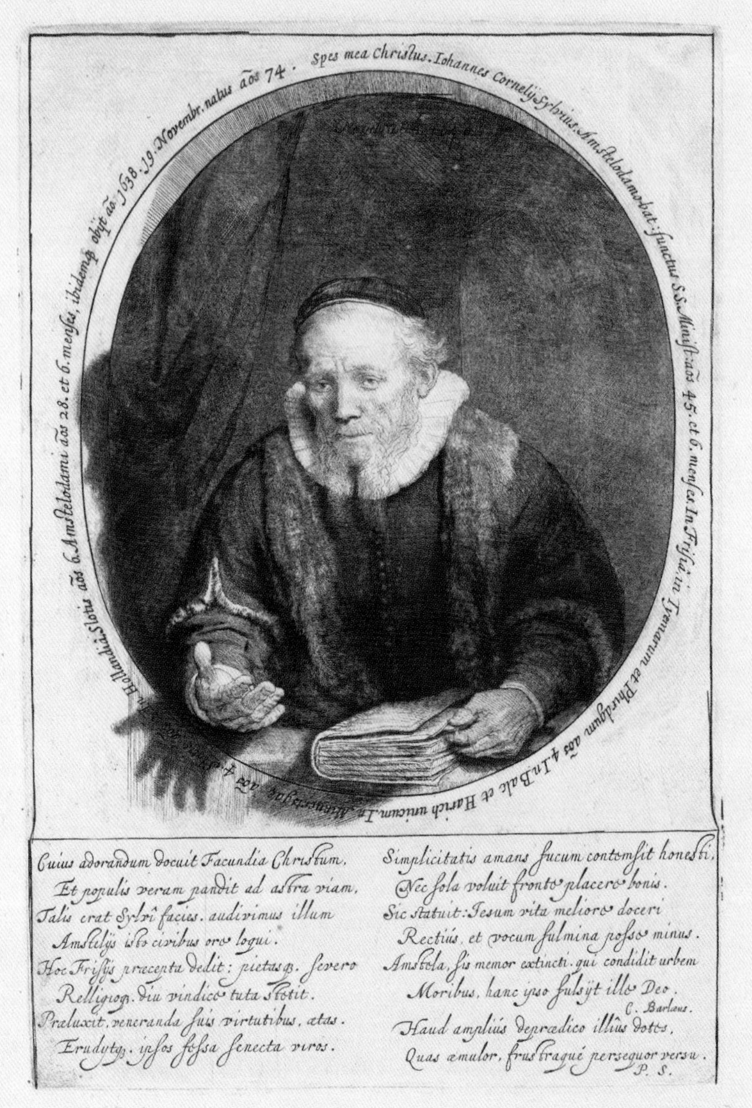

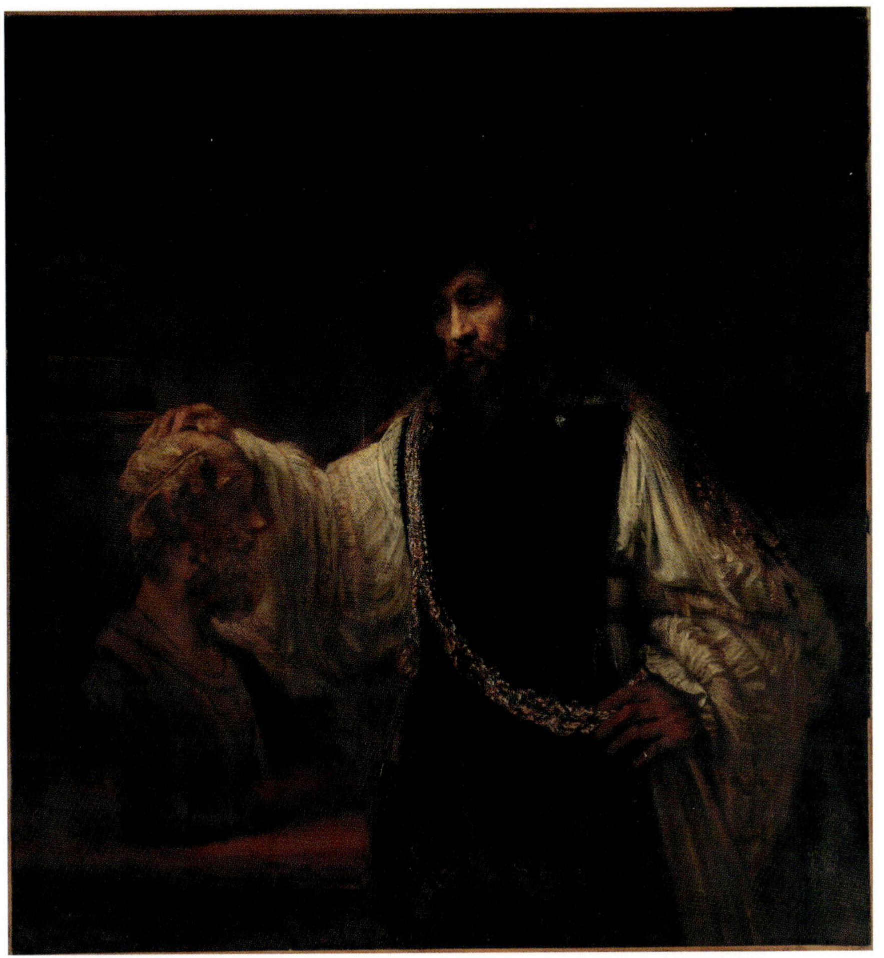

some tough times, as common-law husband and wife until her death.

## FURTHER FINANCIAL PROBLEMS

By the mid-1650s, Rembrandt was undoubtedly being more productive, creating more paintings and etchings. In 1653 he produced two masterpieces, one an oil painting and the other a print. The oil painting, *Aristotle with a Bust of Homer* (The Metropolitan Museum of Art, New York) was commissioned by the nobleman Don Antonio Ruffo, who lived in Messina, Sicily, to where the painting was shipped in 1654. Aristotle, the ancient Greek philosopher, contemplates a bust of the poet he greatly admired: Homer, the author of the *Iliad* and the *Odyssey*. Aristotle places one hand on the bust of Homer, the other on his hip, and holds a chain draped across his body. He is captured deep in thought. Once again, the painting is lit dramatically with an ethereal light that adds to the drama.

In the same year, Rembrandt produced the print *The Three Crosses* (depicting the crucifixion of Christ) and in doing so reached the zenith of his printmaking career. The print was produced using only drypoint – a technique that Rembrandt transformed. It allowed him to create soft velvety lines as the burr left on the incised lines held more ink. On the downside it meant that the plate wore down quickly, so not many impressions could be taken. Once this had happened to this plate, Rembrandt took the unusual step of totally reworking the image, adding numerous diagonal lines, some drawn with a ruler, making it even darker and more dramatic. This would have allowed him to print another edition of the print. Once again Rembrandt created a complex composition, and although he frequently made

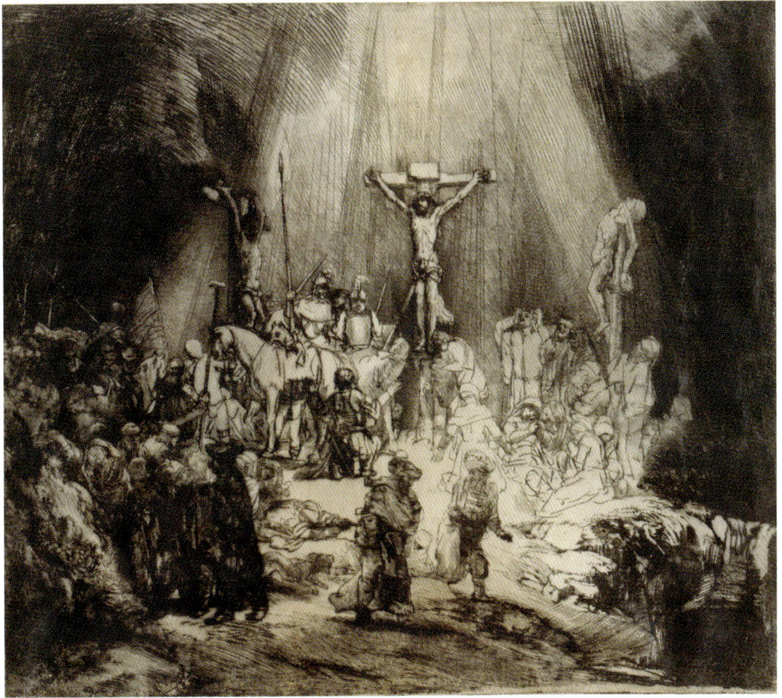

The Three Crosses, *1653.*

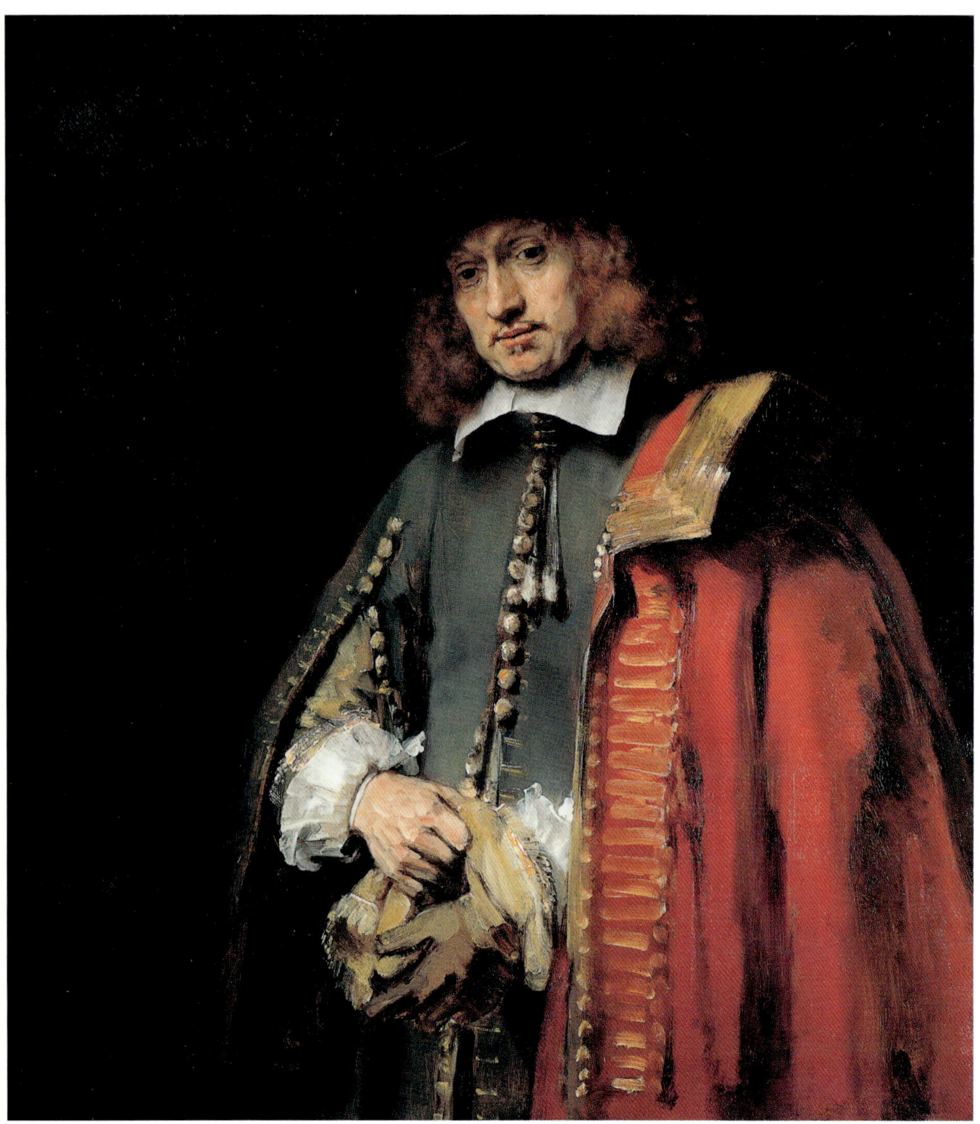

Portrait of Jan Six, 1654. Jan Six was a merchant, magistrate, playwright and an avid patron of the arts and close friend to Rembrandt. He is dressed in a fashionable, long buttoned coat and the low viewpoint means he fills the canvas. Rembrandt painted much of this work with great vigour while also painting some areas, such as the face, in meticulous detail.

changes to his prints, none were as drastic as the alterations he made in the different states of this print.

These commercially successful works could not have come at a better time. Rembrandt was in serious financial trouble. For a decade he had not been taking on lucrative commissions and much of his income was being spent on his art and curiosity collection. By 1649 he had stopped payments on his house and on 11 January 1553 was visited by Christoffel Thijs (1603–80), to whom he still owed over 8,000 guilders. Thijs demanded the outstanding balance for the house, including the taxes that Rembrandt had not been paying. Rembrandt did not have the necessary funds and went to three different friends, including Jan Six (1618–1700), to borrow money, promising each the same security – all his belongings if he didn't pay them back within a year. He borrowed over 9,000 guilders, but paid Thijs only 7,000. Where the remaining money went is unknown, and Rembrandt now owed even more money.

The following year, Jan Six commissioned a three-quarter length, life-size portrait from Rembrandt. This painting is one of the first painted in a much looser manner, often described as Rembrandt's late style. Rembrandt became fascinated with what he could achieve with paint when using a broad brush and leaving brush strokes visible. This is especially prominent on the details of Jan Six's coat. It is a style of painting that he continued to develop for the rest of his career. There are no records of the payment of *Portrait of Jan Six*, which would have cost around 500 guilders, so it is possible it was a gift in lieu of repaying the money he had borrowed.

In the same year, 1654, Hendrickje became pregnant. As a member of the Reformed Church, she was brought before their court on 25 June and accused of living as a whore with Rembrandt. Admitting the arrangement, she was prevented from taking the Eucharist. This was a fairly lenient punishment, but it would still have been a publicly humiliating experience. Rembrandt was not a member of the church. The terms of Saskia's will still prevented him from remarrying, as he was unable to pay Titus's inheritance. She gave birth and their daughter Cornelia was baptized on 30 October. It was the third time that he had named a daughter Cornelia, and this time she survived childhood.

Rembrandt painted a portrait of *Bathsheba at her Bath* (The Louvre, Paris), the infamous adulteress from the Old Testament, in the same year. She is shown having read and still holding King David's letter, deep in thought, her eyes cast down as she contemplated her fate. Perhaps once again, he had painted a subject to reflect his own situation and life from Hendrickje's perspective. In this year he also painted *A Woman Bathing in a Stream*, a tender and intimate painting of a woman up to her shins in a stream. She lifts her slip up high and looks down in delight at the water. A loose curl of hair falls on her neck. There is no official portrait of Hendrickje, but this same model appears in several works and it is likely to be her. If so, it is a sensual, sensitive and informal image of his common-law wife and mother to his child.

In 1655 Rembrandt painted another *Self-Portrait* (Bridgewater Collection, on loan to the National Galleries Scotland), when he was nearly 50 years old. Unlike early self-portraits in which Rembrandt was capturing a likeness, using himself as a model, this portrait seems to be more about the viewer looking into his soul, seeing the person. He looks troubled and he was: in serious financial difficulty, having made some bad decisions. He had loans he couldn't pay back and was trapped, unable to marry Hendrickje. On top of that the economy was in sharp decline due to the First Anglo-Dutch War (1652–54), which meant less demand for works of art and commissions – and less opportunity for Rembrandt to recover from this financial strife.

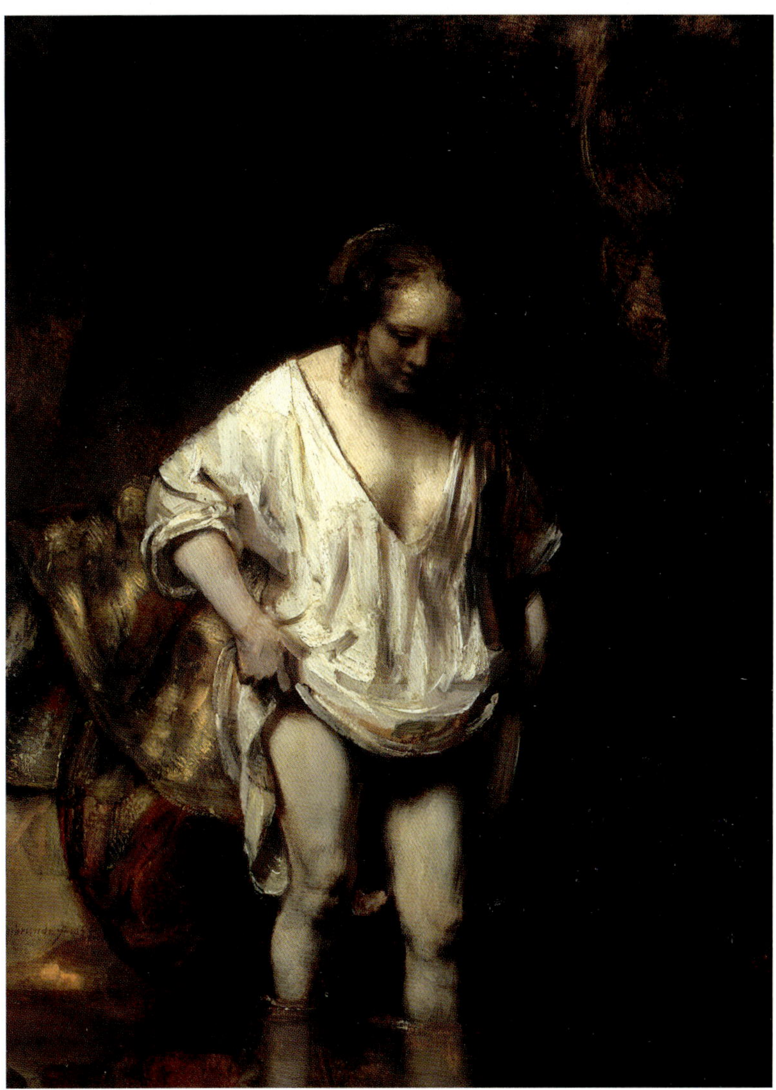

A Woman Bathing in a Stream, *1654. This is a very immediate and affectionate painting that is likely to depict Hendrickje Stoffels. The painting is bathed in a warm light and Rembrandt has successfully captured the effect of the water rippling against her legs.*

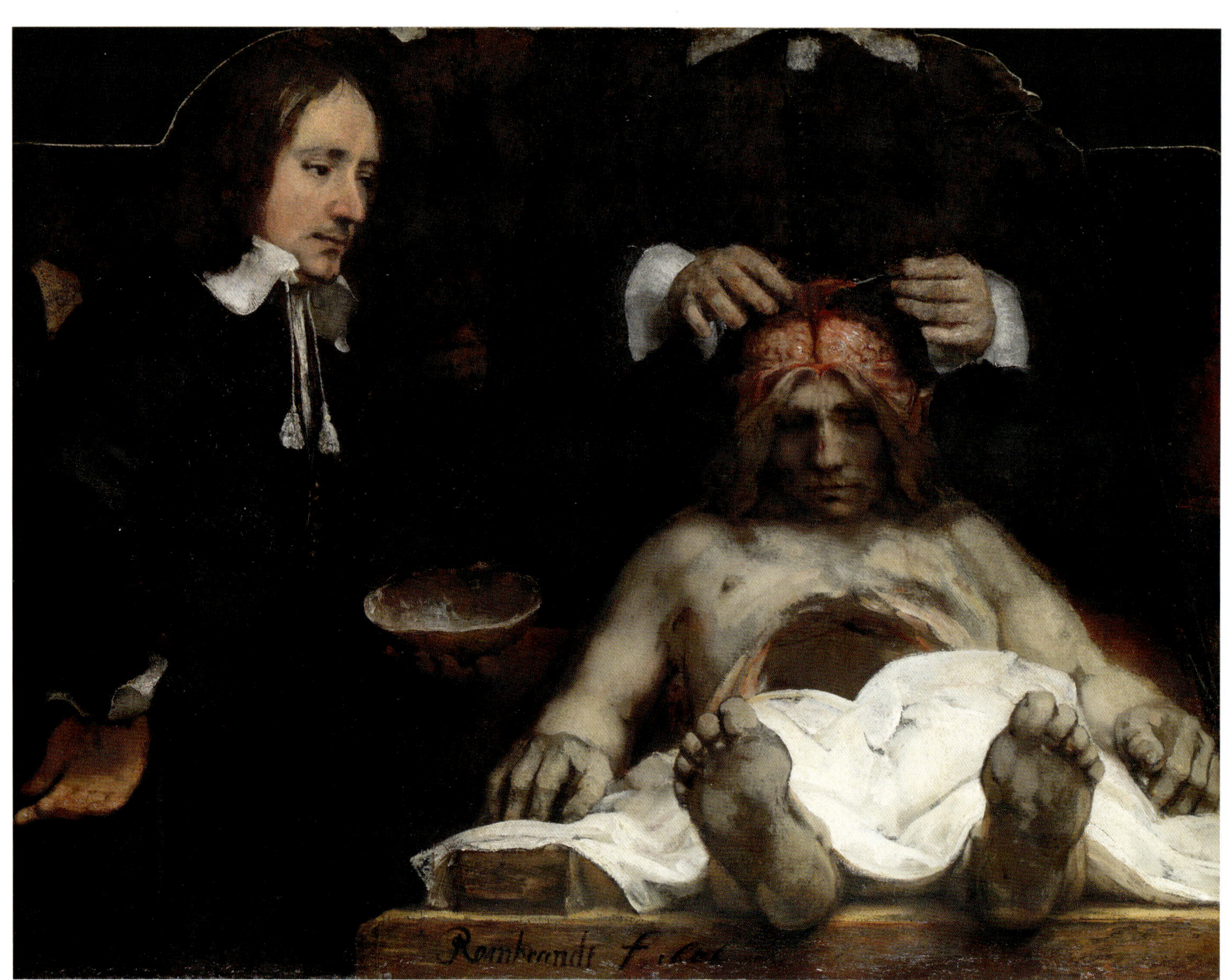

The Anatomy Lesson of Dr Jan Deyman, 1656, *cut down after being damaged by fire in 1723.*

# CHAPTER 4

# The Later Years, 1656–69

## INSOLVENCY

Rembrandt was up to his neck in debt, he had borrowed money that he could not pay back and he was at risk of debtor's prison. In December 1655 he rented a room at an inn and put some of his possessions up for sale – there are no details of what he sold or how much money he made, although he didn't pay the debt for renting the room. He was taking steps to plan for insolvency, and on 17 May 1656 he transferred ownership of his house to his son Titus – in an attempt to protect it, himself and his family, and to pay Titus's inheritance.

Only a couple of months later he went to the town hall in Amsterdam to the Chamber of Insolvency to apply for *cession bonorum*, voluntarily declaring himself insolvent and putting himself in the hands of the city. Although this must have been a shameful occasion for him, it protected him from further personal claims. Rembrandt had to surrender all his property and goods, to be sold to pay off his debtors. On 26 July 1656, a detailed inventory was drawn up of all his assets. This lists all the possessions in his house, room by room, and Rembrandt is likely to have assisted as the inventory is very detailed. For historians this document gives a wonderfully detailed account, of how Rembrandt's house was laid out and used and of the paintings and objects in his collection.

The auctioning off of his possessions took two years to complete. The first sale brought in just 1,322 guilders, a drop in the ocean of what he owed. At one sale in 1658 Titus was sent to buy back at least one object, a large mirror with an ebony frame – perhaps it was an heirloom or the mirror Rembrandt used for his self-portraits. Whatever the sentimental value, the mirror fell to pieces and was destroyed in transit back to his house. Unfortunately, the sales only generated money to repay about a third of his dept and, despite his best efforts, the house was put up for sale at the insistence of one of his debtors. Rembrandt, Hendrickje, Titus and Cornelia moved out of the grand house to a small, rented house at 184 Rozengracht. This was a far less salubrious neighbourhood of Amsterdam, inhabited mainly by tradesmen and retailers.

## LATER PAINTING

Despite all these troubles, upheaval and uncertainty, Rembrandt somehow continued to paint and produced some original and powerful paintings during this period. In 1655 he completed the extraordinary painting *The Slaughtered Ox* (The Louvre, Paris), showing a carcass strung up. It is painted with great energy with short dense brushstrokes and is a very eerie painting (see page 88).

The following year he secured an important commission for an anatomy demonstration, *The Anatomy Lesson of Dr. Jan Deyman*, 1656, (Amsterdam Museum). This was his second such commission, the first being *The Anatomy Lesson of Dr. Nicaolaes Tulp*, 1632 (*see* page 28). The painting was severely damaged in a fire in 1723, so only a small central fragment remains, but it shows just how powerful the painting must have been. A brain is being dissected and the corpse lies heavy, the body at right angles to the picture plane. It is painted with great foreshortening, the feet appearing to stick out of the painting. The body is reminiscent of a dead Christ. If compared to the 1632 painting, it shows just how much Rembrandt's painting style had changed. Like many of his late paintings, his brushwork is much looser and he seems to be conveying much more human emotion.

Rembrandt also painted his son Titus, as he did all his family members, capturing him in a painting called *Titus at his Desk*, 1655 (Museum Boijmans Van Beuningen, Rotterdam), and in a portrait print *c*.1656. He also used him as a model in *Titus in Monk's Habit*, 1660 (Rijksmuseum, Amsterdam), (see page 66), in which he is dressed as a Franciscan monk, perhaps even St Francis. Titus may well have been helping Rembrandt in the studio at this time.

In 1658 Rembrandt painted an extraordinary *Self-Portrait* (Frick Collection, New York). He was now 52 and over the last two years had faced the humiliation of bankruptcy, having to part with his house, paintings and his collection and many of his friends and contacts. Despite all of this, he paints himself as an artist at the top of his game, in the manner of a monarch with golden robes, sitting on a chair like a throne and holding a painter's stick like a sceptre. The painting gleams. It is built up with layers of paint and shows the artist sombre but still prominent, full of life. He painted in thick dramatic strokes, leaving the brushwork visible. No other artist was painting in this way at this time.

Still at risk from creditors, the family came up with a plan in 1660 to further protect any income. Titus and Hendrickje formed an art company 'in paintings, graphic arts, engravings and woodcuts, as well as prints, curiosities, and all related objects' and their sole employee was Rembrandt. This protected any money from sales and commissions, and may not have been totally legitimate, but was an attempt to protect his family.

It is probable that Rembrandt's printing press was sold in the insolvency auctions: he did not produce as many prints after moving out of his grand house. It is also likely that he sold his copper printing plates. Many of these would no longer have been any good for printing because they would have been too worn down, but they would still have been collectors' items to print specialists.

Rembrandt was no longer the fashionable artist he had once been, though he was still highly respected in many circles and could still command commissions from important patrons. His patrons had aged with him and now many were from the older generation

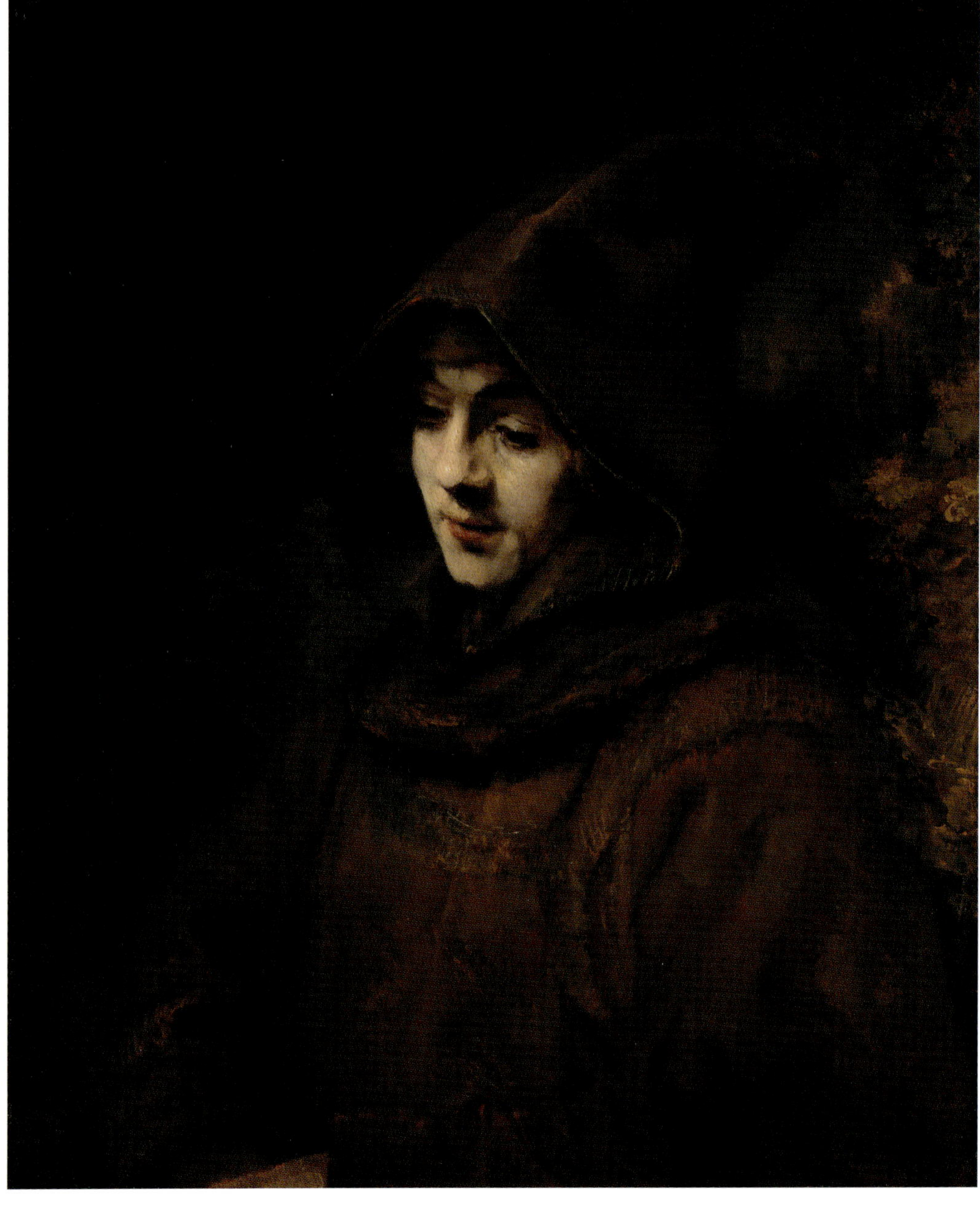

Titus in Monk's Habit, 1660. *Titus wears a brown habit with a peaked hood worn by Franciscan monks. It is one of a number of single-headed religious paintings from this time.*

in Amsterdam. In 1661 he was commissioned by the prominent Trip family for two large-scale likenesses, *Portrait of Jacob Trip* and *Portrait of Margaretha de Geer*, 1661 (National Gallery, London). They had been married for 60 years and were among the wealthiest people in the Netherlands. Rembrandt had previously been commissioned to paint other members of the family, and these new commissions were to be hung together in a palazzo being built in Amsterdam for their sons. It was usual for companion portraits, such as these, to be symmetrical, each sitter in a mirrored pose and gesturing to the other. Jacop is painted turning to the right, but Rembrandt decided to paint

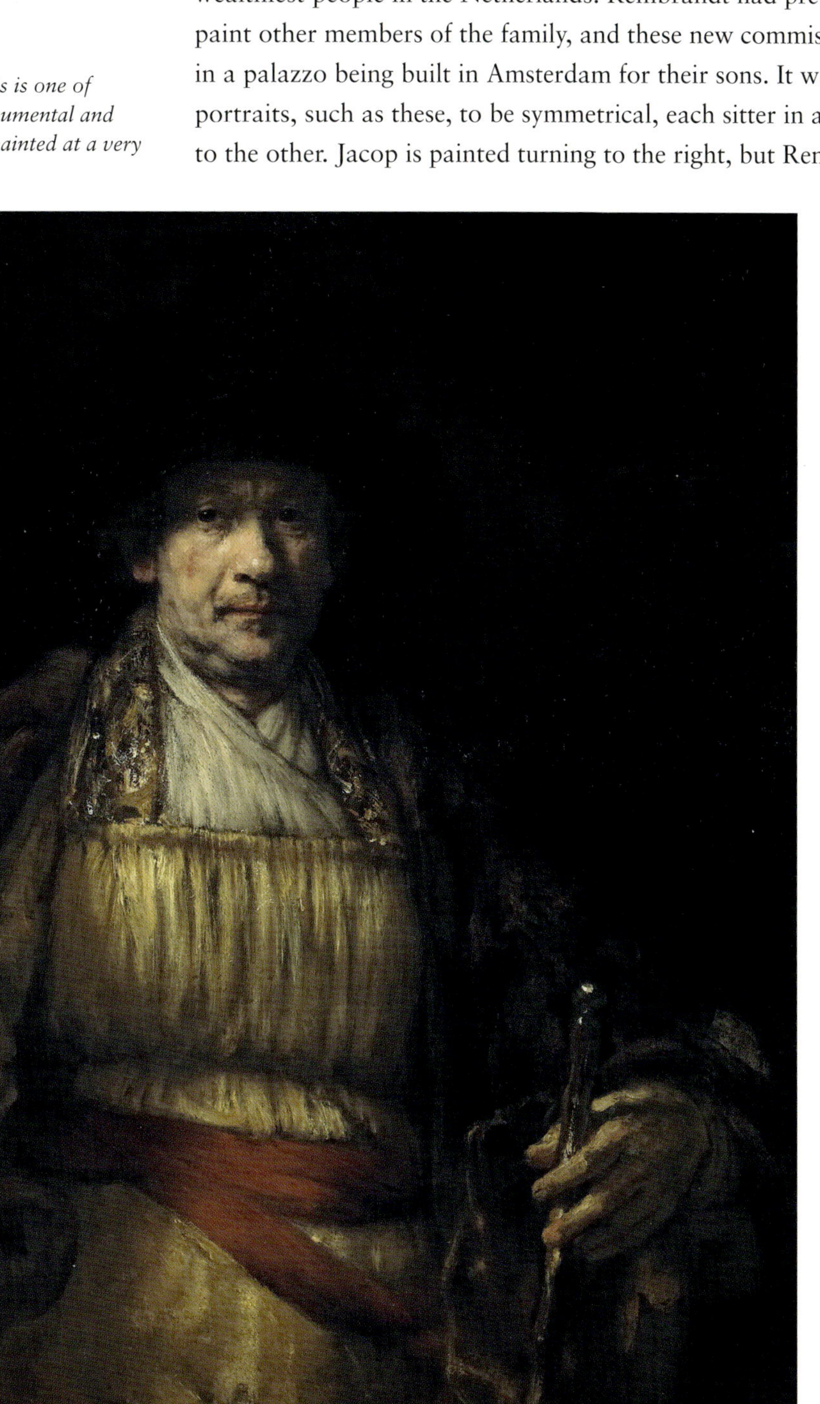

Self-Portrait, 1658. *This is one of Rembrandt's most monumental and majestic self-portraits painted at a very difficult time in his life.*

Margaretha face-on, looking directly at the viewer. She is painted with an air of authority and gravitas, but Rembrandt has not shied away from depicting her age; she was about 78 and her face shows the effects of the ageing process. Rembrandt was particularly skilful at capturing the face, with all the lines and wrinkles and inevitable sagging, and was able to paint skin realistically. This is one of many portraits of women that he painted with great empathy, depicting them as individuals with their own characters. He almost seems to champion the women in his portraits.

As part of a series of works of individual portraits of biblical figures that included St Batholomew and St James, Rembrandt painted himself as an apostle, *Self-Portrait as Apostle Paul*, 1661 (Rijksmuseum, Amsterdam). Although he was using himself as a model, this painting is certainly a portrait of the artist. He sees the ageing process in his own face with sagging cheeks and

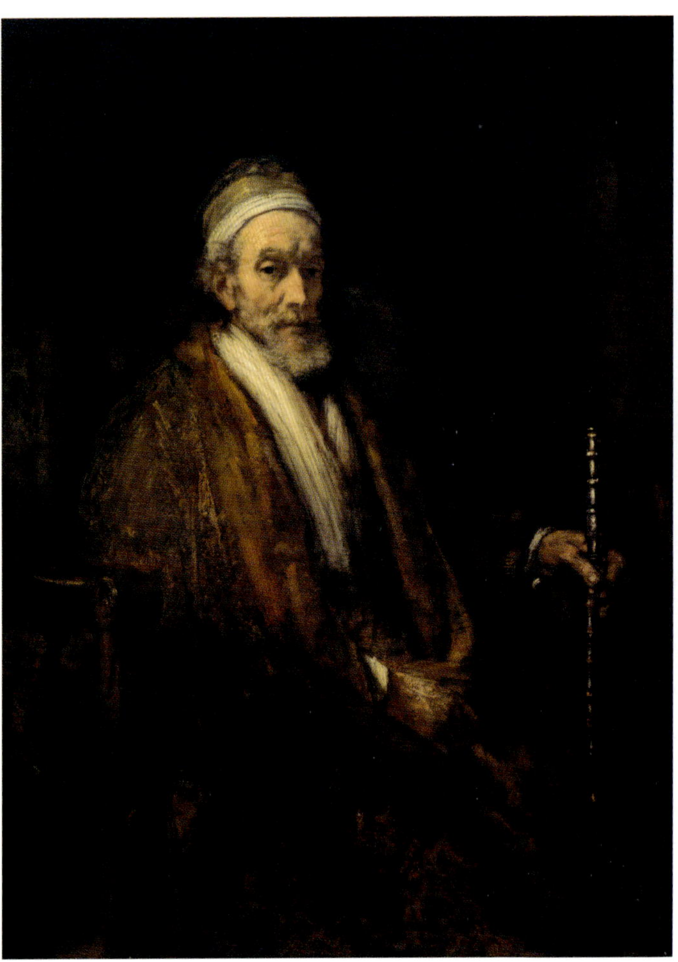

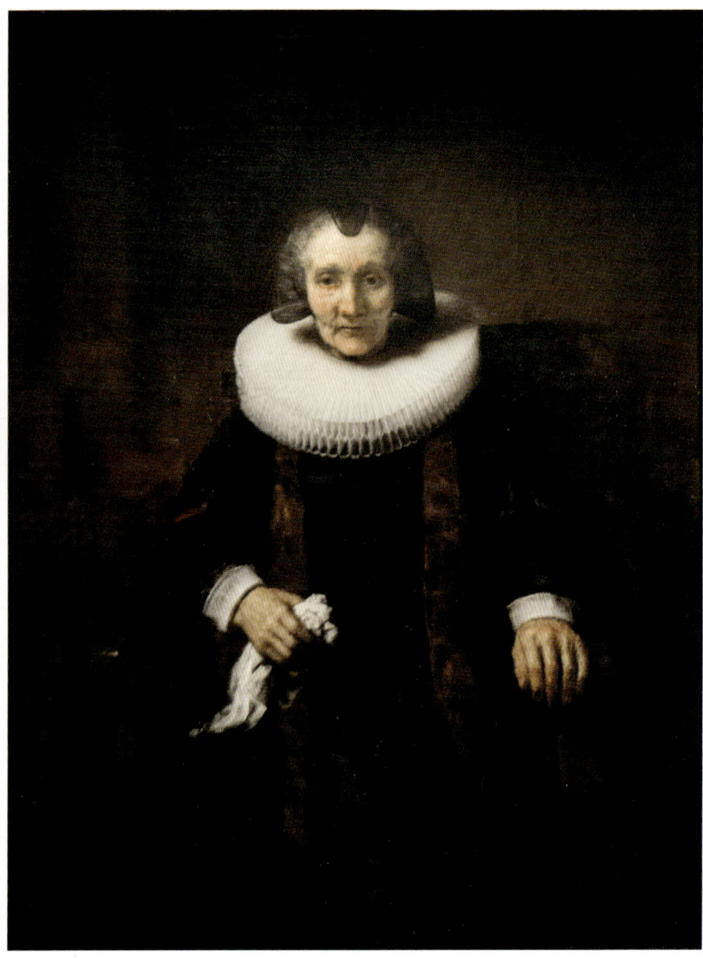

greying hair. In areas, the painting appears swiftly painted – the turban is captured in only a few brush strokes – but even so, the painting has depth. Rembrandt is inviting the viewer to see him as he is, to see the truth.

## THE CONSPIRACY OF THE BATAVIANS UNDER CLAUDIUS CIVILIS

In 1656 Rembrandt had missed out when authorities were looking for artists to decorate the rooms of the newly built City Hall. It was a wonderful opportunity at a time of economic downturn and some of his past pupils were more successful in securing these important commissions. They were painting in styles much more akin to Rembrandt's early painting style, creating highly finished, Rubenesque works.

In November 1659, Rembrandt again missed out on a very prestigious contract for eight enormous canvasses for the building, which instead was given to his pupil Govert Flinck. Flinck died of the plague in 1660 when the work was still in the planning and design stage, so the burgomasters decided to hand out commissions for the individual paintings at 1,200 guilders a painting. Rembrandt got the contract to paint one of the works in the series, *The Conspiracy of the Batavians under Claudius Civilis* (National Gallery, Stockholm). This was the first painting in the series from the Batavian Rebellion when a small group of Batavians rose against the Romans, a romanticized story regarding the very beginnings of the Netherlands. The one-eyed chieftain Claudius Civilis led the chiefs and the 'boldest spirits of the lower class' to swear an oath to join in rebellion. The commission was a wonderful opportunity and the chance to have a painting in a new, prestigious location. The greatest commission for Rembrandt since *The Night Watch*, it was certainly the largest at 5.5 × 5.5 m (18 × 18 ft). Unfortunately, it proved a total disaster. Rembrandt delivered the painting, which was hung in place sometime before 21 July 1662, only to be taken down again a couple

*Opposite left:* Jacop Trip, 1661. *Tripp made his fortune as an arms dealer. Here he is shown dressed informally and has a quiet, contemplative, wise aura. He died around the time that this painting was commissioned.*

*Opposite right:* Marguerite de Geer, 1661. *In contrast to her husband, Marguerite's portrait has much more energy and she meets the viewer's gaze head on.*

of months later, on 24 September 1662 and replaced by an earlier watercolour and charcoal work on the same theme by Flinck. Either the Burgomasters were so disappointed with the final product that they didn't even ask for alterations, or Rembrandt was unwilling to make them. There is no record of him receiving payment.

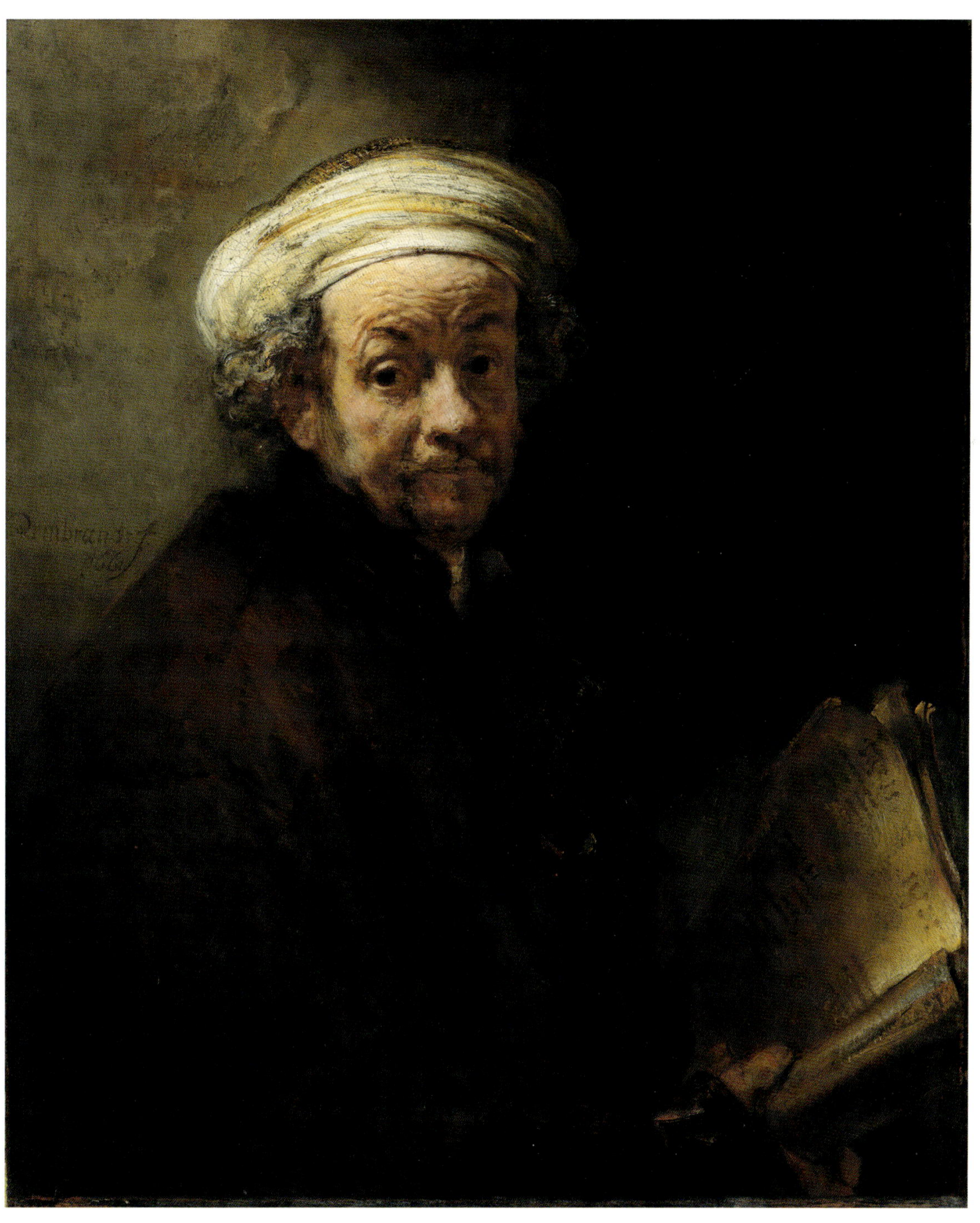

Self-Portrait as the Apostle Paul, *1661. This painting belongs to a series of portraits of biblical figures from the late 1650s to the 1660s. Rembrandt had a particular interest in the Apostle Paul and painted numerous representations of him. Here, he has depicted himself in the role, holding a manuscript and a sword, the saint's attributes.*

We can only speculate about why the painting was rejected. It was probably a combination of reasons: the lack of grandeur in his treatment of the subject, the painting's style and technique, and the composition. Instead of the usual grand and noble paintings, Rembrandt chose to paint the scene realistically, showing Claudius Civilis with only one eye – a detail that was factually correct, but which most artists chose to ignore. He also showed the Batavians not as heroes but as ordinary, real people, each with different facial expressions and poses. This painting was in a very different style to the other paintings commissioned, loose and painterly rather than polished and highly finished. Against the other works it might have looked unfinished. The composition may also have been seen as unsuitable for the intended location of the work, high up on a large wall: the figures around the table were in the centre of the painting and not large at all in relation to the size of the canvas. Some time after it was returned to him, Rembrandt cut the painting down, probably to make it more saleable. Just the central table and figures now remain. It

was a huge opportunity missed. Rembrandt's painting was certainly unique and experimental, but too much in the end for the commissioners.

In 1662 Rembrandt was also commissioned to paint another group portrait known as *Syndics of the Draper's Guild*, or *The Sampling Officials* (Rijksmuseum, Amsterdam), a portrait of the sampling officials of the Amsterdam Drapers Guild. These officials met three times a week to check the quality of the blue and black dyed cloth sold by members. Rembrandt made numerous alterations to the composition of the figures in this work until the final positions were decided upon. All the figures stare directly out as if the viewer has interrupted their meeting. The viewer becomes part of the narrative. So different to *The Conspiracy of the Batavians under Claudius Civilis* is this painting in both style and finish, that they could have been painted at totally different times, not in the same year. This painting is realistic, the figures looking like they live and breathe. The table is very foreshortened and appears

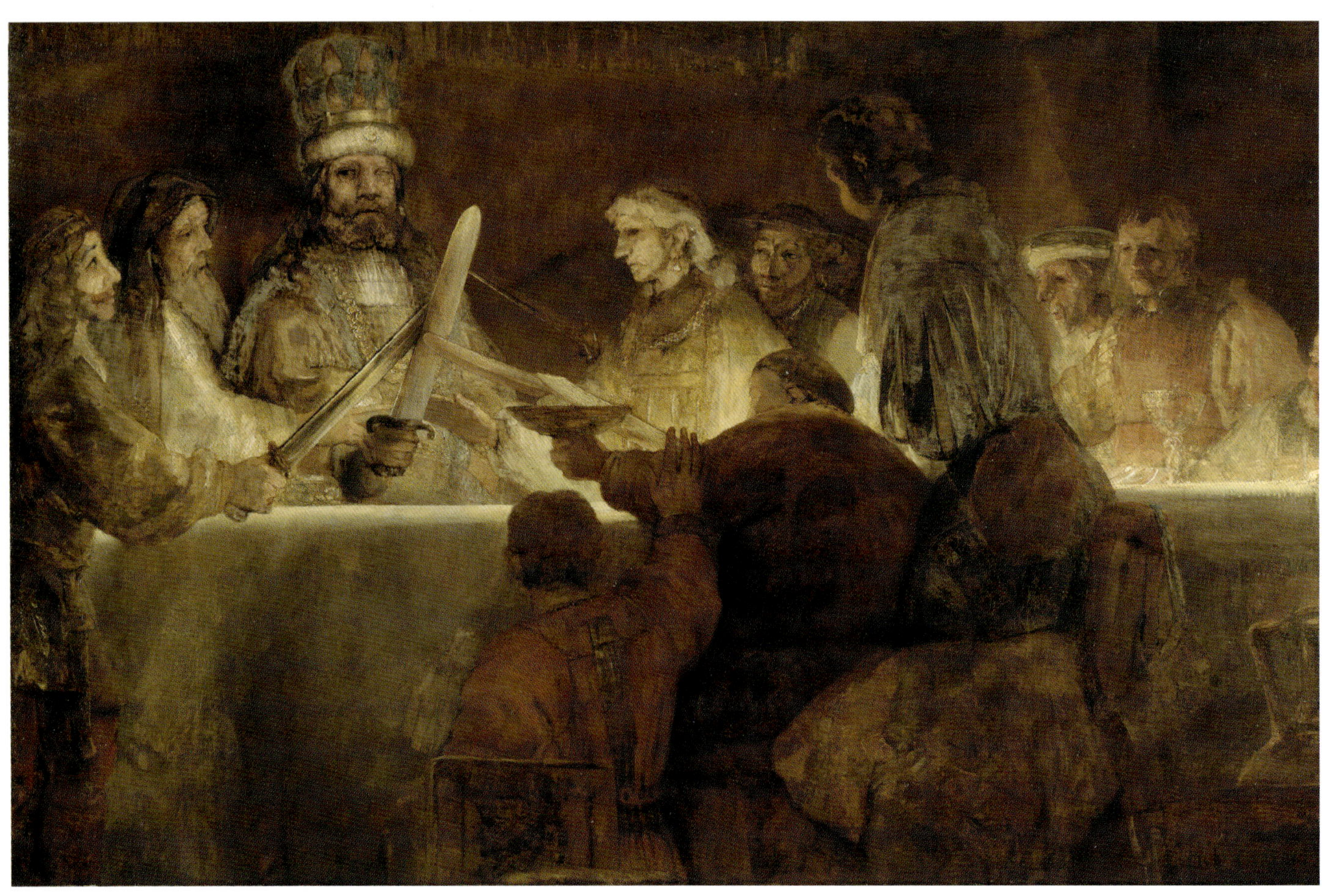

to jut out into the viewer's space. We can almost sense the thickness of the table carpet. This painting had a much more successful outcome for Rembrandt.

Rembrandt secured further important commissions at this time. In particular, he must have been pleased when his Sicilian patron Don Antonio Ruffo, who had purchased *Aristotle with a Bust of Homer*, 1653, commissioned two further paintings in 1661 and 1663, both of which were shipped to his palazzo in Sicily. The painting *Alexander the Great*, 1662 was lost in a fire that also seriously damaged the second commission, *Homer Dictating to His Scribes* (Mauritshuis, The Hague)

*Opposite: The Conspiracy of Claudius Civilis: the Oath, 1661–2. It was significantly cut down from the original vast canvas.*

*Below: The Sampling Officials of the Drapers' Guild (The Syndics), 1662.*

## DEATH OF HENDRICKJE STOFFELS

Financially Rembrandt was still struggling: he owed money to many people, and had taken another loan of 537 guilders from Harmen Becker, who specialized in loans to struggling artists. In 1660 Hendrickje wrote a will appointing Rembrandt as Cornelia's sole guardian in the event of her death. In 1662 Rembrandt sold Saskia's grave in the Oude Kerk, to raise funds, but only a year later he was burying the second love of his life, Hendrickje, who died of the plague that swept through Amsterdam that year. She was buried on 24 July 1663 in a rented grave that cost 10 guilders. Hendrickje and Rembrandt had been together for 15 years and she had stood by him throughout all his troubles, been a mother to Titus and their own child Cornelia, but had never been able to marry him due to the restrictions of Saskia's will.

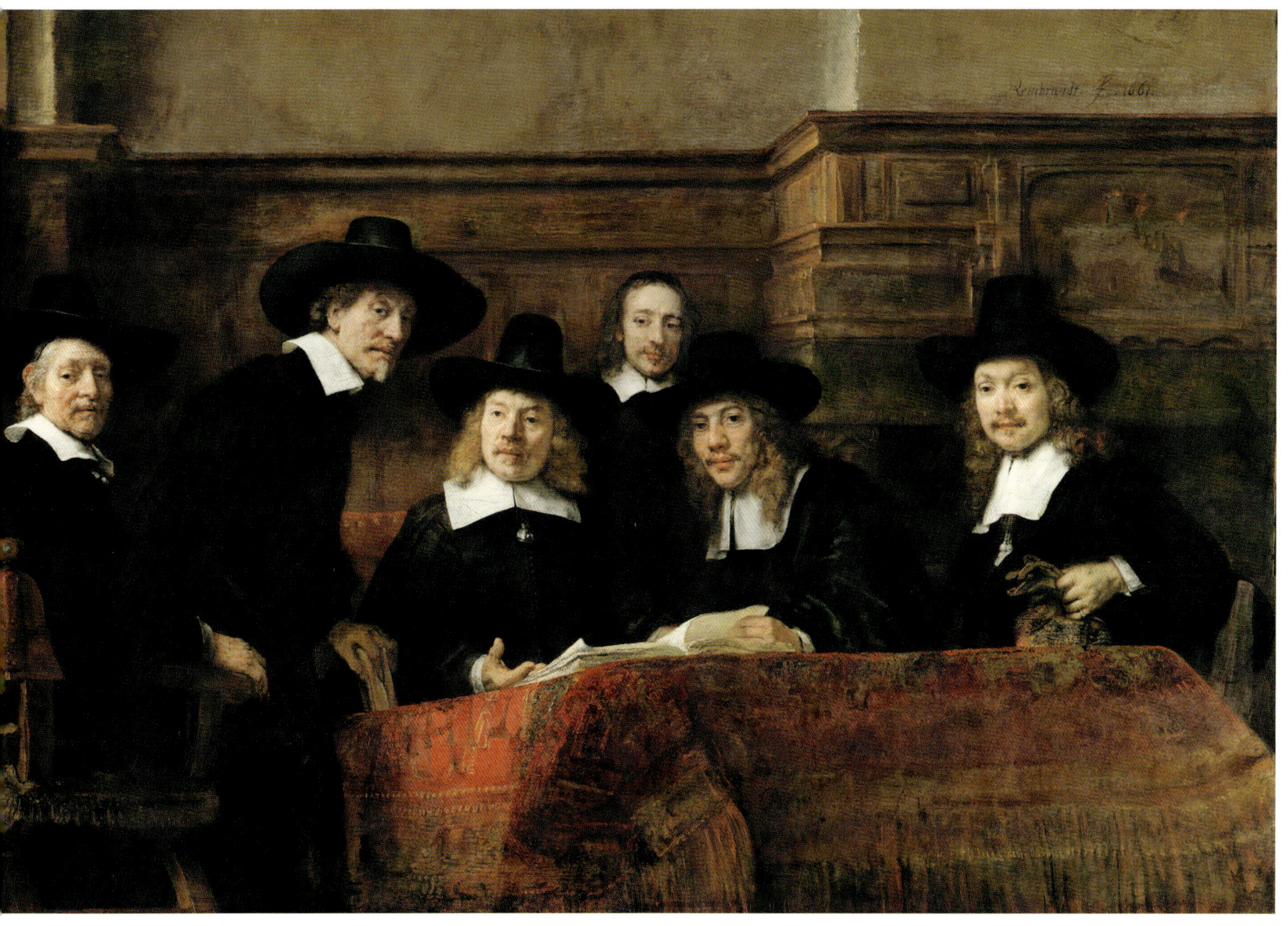

# THE JEWISH BRIDE

The sitters in this poignant painting are unknown, but is thought that they may have wanted to be painted as historical figures within a marriage portrait. It is believed to be a depiction of Isaac and Rebekah, who feared for their lives in a land ruled by King Abimelech, and pretended to be brother and sister. But Abimelech looked out of a window and saw them touching. Nonetheless, he ordered his people not to lay a hand on the couple. As the king is not included in the painting, the viewer is involved in the narrative, perhaps taking on this role. The painting captures an instinctive, tender moment between a couple as the man places his hand on his wife's breast and she brings her own hand up to touch his. When Vincent van Gogh first saw the painting in 1885, he is reported as saying that he would gladly give

The Jewish Bride, *c.1665.*

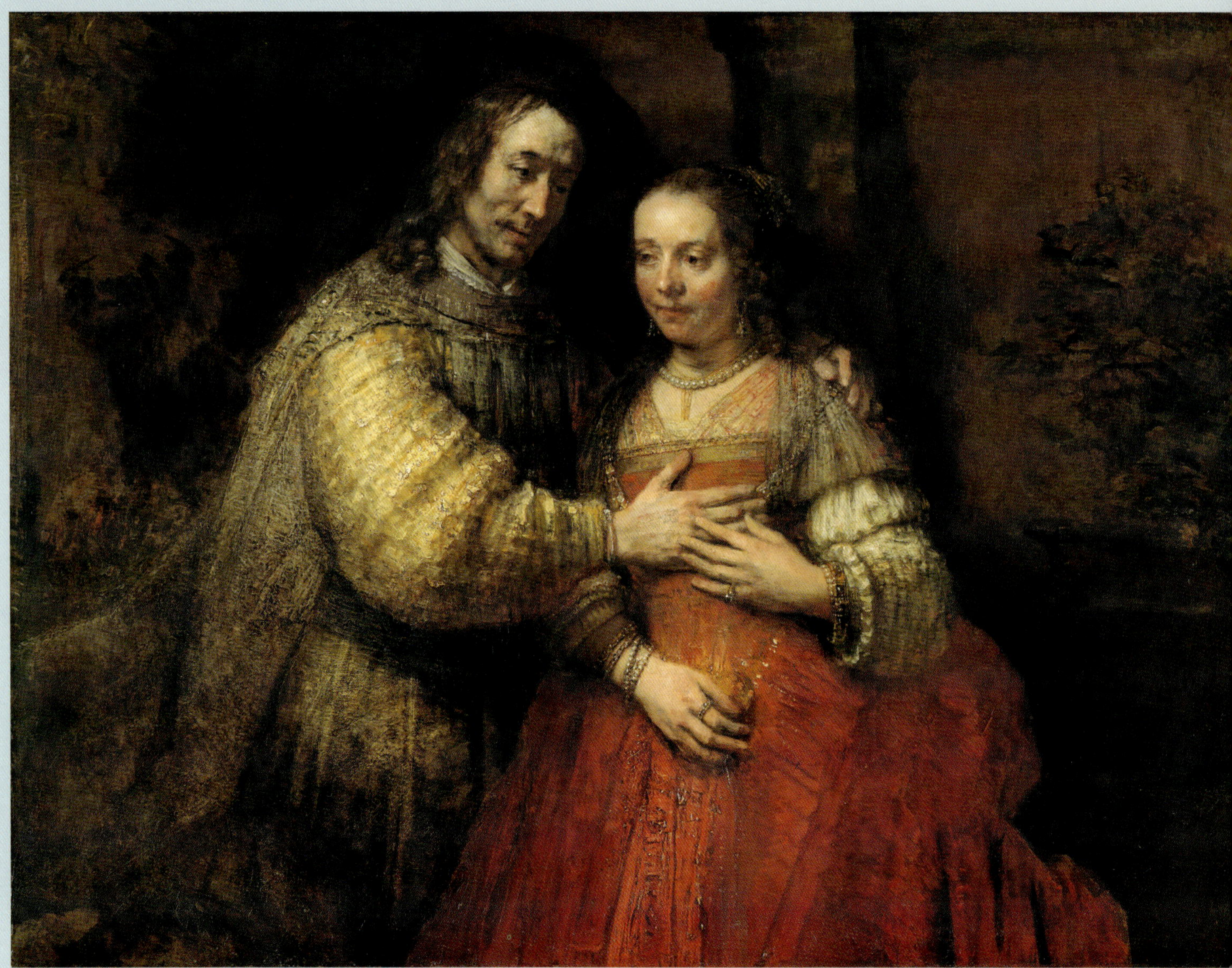

up 10 years of his life to be able to sit in front of it for a fortnight with only a crust of dry bread to eat. He wrote to his brother Theo: 'What an intimate, what an infinitely sympathetic painting.' The intimacy is all in the touch of the hands, that is brilliantly framed by the other hands, the man placing his on her shoulder and she placing her own on her hip. He painted the same couple again *c.*1666 in *A Family Group* (Herzog Anton Ulrich-Museum, Braunschwig), which includes the couple's three children. The tender touch is now not between man and wife but between mother and child. Rembrandt has expressed so much meaning and love in such a simple gesture.

The painting of *The Jewish Bride* must also have brought up thoughts of Rembrandt's own relationship with Hendrickje. Isaac was 40 and much older than Rebekah when they married just as Rembrandt was 40 and 20 years older than Hendrickje when they had met.

The painting was executed in a remarkable way, creating a richly textured painting. As well as scratching into wet surface, Rembrandt seems to sculpt the paint with a palette knife, creating areas of deep impasto. This technique is particularly prominent in Isaac's sleeve: looked at closely, it appears abstract and impressionistic and was well advanced of its time. Rembrandt continued to experiment in his paintings and was painting some of his most expressive paintings at this late point in his career.

A Family Group, *c. 1666–68.*

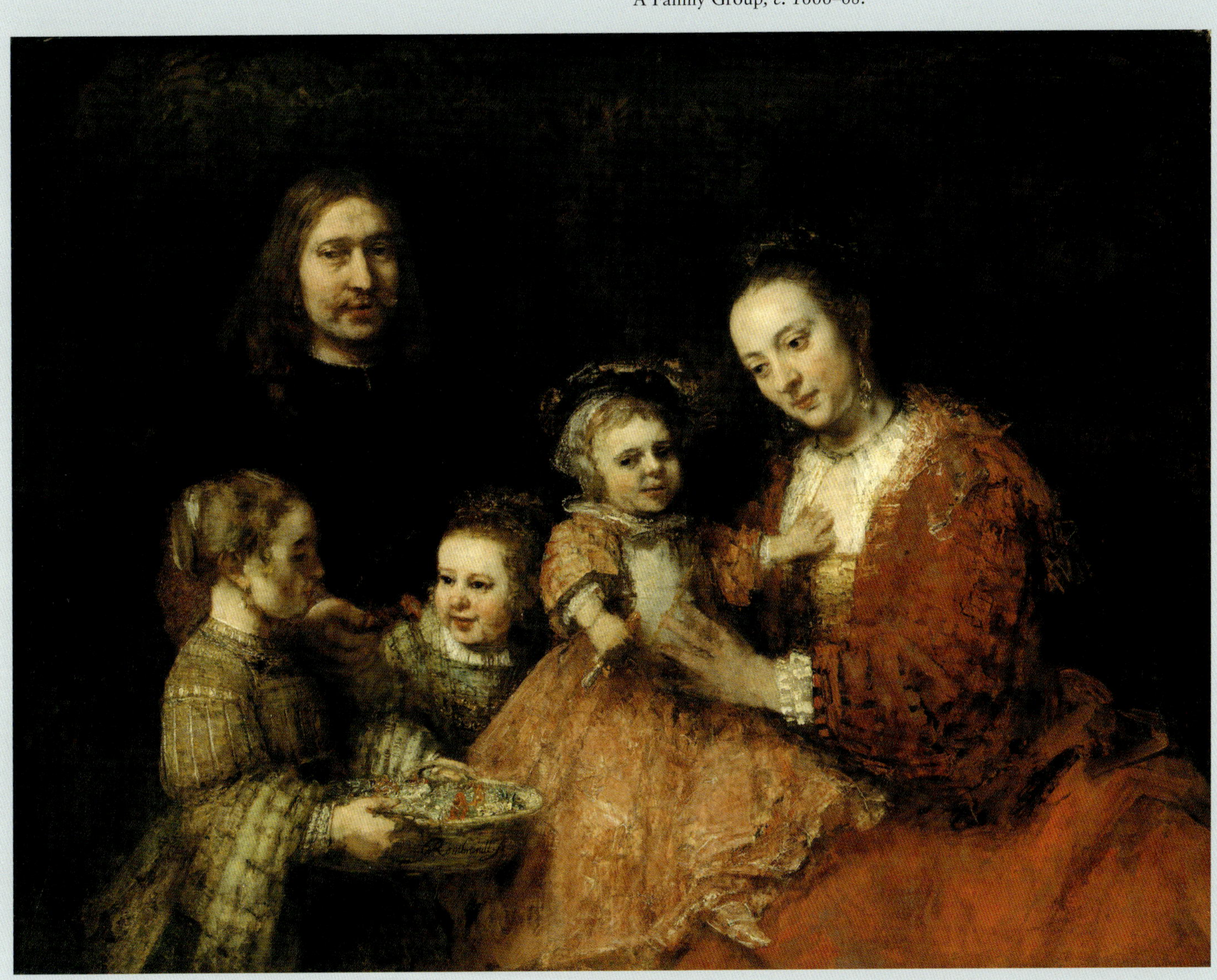

Rembrandt continued to paint and was completing a significant number of paintings at this time, including an extraordinarily moving and beautiful painting, *The Jewish Bride*, c. 1665–1669 (Rijksmuseum, Amsterdam). In 1665 he painted one of the largest and most mysterious of his self-portraits, *Self-Portrait with Two Circles* (Kenwood House). Like many of his late self-portraits this work is less about the form: gone are the costumes of his early portraits, in favour of simple clothes and a plain white hat. In this painting he is presenting himself as the artist, holding the tools of his trade – a palette, brushes and mahlstick. He stares directly out, with a brutally honest depiction of his ageing face. Behind him are two incomplete circles, the reason for these unknown. Always the innovative painter, this work combines some areas where the paint has been swiftly applied, with other areas where it is thick and textured.

Perhaps this is how Rembrandt looked on 29 December 1667, when Cosimo de'Medici, the 25-year-old prince and future Grand Duke of Tuscany, visited him at his home in Amsterdam. The young man described the artist in his diary as a *pittore famoso* ('famous painter'), which may indicate that Rembrandt was still held in high esteem, even if his art did not fit with the new fashion for Classicist art that had developed in Dutch Republic. The Grand Duke may have bought a late self-portrait by Rembrandt on a return visit to the city.

## TITUS

Rembrandt never recovered financial stability, and in 1666, after he failed to pay his rent, his landlord took action. There was good news for Titus, though, who had been of great assistance to his father. On 9 September 1665 The Chamber of Orphans awarded him 7,000 guilders for the grand house that Rembrandt had put in his name. This overruled the previous decision to sell the house to pay Rembrandt's creditors, who were

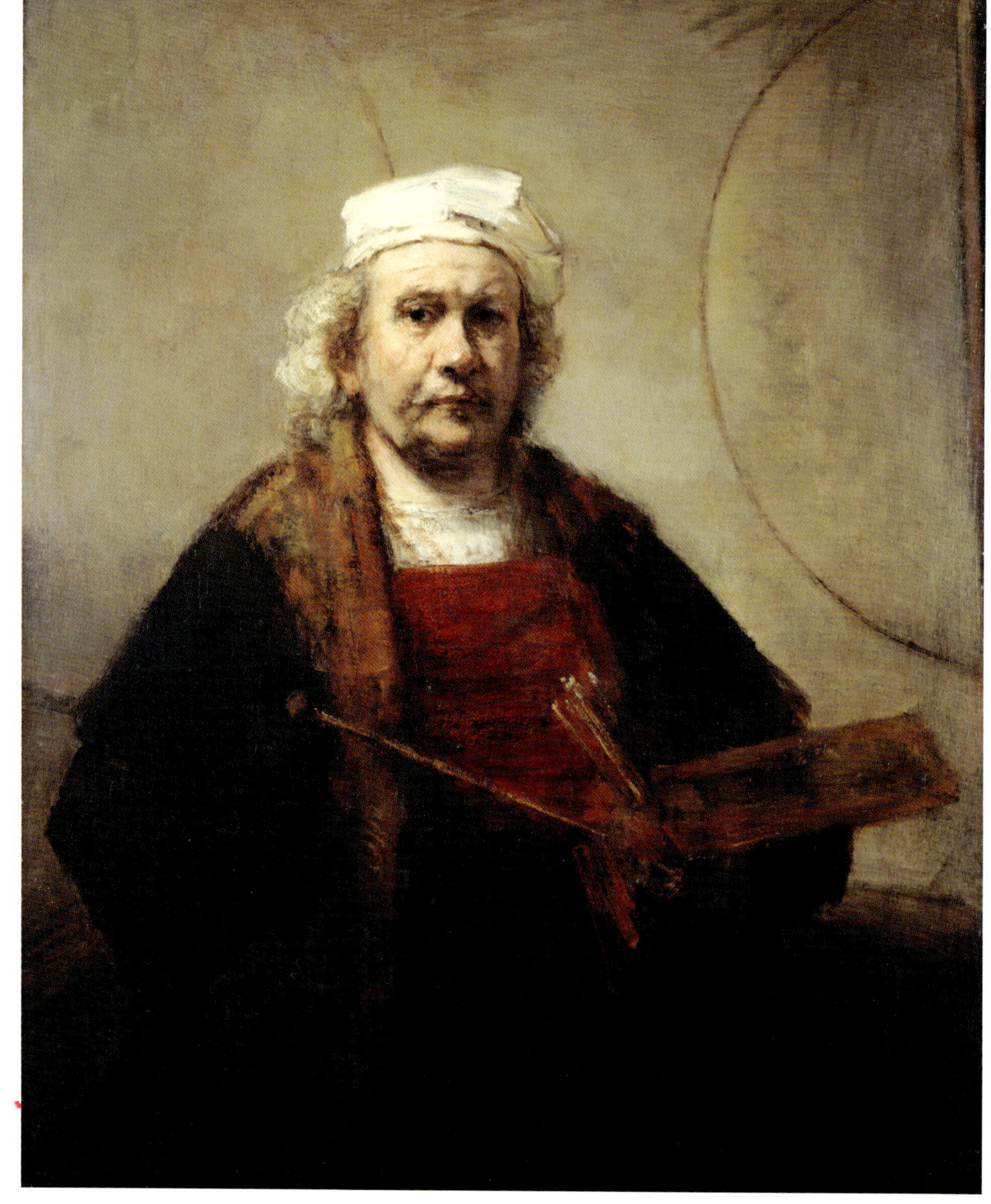

*Self-Portrait with Two Circles, 1665. This monumental late self-portrait is expressively painted, but with it Rembrandt also seems to convey his aims and aspirations as a painter.*

then ordered to pay back the money so it could be allocated to Titus. With the dept to Titus paid, Rembrandt was now free to marry, three years after Hendrickje had died.

On 28 February 1668 Titus married Magdalena van Loo, the daughter of a family friend and a childhood friend of Titus. He moved out, but once again tragedy struck and only six months later Titus was dead, taken ill on a trip to Leiden. On 7 September 1668 he too was buried in a rented grave in Westerkirk, but was later moved by his wife's family. It is unlikely that he knew that his wife was pregnant, and their daughter Titia was baptized on 22 March 1669. Rembrandt became a grandfather and was also one of the godfathers. That year, in another extraordinary example of his paintings reflecting his life, Rembrandt painted *Simeon in the Temple* (Nationalmuseum, Stockholm). The elderly Simeon gently cradles the baby Jesus, having been promised that he wouldn't die before seeing the saviour. It is hard not to make the comparison to Rembrandt holding his new granddaughter.

## DEATH OF REMBRANDT

Rembrandt died on 4 October 1669 from causes unknown and he too was buried in a rented grave in the Westerkerk, in a simple service with hired pallbearers. There was no public commemoration of his death, as there had been for his teacher Lastman, his pupil Flinck and his inspiration Rubens. Nor was there a monument, not even a headstone.

When he had painted his *Self-Portrait* (Mauritshuis, The Hague) in 1669, he was probably unaware it would be his last, but it was painted very quickly with little or no drawing. His dress is simple as he concentrated on the depiction of his face. Once again he captured the skin on his ageing face brilliantly. His face perhaps reveals a life of both triumph and hardship, but it was a life in which he continued to experiment and search in his art right until the end.

Simeon in the Temple, 1669. *This painting was left unfinished in Rembrandt's studio when he died. This may account for its free style. The old Simeon, with his eyes half open, tenderly holds the baby Jesus.*

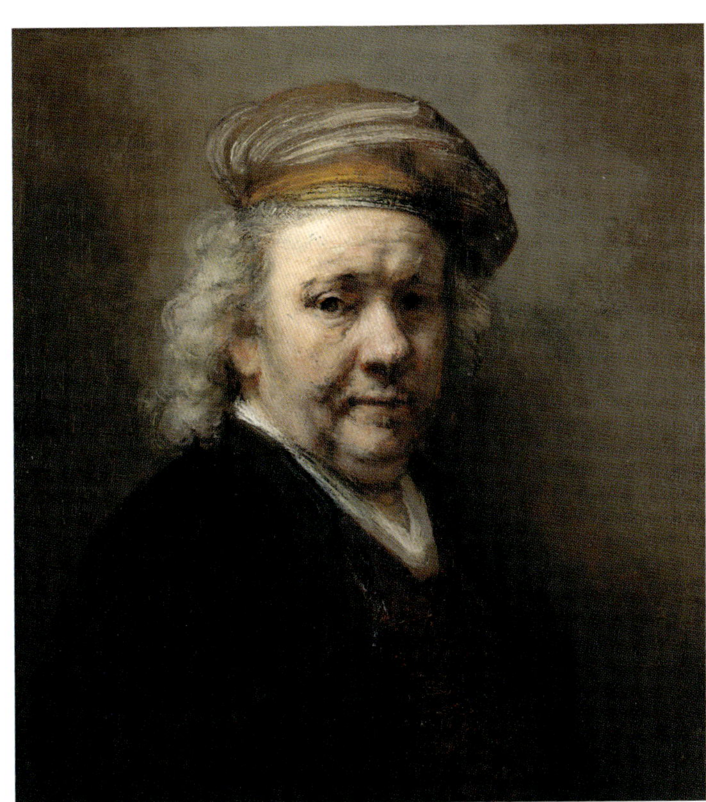

Self-Portrait, 1669. *Rembrandt continued to paint Self-Portraits until his death, and this is one of a few that date to the year of his death.*

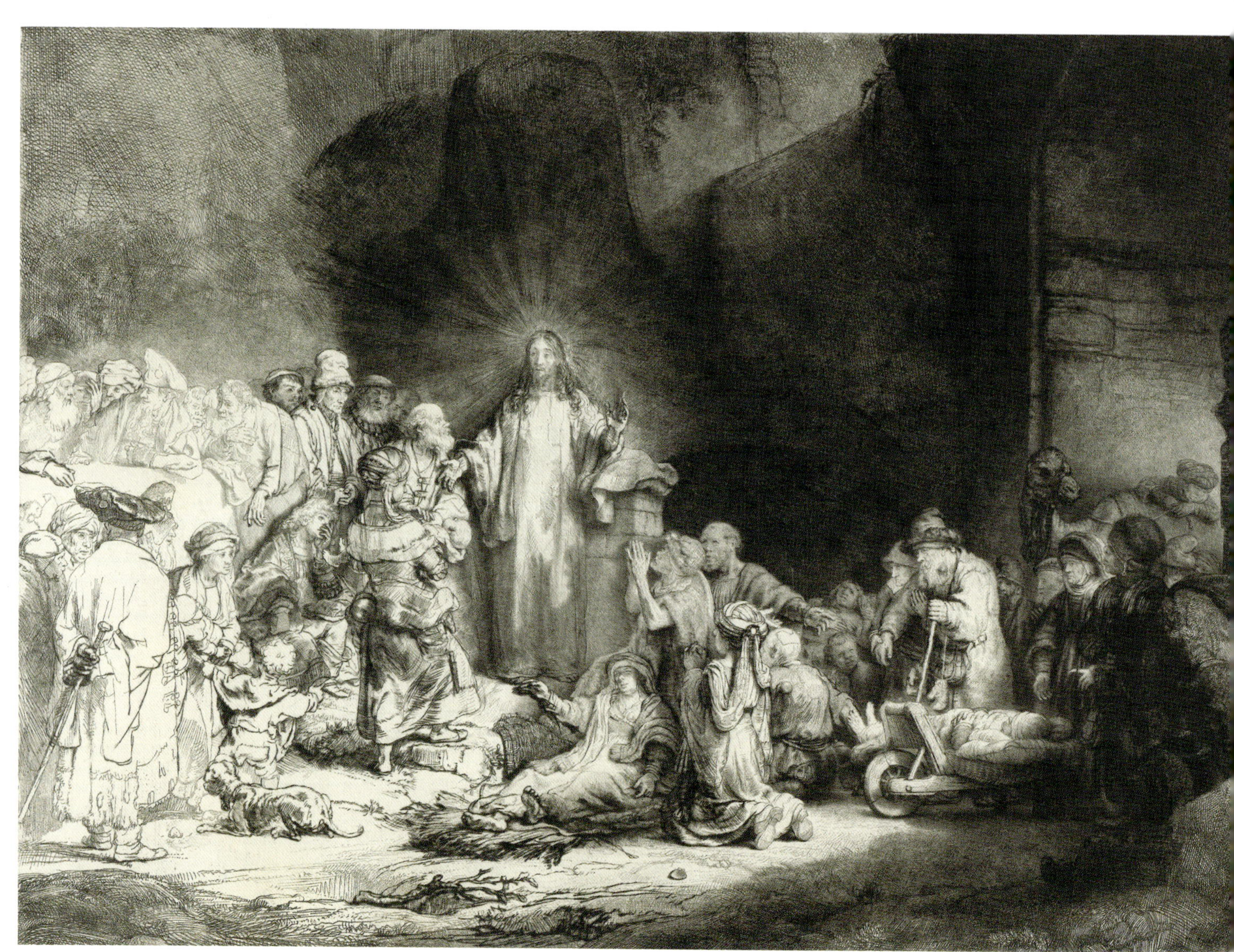

Christ Healing the Sick, also named The Hundred Guilder Print, *1648/9, etching. Rather than portray a single event, this print combines several biblical episodes. The design is also complex with numerous figures and different poses.*

# CHAPTER 5

# Rembrandt the Printmaker

Rembrandt was a prolific printmaker and produced as many prints as paintings in his career. It was an important part of his output and he is undoubtedly the most innovative printmaker of the seventeenth century, and perhaps of all time. Rembrandt did not use prints to create reproductions of his paintings; he used the medium to create original images. It is thought that he did not receive any formal training in printmaking techniques but was self-taught – although it is interesting to note that his hometown Leiden was renowned for its printing businesses.

If he had received lessons, Rembrandt would no doubt have been taught the usual method of apply the etching lines: in a regular way with hatching. Instead Rembrandt's etchings are, from the start, created in a much freer style, and that led to him adopting a much more sketch-like, or painterly, appearance in many of his prints. He was pushing the possibilities of what was achievable in the medium and learning by experimenting.

He captured many different subjects in his prints, all showing what a keen observer of life he was and how he became a master at using light and shade. Many of his prints are much more informal than his oil paintings and they allow the viewer a more intimate view of Rembrandt and how he looked at the world around him. Some years, Rembrandt produced many etchings, 15 or more and of different subjects; in other years, he produced only a couple of images. He continued, however, to print throughout his career. Just as he experimented with his paintings, he also experimented with techniques in etching and how to achieve different effects. This included combining different printing methods on one plate and leaving tone on the plate instead of wiping it clean. He transformed the way that drypoint could be used, raising it from a technique used only for making alterations to a valid print technique in its own right. He experimented with reusing plates and cutting them up. He also tried different types of papers, using both laid and woven paper, coarse oatmeal cartridge paper and Japanese paper. Sometimes it looks like some prints are unfinished: Rembrandt deliberately leaves some areas as sketches or outlines, while fully working other areas of the print, such as the details of a face.

Rembrandt's prints would have been an important source of income and also a way for the artist to raise his profile and reputation among the art-buying public. Prints were more readily available and more widely disseminated to those unable to afford one of his paintings. Rembrandt's prints also became highly desirable to print collectors across Europe during his lifetime and as his reputation as a printmaker grew, so too did his fees. A highly finished portrait etching could cost as much as 400 guilders, when some oil portraits cost 500 guilders. Rembrandt's prints continued to be highly collectable after his death, and still are. This led to his plates being falsified after his death. Dealers created false states from his original plates and in some instances even created new prints by printing two plates together.

## HOW TO MAKE AN ETCHING

To make an etching, a copper plate is covered in wax, onto which the artist can easily draw with a needle, scratching away at the wax and exposing the plate. The plate is then dipped in an acid bath or acid is poured over, and where the metal is exposed the acid bites into the metal, creating the etched lines. Once the artist is satisfied with the lines, the wax is removed by heating the plate and the plate then thoroughly cleaned. It is now ready for printing. This involves rubbing a sticky black ink over the plate so that it fills the etched lines. The copper plate is then cleaned and placed on a rolling press. A damp sheet of paper is placed on top and the plate is rolled through the press. The image that is transferred on to the paper is in reverse, so the artist must always work in reverse when scratching into the plate.

Often, Rembrandt would make alterations and continue to work on the image, so the plate could be worked on again and printed again – each printing stage is called *a state*. Sometimes Rembrandt worked directly on to the plate, scratching it with a needle in a technique called *drypoint*. This allowed him to make swift alterations and often resulted in a stronger line with jagged edges, the *burr*. When he was satisfied with the image it would then be issued in an edition of probably around 20 to 25 prints. As the interest and demand for his prints grew, the early states became particularly desirable to collectors and still are today.

## FORMAL SUBJECTS

Rembrandt's first etchings are dated to 1626, a year later than his first signed oil painting. Like his oil paintings these were historical works, images from the Bible: *The Rest on the Flight into Egypt* and *The Circumcision*. Rembrandt produced prints with religious subjects throughout his career and they form the majority of his output. He often returned to the same subjects, including *The Rest on the Flight into Egypt*, *St Jerome* and *the Raising of Lazarus*. Perhaps his most revered print in this genre is from 1648/9, *Christ Healing the Sick*, also named *The Hundred Guilder Print*, (see page 76) a name which derived from the high price this print is purported to have fetched in Rembrandt's lifetime. It is a complex composition that was created by combining several techniques, including etching, drypoint and engraving. The work magnificently showcases Rembrandt's use of light and shade, the light falling on the figures around the central Christ, who shines almost

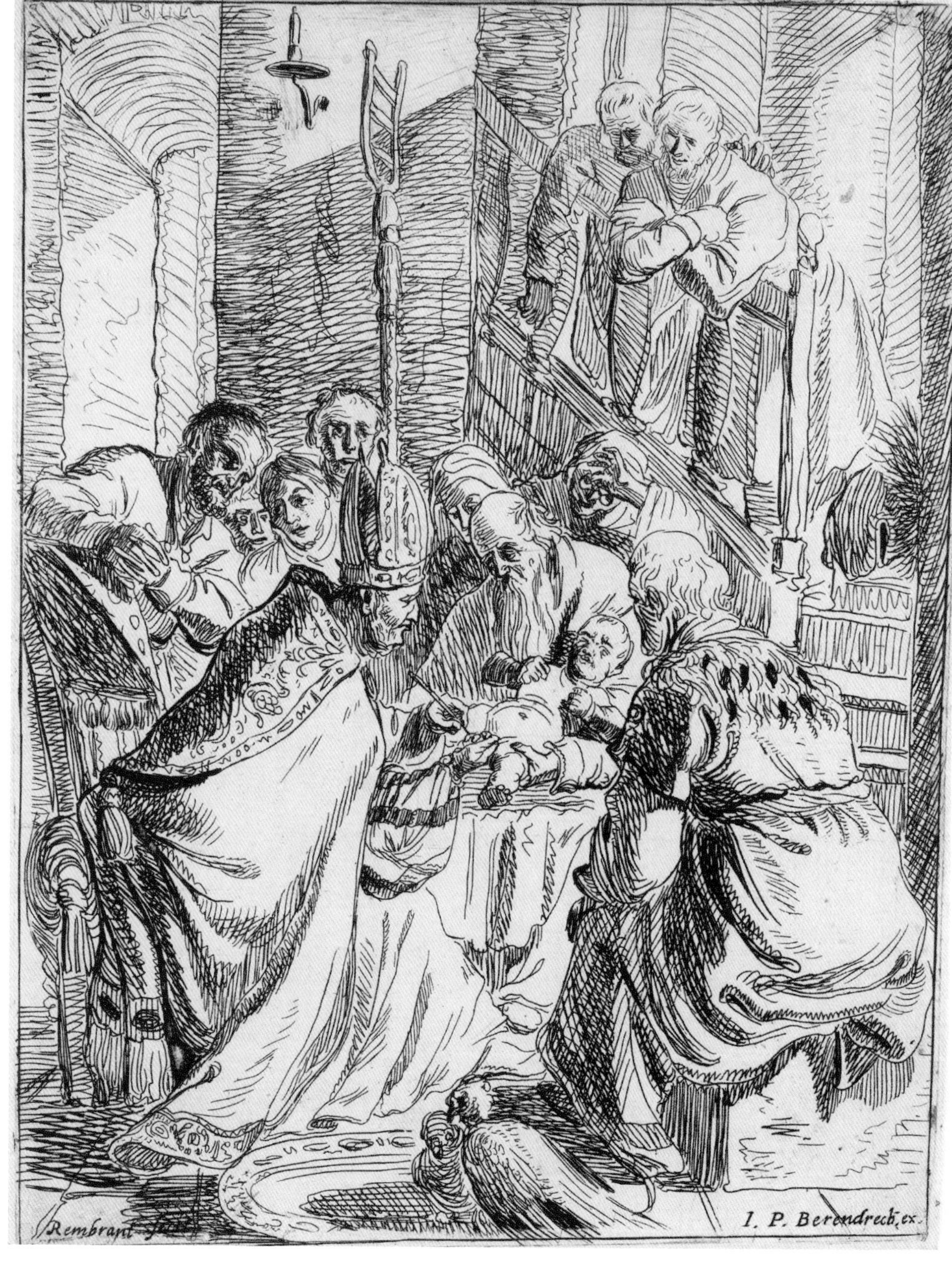


The Circumcision, *c.1624–16. This is perhaps Rembrandt's first print and shows great ability in the complex design with numerous figures. It was published by the print seller Beerendrecht in Haarlem.*

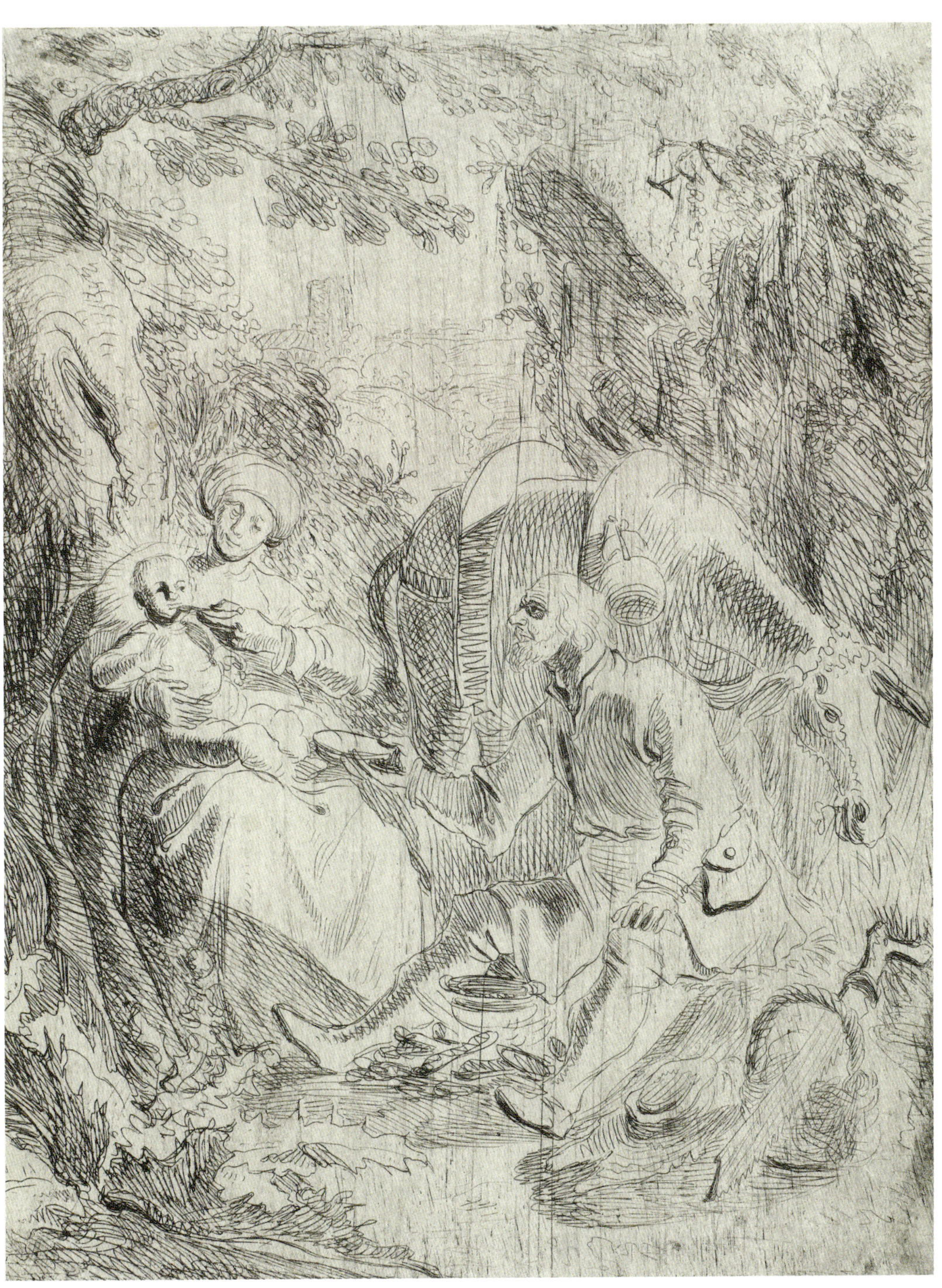

The Rest on the Flight into Egypt, c.1626. *Mary feeds the baby Jesus as they rest on their journey. Rembrandt is experimenting with the use of light and shade.*

like a beacon. To the left of the image a woman holds up a baby to him, while others are clearly sick and being brought to Christ. Rembrandt chooses a dramatic story and enhances it with the theatrical use of light and shade.

## SELF-PORTRAITS

As a young artist, Rembrandt made numerous self-portraits in paint and also in print. In many of his early self-portraits he uses his own face to explore facial expressions such as anger, astonishment, smiling, shouting and frowning. These prints, dating to 1630, are small and were probably drawn directly onto the plate. Their purpose is not clear: it would be easy to assume that they were for personal study, to develops skills for future works, yet they are signed and dated, so they may well have been distributed. History painters were revered for their ability to express emotions in the figures in their work, so perhaps these were demonstrations for clients of his skill in this area.

Rembrandt had the wonderful ability of capturing textures in his prints. This is very much in evidence in his *Self-Portrait in a Velvet Cap with Plume*, 1638, where he has brilliantly contrasted the smooth texture of the velvet with the feather in his cap and his unruly, curly hair. In 1648 he also produced the work *Self-Portrait Etching at a Window* (see page 54), which is an indication of how important he saw his printmaking. The light floods through the window, casting the left side into light and the right side into shadow. He stares out at the viewer, etching needle in hand.

Self-Portrait with Beret, Wide Eyed, *1630*.

Self-Portrait, Laughing, *1630*.

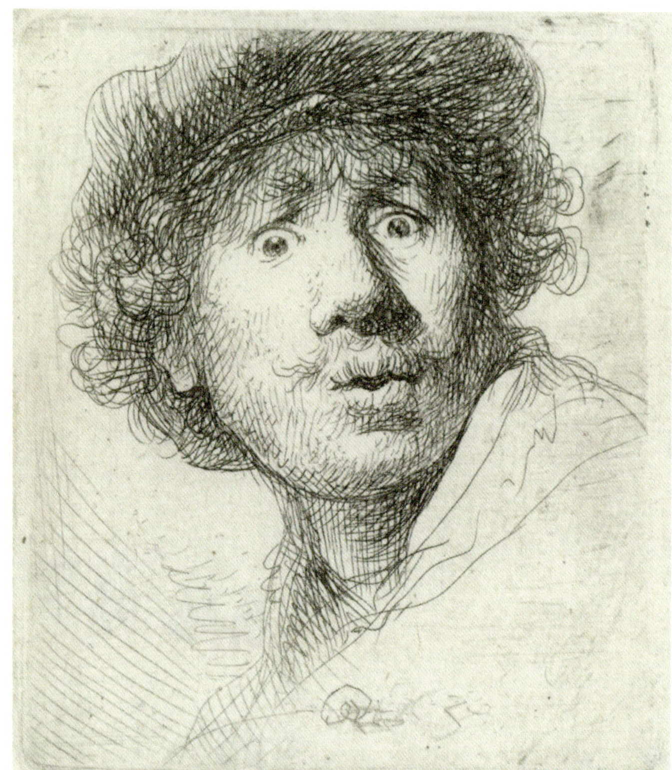

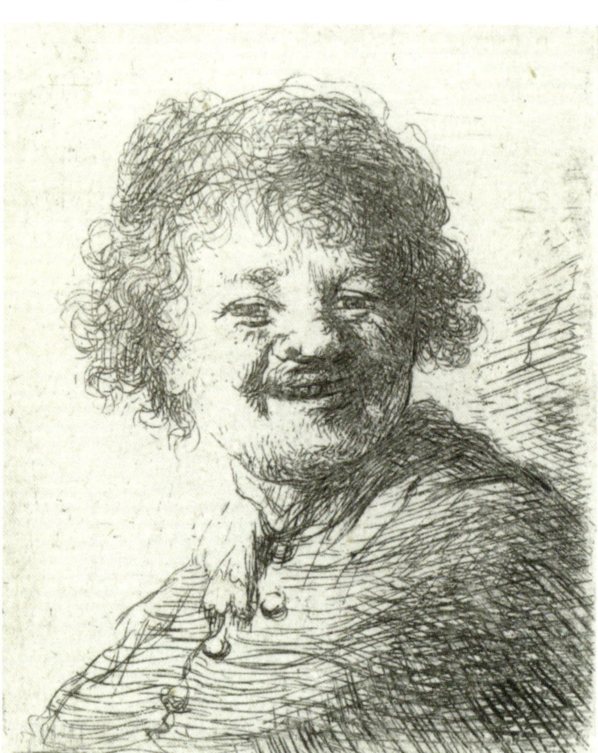

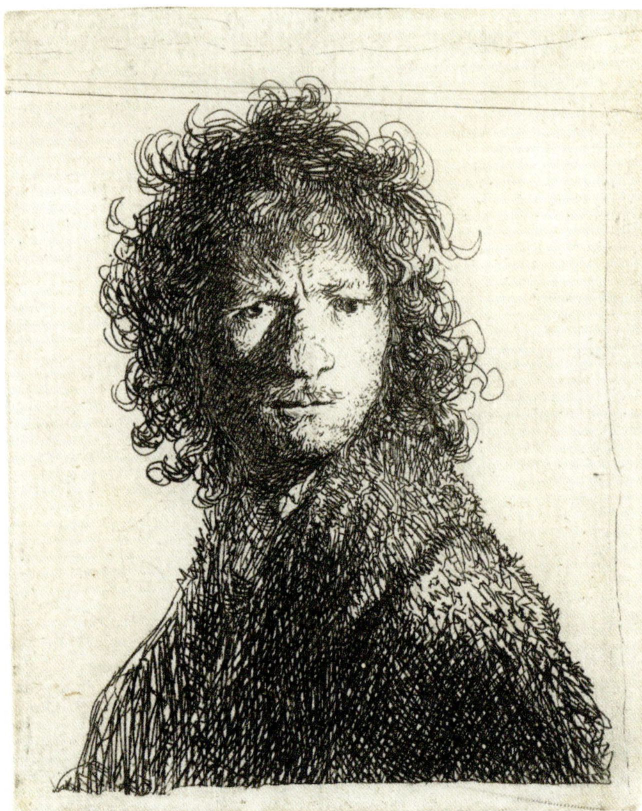

Self-Portrait, Frowning, *1630*.

Self-Portrait, Open-mouthed, *1630*.

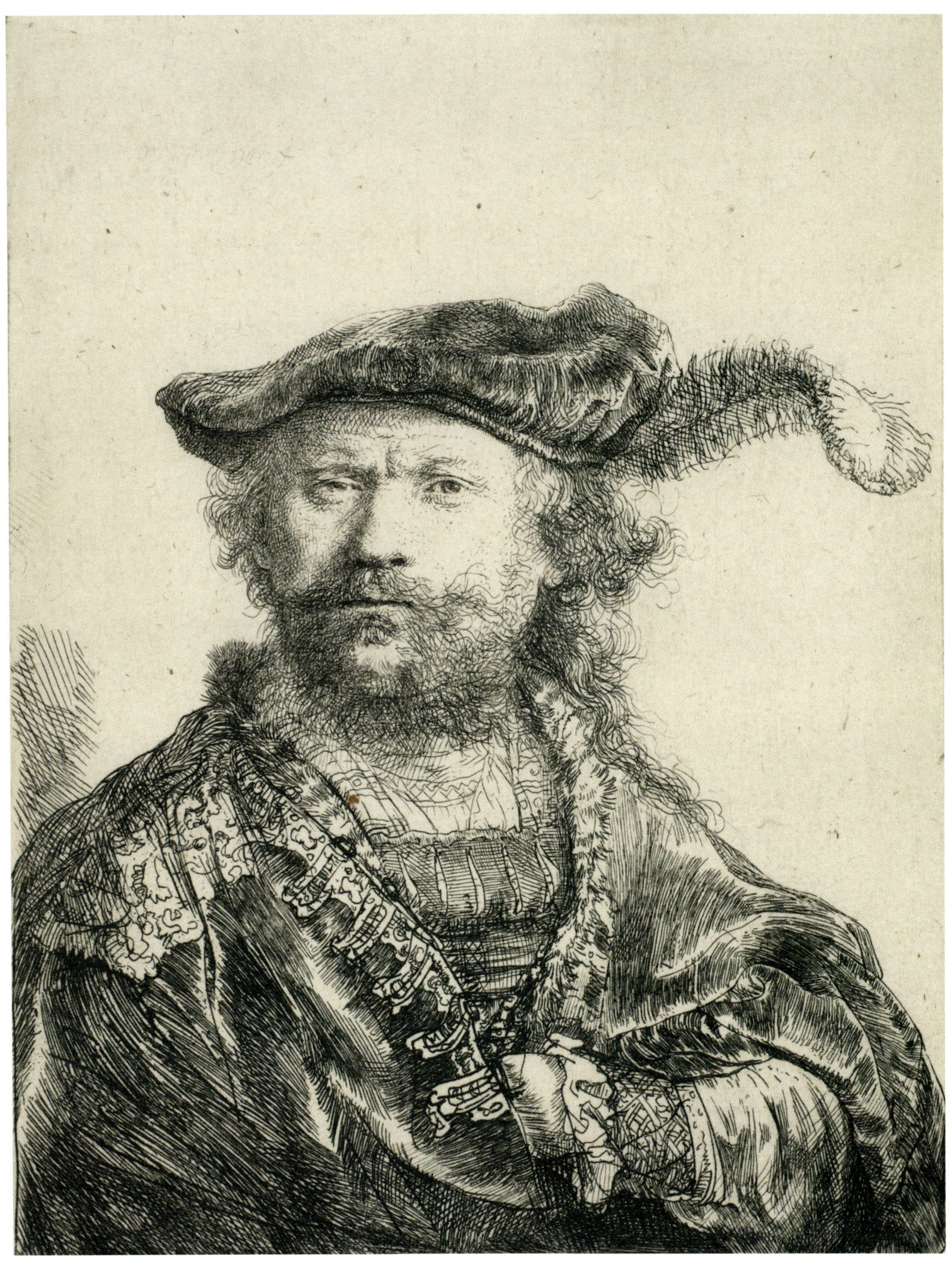

Self-Portrait in a Velvet Cap with Plume, *1638*.

## PORTRAITS

In other prints he used his family as models, such in as *The Artist's Mother: Head and Bust* dated 1628, printed when he was still living in Leiden. After he married Saskia van Uylenburgh (1612–42), she too regularly appears in prints, sometimes as herself as in the double portrait with Rembrandt in *Self-portrait with Saskia*, 1636 (page 32) and at other times dressed in character and used as a model, such as *The Little Jewish Bride (Saskia as St Catherine)*, 1635. He also later captured his son Titus in an intimate etching of him as a teenager, *The Artist's son, Titus van Rijn*, 1656.

Rembrandt made numerous studies of heads, of old people with beards, in hats, bald men, women reading, young children or *tronies* – portraits of people in character, often dressed in fanciful or oriental costumes, such as *The Persian*, 1632.

From 1633 Rembrandt was making portrait prints, some of which were commissions. He is revered for capturing realism in his portraits and for portraying the sitters' character as opposed to flattering them. His portraits include *Lieven Willemz van Coppenol*, 1658, the painter *Jan Asselyn*, 1647, the print-seller *Clement de Jonghe*, 1651, and the apothecary *Abraham Francen*, 1657. The portrait of *Jan Uytenbogaert (The Goldweigher)*, 1639 shows his friend depicted at work as a tax collector, seated by a carpet-covered table with his scales and book. A young assistant hands him a bag of coins for weighing, while clients wait by the door. Rembrandt has depicted the whole room, including a painting on the wall behind. The work has a compelling use of light and shade, taking the viewer's eye around the work. The artist may have met the sitter when they both studied in Leiden, and Uytenbogaert assisted Rembrandt in collecting outstanding payment for some paintings.

The Artist's Son, Titus van Rijn, *1656, etching.*

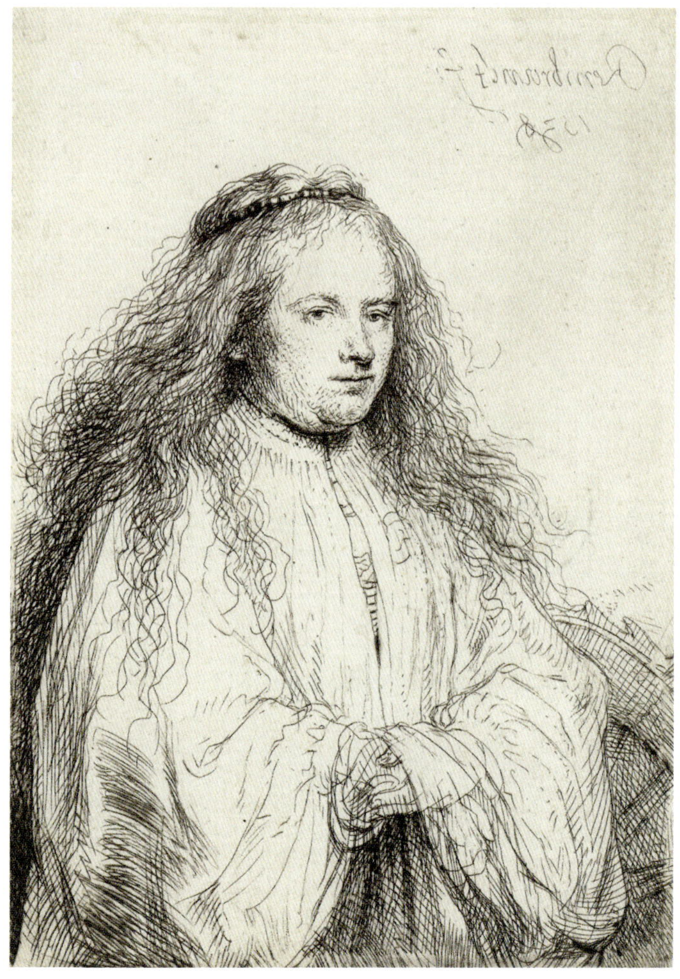

The Little Jewish Bride (Saskia as St Catherine), *1635.*

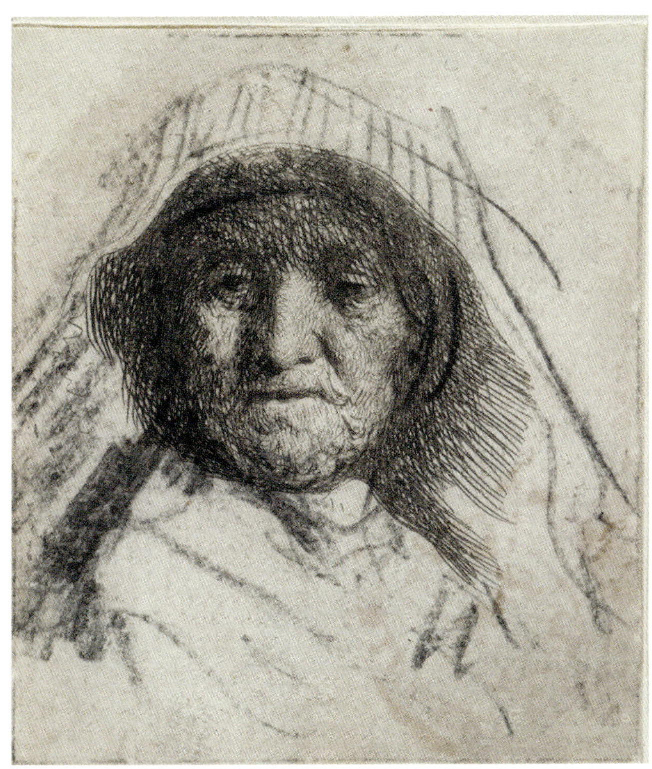

The Artist's Mother, Head and Bust, *1628 etching. Rembrandt repeatedly used his mother, Neeltgen Willemsdr van Zuytbroeck, as a model and made several prints of her. Here he has concentrated on her face and capturing her aging features.*

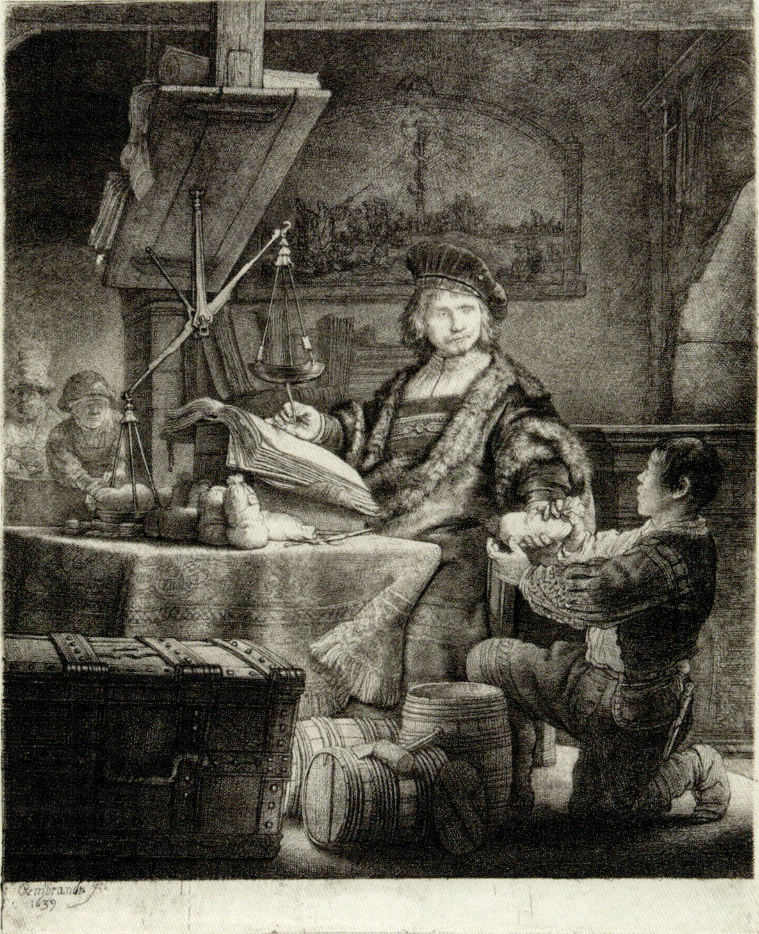

Portrait of Jan Uytenbogaert, The Goldweigher *(1608–80), 1639. Uytenbogaert acted as an intermediary between Rembrandt and Stadholder Frederik Hendrik when he was chasing payments for a commission.*

Portrait of Jan Asselyn, *1647.*

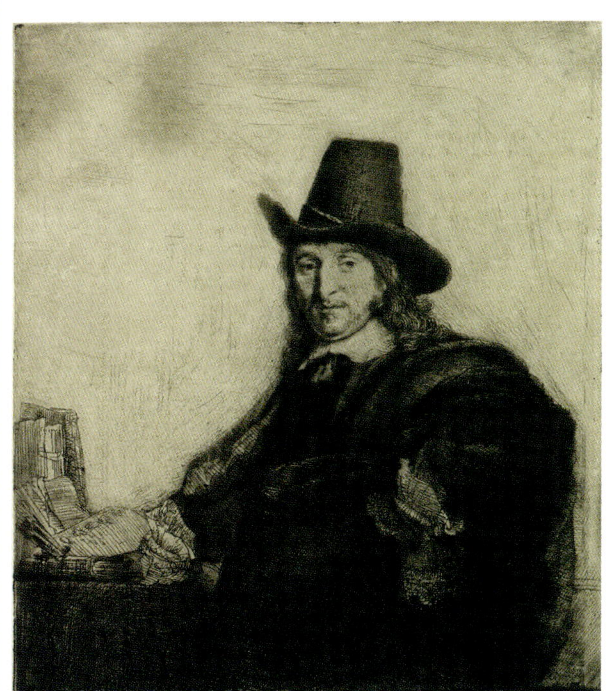

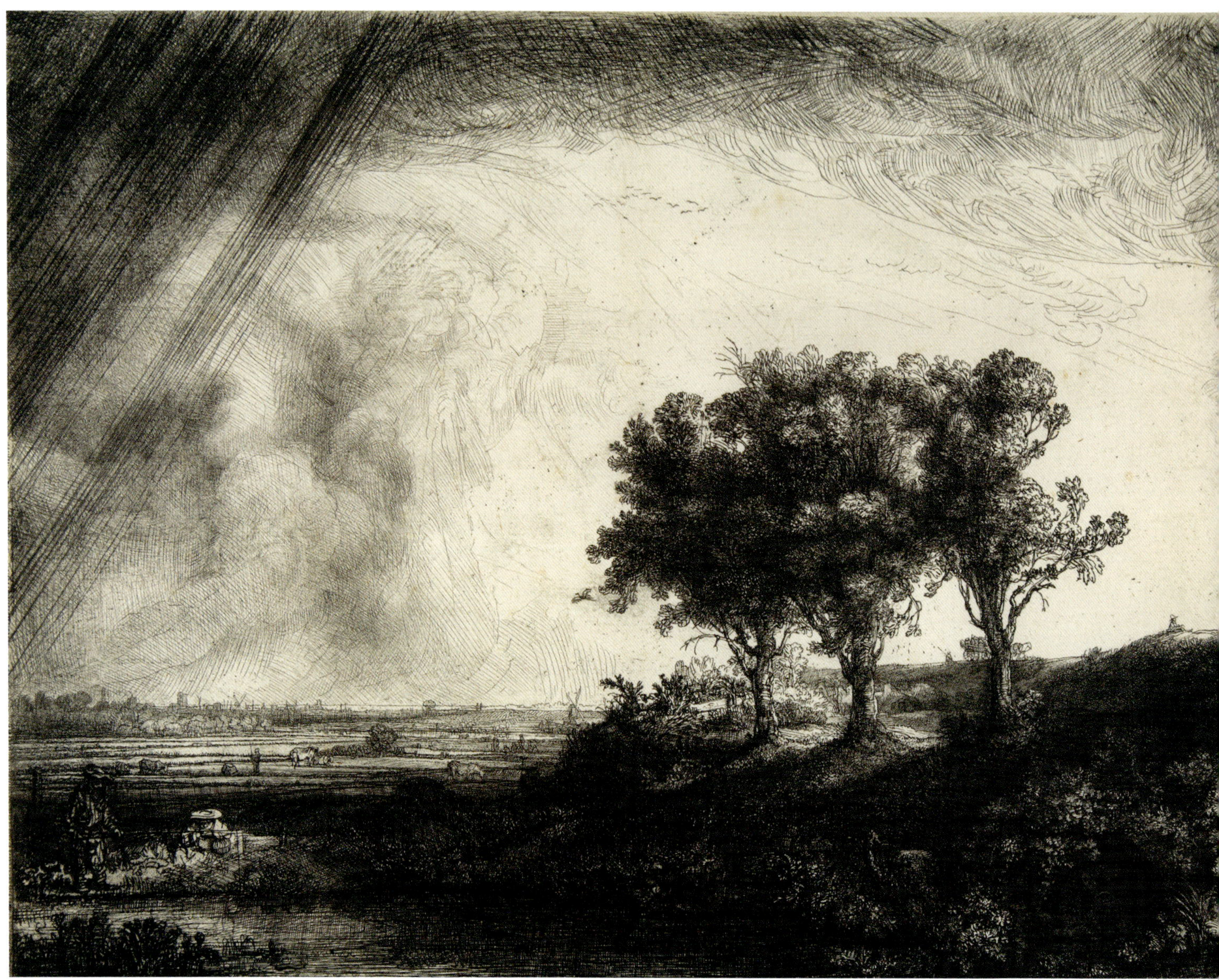

## LANDSCAPES

From about 1640, Rembrandt made a group of prints of the landscape around
Amsterdam. Many of the features, such as bridges and churches in the landscapes, are
recognizable and they certainly reflect the flat, low horizon of the Dutch landscape.
Rembrandt went out walking and sketched the landscape he saw, which he could use
back at the studio to create these prints. However, Rembrandt was as concerned about
capturing an atmosphere as depicting a specific location in these works, so they are a
combination of reality with imagination. The drama and dark, brooding atmosphere
created in *The Three Trees*, 1643, is not reflected in its very simple title. The trees on the
hill have often been said to represent the three crosses at Jesus's crucifixion. The sky is
dynamic, a rain shower just passing, and Rembrandt has left ink on the plate to create
the areas of tone. The more the viewer looks, the more details can be found, such as the
artist on this hill sketching, a couple fishing and even lovers hidden in the bushes.

The Three Trees, *1643. This large,
painterly print is lit by the light of a
sun that gone down on the right. The
drama is not in the subject but in the
stormy sky and dramatic use of light
and shade.*

## EVERYDAY SCENES

Some of the most compelling prints that Rembrandt made, and which certainly appeal to a modern audience, are the prints of ordinary scenes and people. While in Leiden, he made numerous prints of peasants and beggars, sometimes even using himself as the model, as in *Beggar Seated on a Bank*, 1630. Rembrandt was said to do 'portraits of the wealthy and etchings of the poor'. His subjects ranged from *Strolling Musicians*, 1635 to *The Rat Catcher*, 1632, *The Pancake Woman*, 1635 and *The Ringball Player*, 1654.

In *The Hog*, 1643, the image of the pig is worked quite extensively and is drawn using many lines, but in the background the figures are only suggested, with a few, lightly etched lines. This is quite typical of many of his prints: he concentrates on certain areas, but is not afraid to leave other areas merely suggested with sketches.

Rembrandt produced a number of prints that look like pages from a sketchbook, as though he has drawn free hand directly on to the etching plate. *Three Heads of Women, One Asleep*, 1637 shows three different studies, seemingly not connected to one another on one sheet. In *Sheet of Studies with a Woman Lying Ill in Bed*, 1641–2, the plate has been drawn on in one direction and then turned by 90 degrees and another figure drawn. These informal prints were very unusual and are representative of how experimental Rembrandt was with this printmaking.

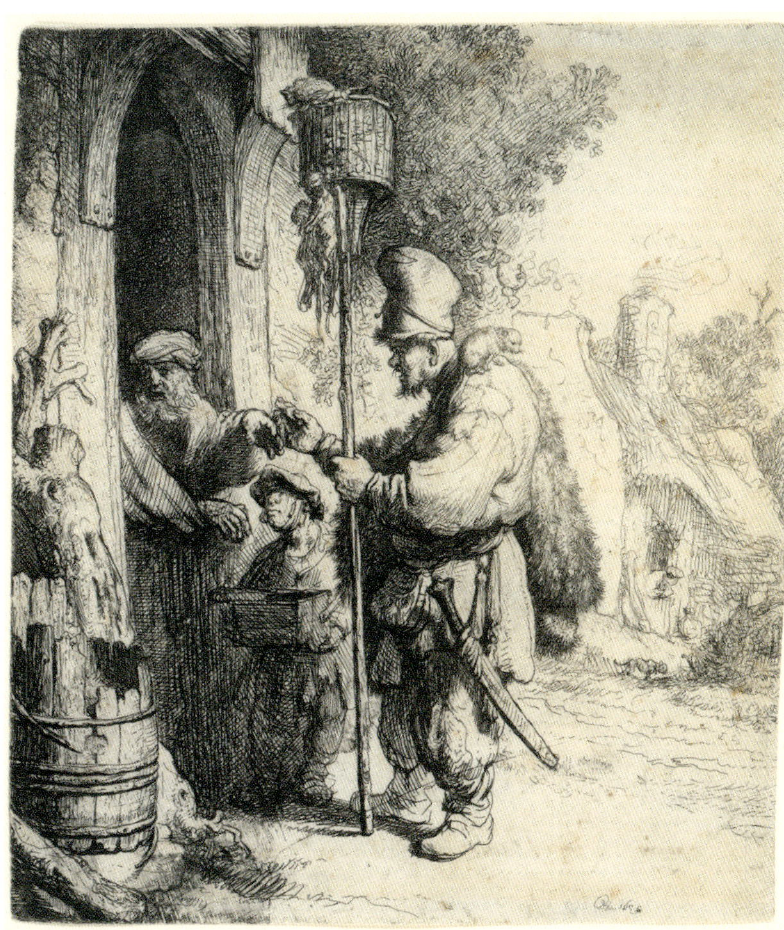

The Rat Catcher, 1632. *The rat catcher and his assistant call at a house.*

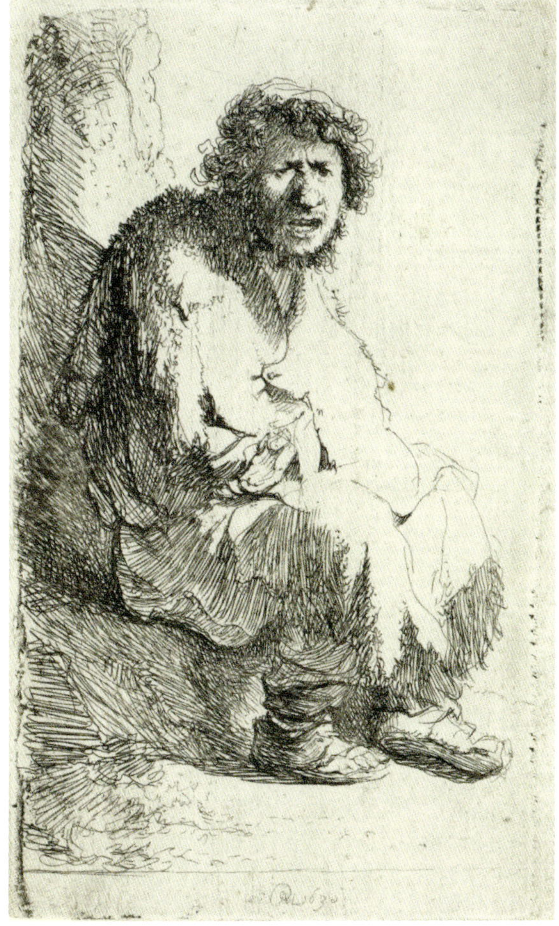

Beggar Seated on a Bank, 1630. *Rembrandt was sympathetic in his images of beggars rather than ridiculing them or moralizing. He has even used his own face for this figure.*

The Hog, 1643. *The fattened hog appears to be unaware of its imminent slaughter as the butcher in the background is preparing his equipment.*

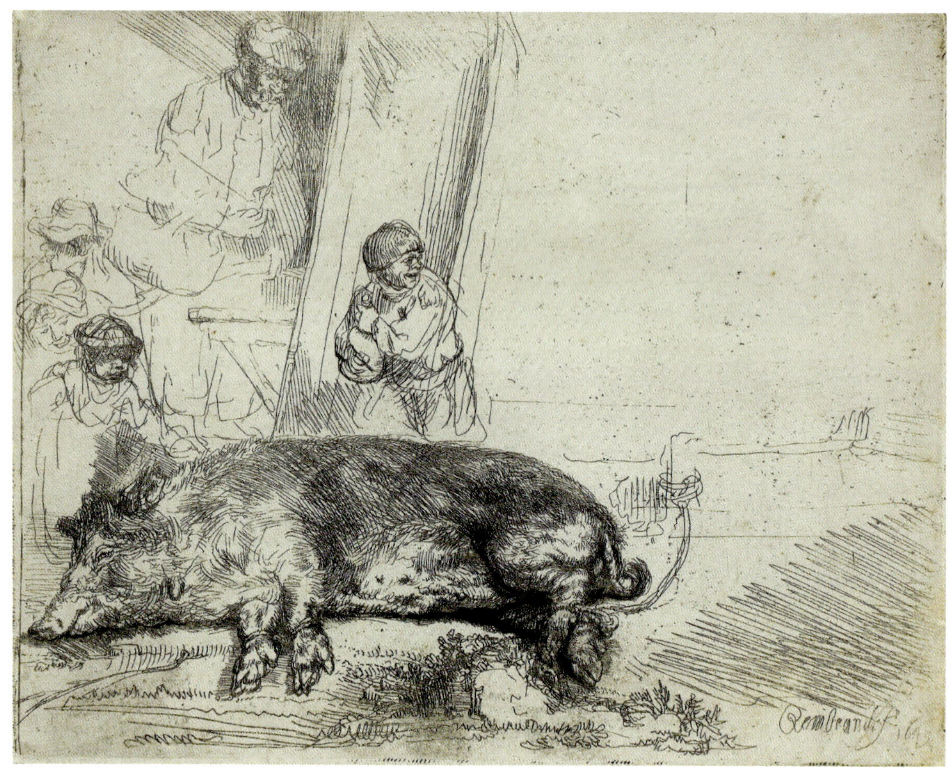

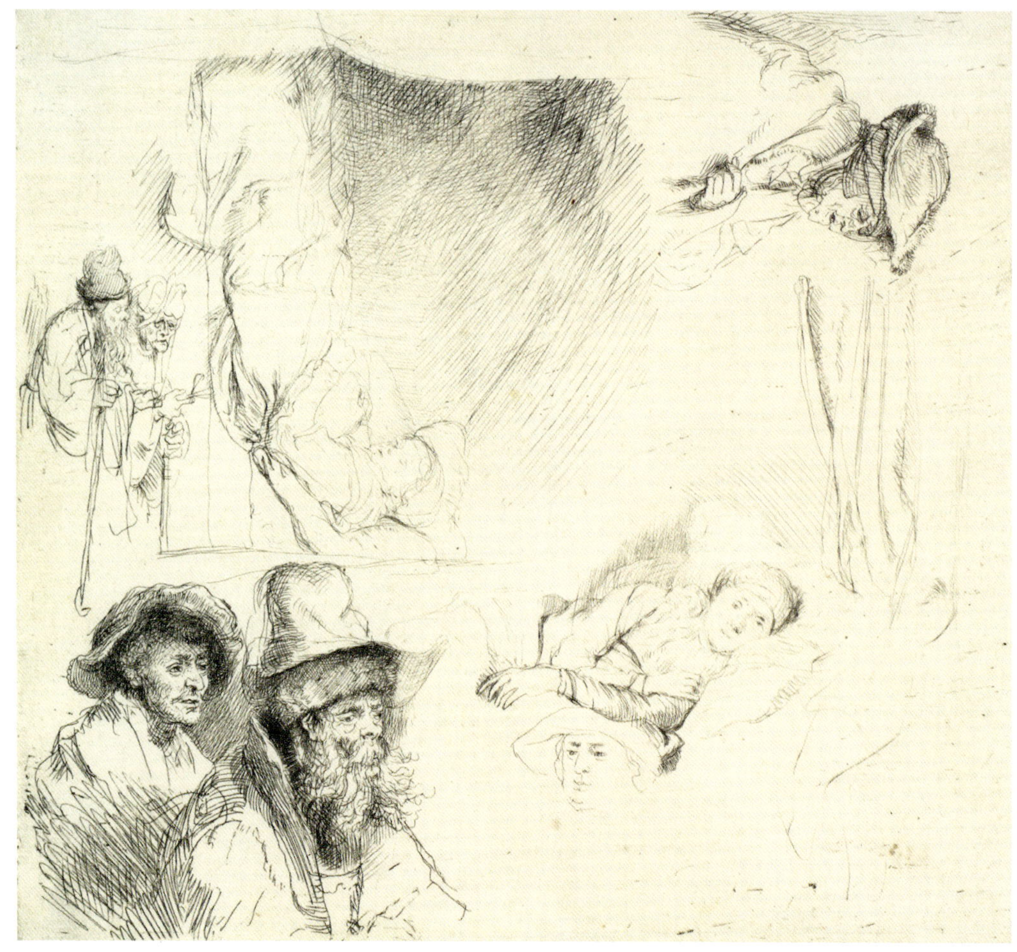

Sheet of Studies, with a Woman Lying Ill in Bed, *1641–2. The woman depicted twice in bed, once asleep and the other time gazing out, is no doubt his wife Saskia. The other figures are unrelated, making the plate feel like a sketchbook page.*

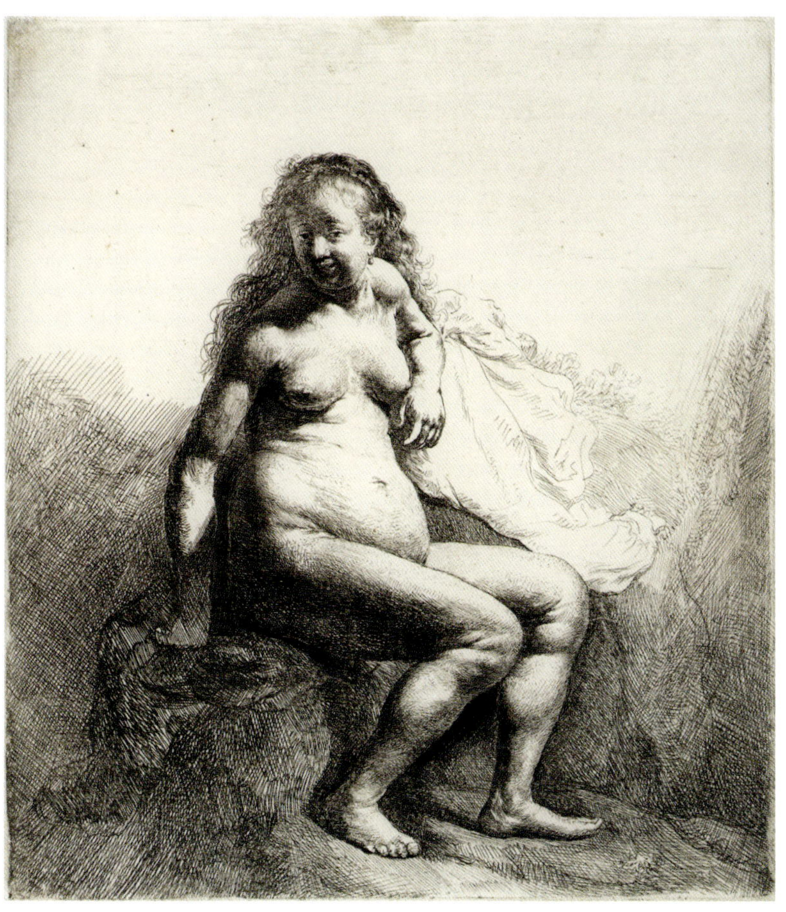

Naked Woman Seated on a Mound, *1631. The woman may be a representation of a biblical or historical bather. Her figure is extensively modelled in light and shade creating a three-dimensionality.*

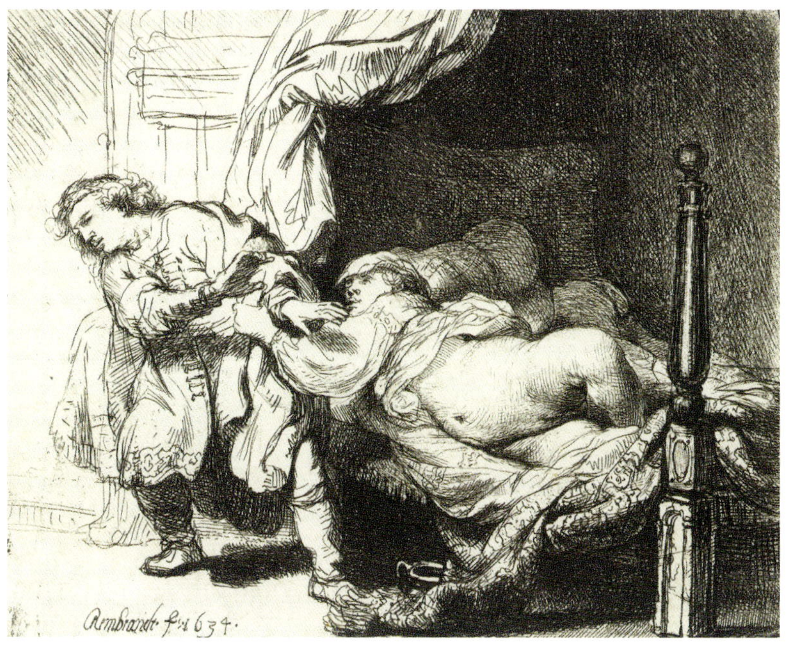

Joseph and Potiphar's Wife, *1634. In a scene from the Old Testament Potiphar wife's is shown seducing Joseph, she is in danger of falling out the bed as she holds on to him.*

## NUDES

Nude figures sometimes appear in biblical or allegorical prints such as *Joseph and Potiphar's Wife*, 1634, but Rembrandt was unusual in also depicting both men and women nudes as images in themselves. He produced a couple of prints depicting lovers, in the bedroom and in a field. He also employed models and produced several men and/or women posing, the men usually wearing loincloths, as in *A Nude Man Seated on the Ground With One Leg Extended*, 1646. His nudes are true to nature and tend to show all the curves and imperfections of each model, as in the print *Naked Woman Seated on a Mound*, 1631. He also etched nudes in domestic scenes such as the much later print *Woman Sitting Half-dressed Beside a Stove*, 1658.

Rembrandt only received one known commission to illustrate a book. Instead, he sold his prints as individual sheets, as art works. Some collectors would have framed the prints and hung them on walls, but most collectors would have pasted them into albums (*constboeken* or *prentboeken*) or kept them in portfolios in their libraries, where they would be viewed and studied.

Rembrandt's last print is dated 1665, it is a portrait *Jan Antonides van der Linder*. It was one of only two prints he produced after 1660. Up until this point his printmaking ran parallel to his paintings and he was just as experimental and innovative in this medium as he was in oils. However, it seems his printmaking was more of a personal endeavour and there is no evidence that he shared his printmaking skills with his many pupils. He certainly valued the importance of prints, he was a collector himself and drew much inspiration for his own work from prints by earlier masters.

## EPILOGUE: REMBRANDT'S INFLUENCE AND LEGACY

Rembrandt produced a body of artwork that has never ceased to attract acclaim and investigation. He is one of art history's most important artists and had an impact on the development of Western art like very few artists have. He is one of the most researched artists from his age and is still the subject of exhibitions, books and catalogues. Authenticated works sell for millions of pounds.

In his lifetime, Rembrandt attained both recognition and influence across Europe. He had great influence on his contemporaries and in particular on the many pupils who passed through his studio, learning their trade and how to paint like their master. Some went on to have successful careers of their own. He became the most famous artist in the Dutch Republic and, though he never travelled abroad, his paintings found their way to collections around Europe, to the English court and Italian palazzos.

Yet, he also fell out of fashion within his own lifetime, and certainly received criticism as well as praise. What is perhaps now most admired about Rembrandt's art is what was criticized in his later life and at the time of his death. The Dutch poet Andries Pels (1631–81) said that Rembrandt chose to represent 'vulgar peasant women' in place of a 'Greek Venus'. Yet following generations have admired him specifically for this realism in his art, as well as for his unending desire to experiment and develop, and his ability to convey emotion and to capture the human detail, which made him stand out from his contemporaries.

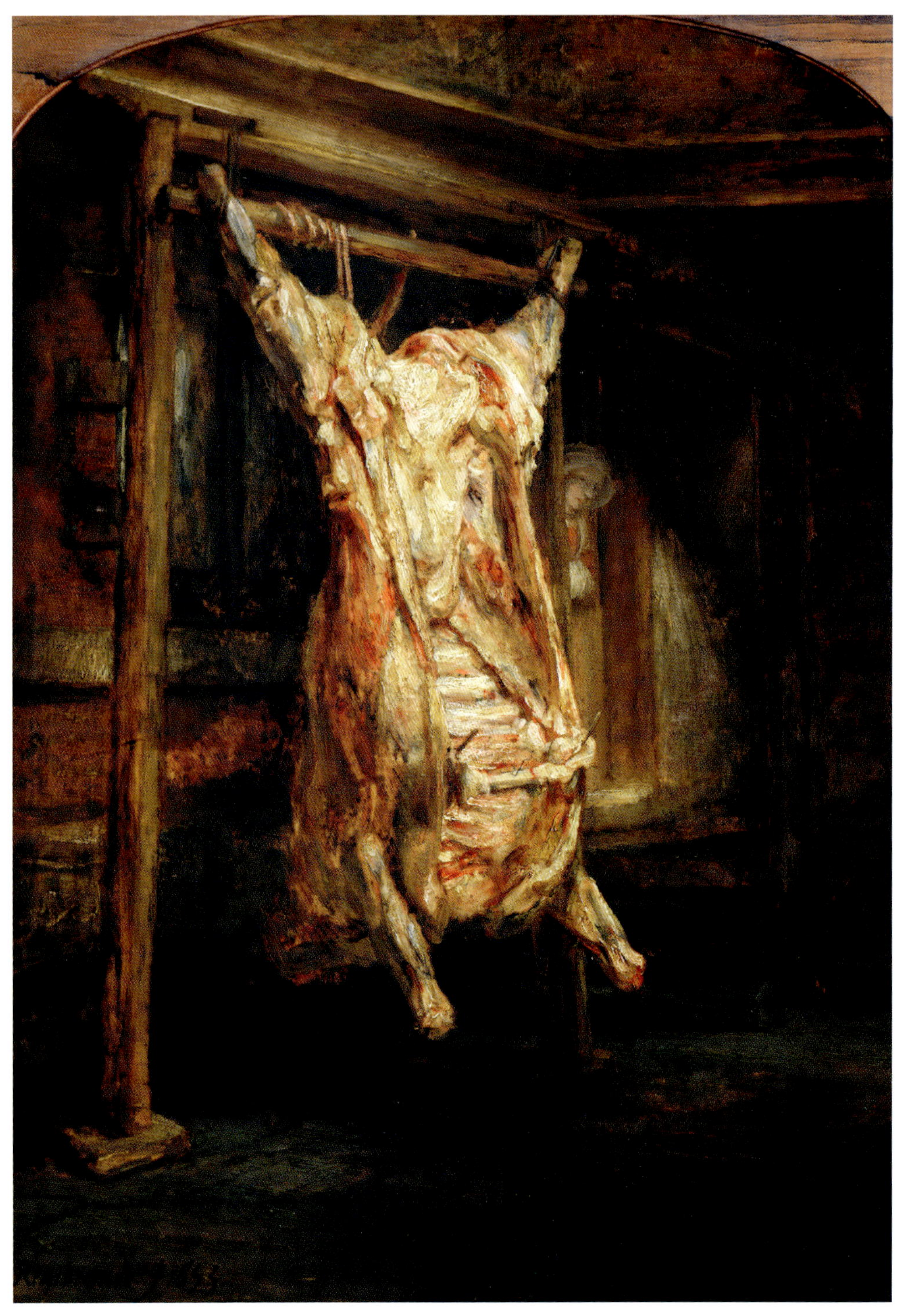

The Slaughtered Ox, *1655*.

His influence can be found across generations and countries. His popularity grew in Europe, particularly in France and Britain in the 18th century. In Britain, the art of William Hogarth (1697–1764) for example, is indebted to Rembrandt whilst Joshua Reynolds (1723–92) President of the Royal Academy and leading portraitist studied, admired and collected

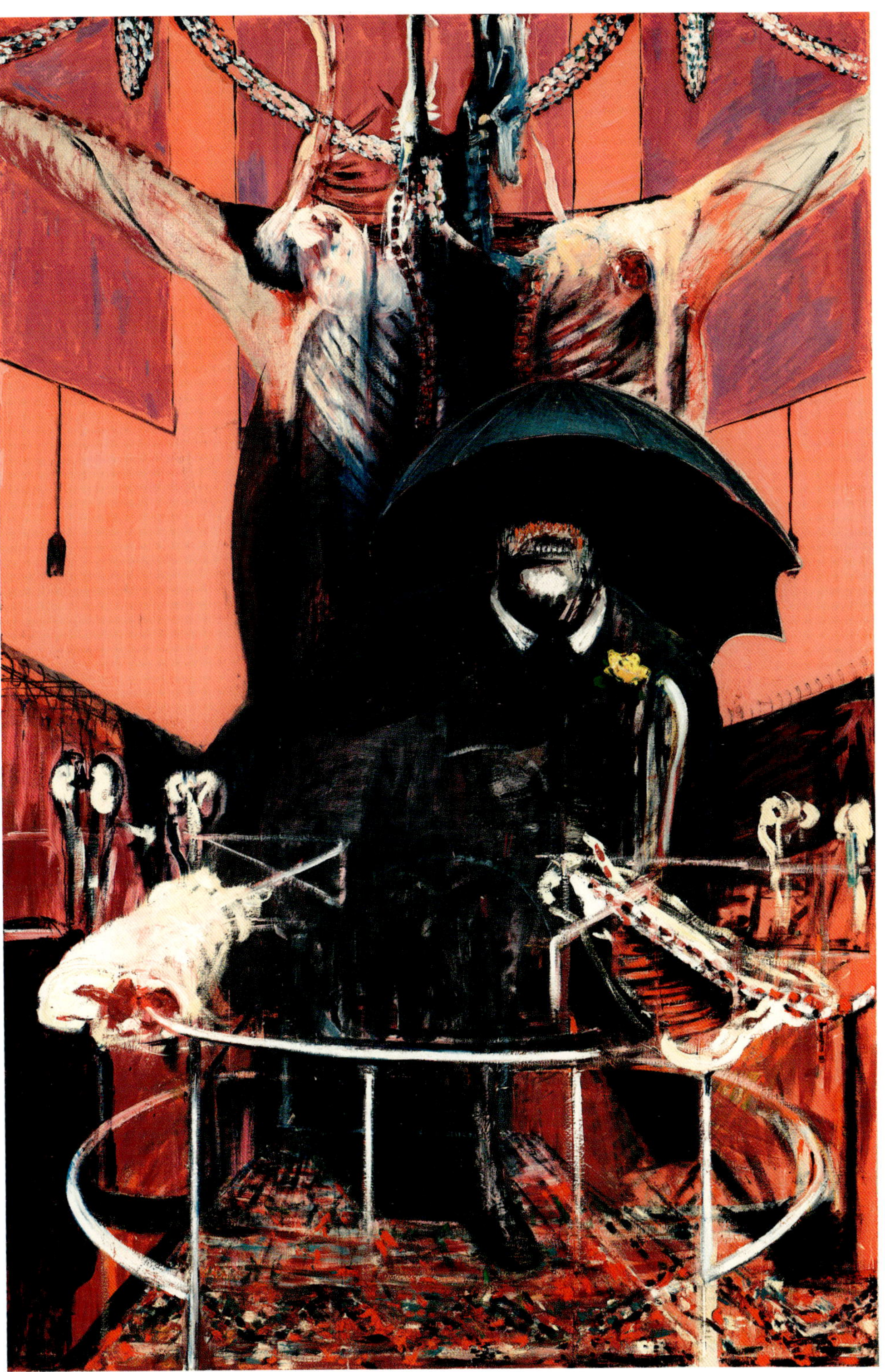

Painting 1946, 1946, *Francis Bacon.*

Rembrandt's work yet also publicly decried his technique. Later renowned artists such as J.M.W. Turner (1775–1851) and John Constable (1776–1837) were also much inspired by his art. It was not until the 19th century that there was a particular revival of interest in his art in the Netherlands and the first statue of Rembrandt was erected in Amsterdam in 1852.

Despite this interest the Rijksmuseum were slow to acquire his work and it was not until the twentieth century that they put together what is now the largest and most representative collection of his work.

French Realist and Impressionist artists looked to Rembrandt for inspiration and Edouard Manet (1832–83) even painted a copy of *The Anatomy Lesson of Dr Tulp* in 1856.

Van Gogh (1853–90) wrote about *The Jewish Bride*, 'What an infinitely sympathetic painting. This is the essence of Rembrandt's genius. It's his sympathy for humankind which makes his art eternal.' When busts by Auguste Rodin (1840–1917) were compared with Rembrandt's portraits, the French sculptor is quoted as saying: 'Compare me with Rembrandt? What sacrilege! With Rembrandt, the colossus of Art! What are you thinking of, my friend! We should prostrate ourselves before Rembrandt and never compare anyone with him!' The German painter Max Liebermann (1847–1935) said: 'Whenever I see a Frans Hals, I feel like painting; whenever I see a Rembrandt, I feel like giving up.'

Modern and contemporary artists, including Frank Auerbach (b. 1931) and David Hockney (b. 1937) continue to be influenced by Rembrandt's art. Francis Bacon (1909–1992) was fascinated both by the late self-portraits, and by portraits such as *Margaretha de Geer, Wife of Jacob Trip*, *c.* 1661, which he knew from visiting the National Gallery, London and *Slaughtered Ox*, 1655, which can be related to his *Painting 1946*. Rembrandt's technical skills are still admired, and direct comparisons can be made with Bacon's paint application, specifically the use of thick impasto.

Rembrandt's prints were highly prized and collected in his lifetime both in the Netherlands and across Europe. As early as 1641 a German book describes Rembrandt as one of Europe's greatest contemporary etchers. His technical abilities had a lasting effect on printmakers for centuries. Artists such as the British painter and printmaker Augustus John (1878–1961), were influenced by his work. John won a scholarship at the Slade School of Art to go to Amsterdam, where he studied the work of Rembrandt. He made a series of prints showing the direct influence of Rembrandt in both technique and subject.

Rembrandt remains one of the most deeply admired and influential masters of art. Many of his works once criticized for not conforming are now widely admired. His paintings have intensity and mystery, but also show humanity, sympathy and realism. His influence was felt during his lifetime, through his pupils, and in the following centuries many artists, across counties have been intrigued and fascinated by his art.

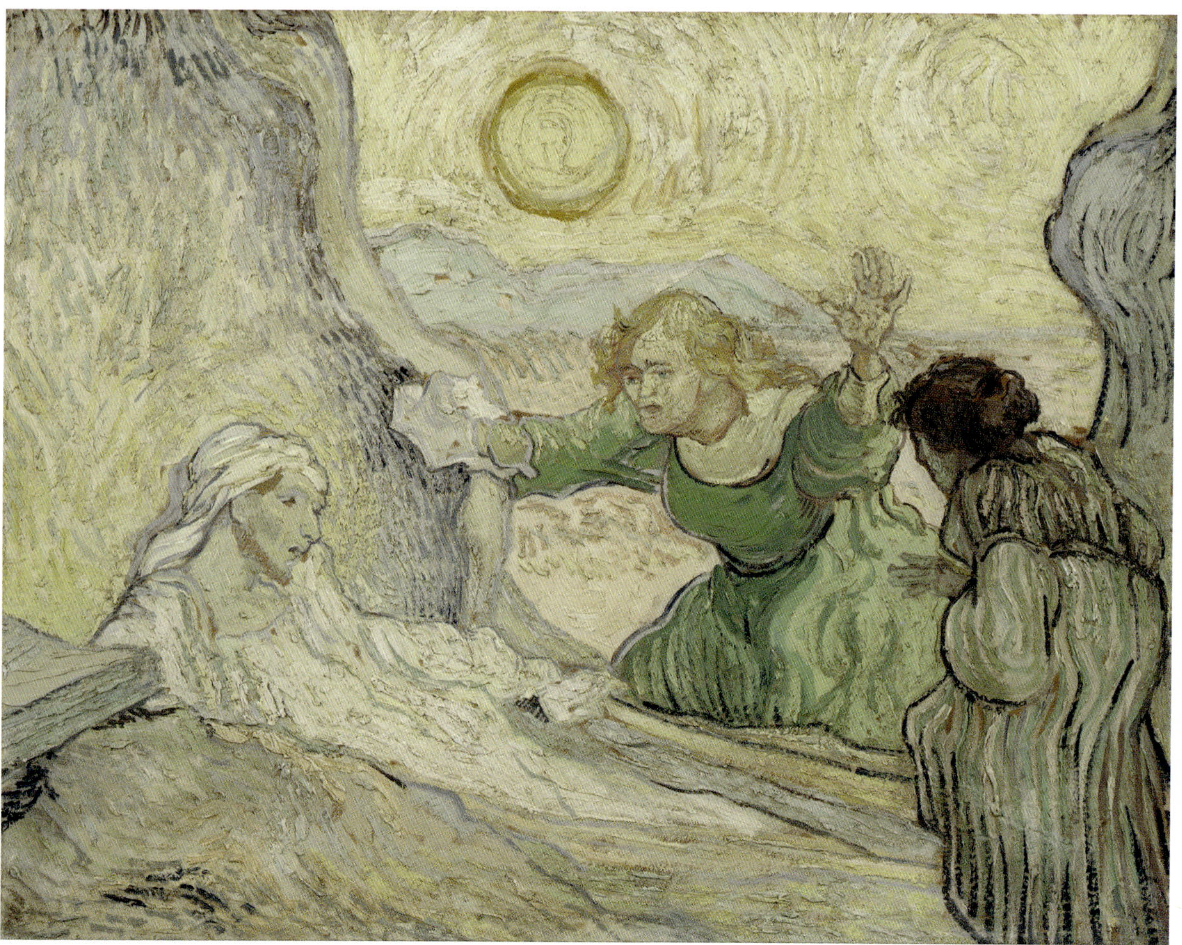

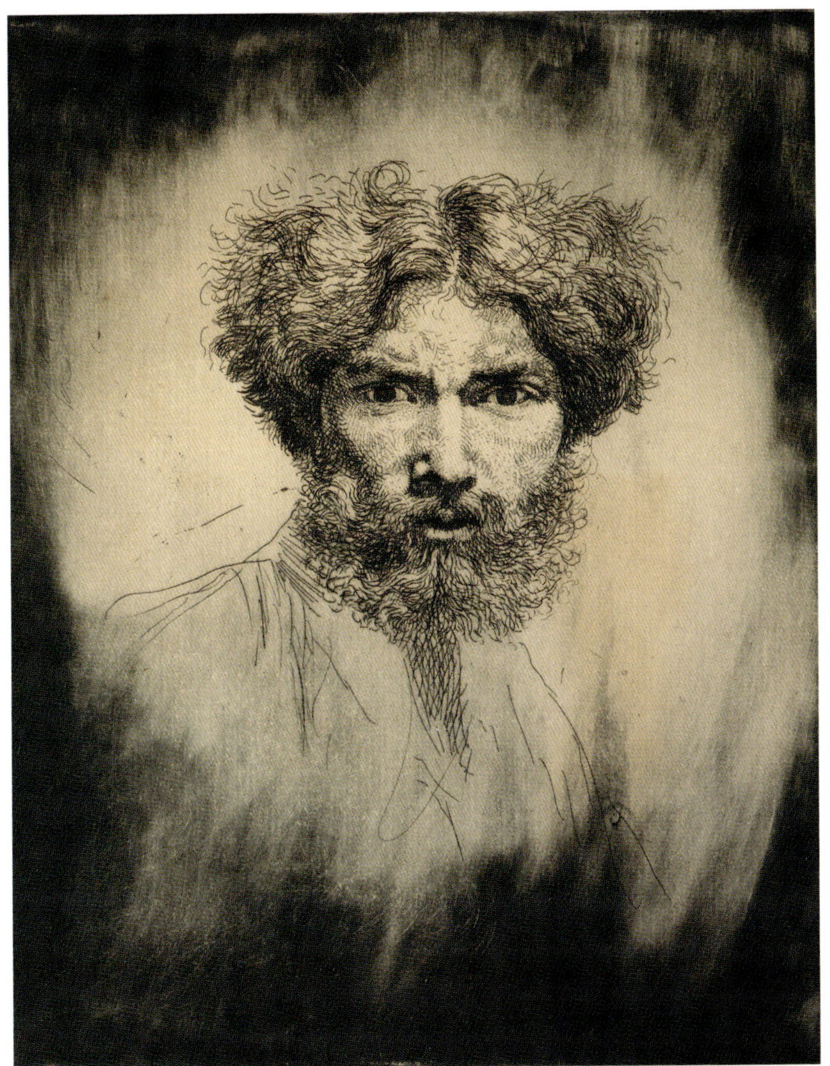

Portrait of the Artist: 'Tête Farouche', *Augustus John, c.1902*, First exhibited with the French title meaning 'wild looking head' this is one of a series of self-portraits. At the Slade School pupils were taught to draw and study old masters. John was an exceptional draughtsman and has examined his own face with a penetrating gaze, as Rembrandt did. Created early on in his career, he is presenting himself as the exciting, bohemian artist. He later reworked the plate to make it even darker and more dramatic.

Copy of The Anatomy Lesson of Dr Tulp, *1856, Edouard Manet. Manet, like many of his contemporaries, greatly admired Rembrandt's ability to capture the world around him and his individuality. Rembrandt's expressive late painting style must have been of particular interest. This copy is evidence that Manet directly studied his work. He was also inspired to take up etching and was part of a wider revival of the medium.*

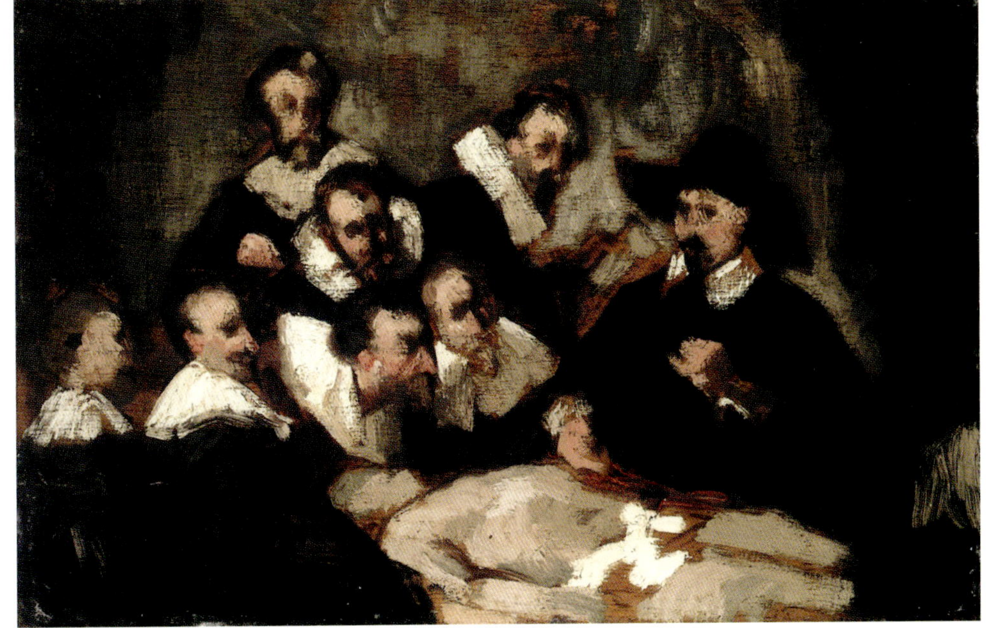

*Opposite:* The Raising of Lazarus (After Rembrandt), *Vincent Van Gogh, 1890. This work is directly inspired by Rembrandt's print of the same subject. However, after discovering his work in the mid-1870s Rembrandt's influence on van Gogh is not always so direct. It was what Rembrandt aimed to achieve in his art that fascinated van Gogh. He came to admire him for his ability to say things with his art 'for which no words exist in any language'.*

# TIMELINE

## 1600s

**'06** 15 July Rembrandt Harmenszoon van Rijn is born in Leiden.

## 1620s

**'22** Begins a three-year apprenticeship with the painter Jacob Isaacszoon van Swanenburg (1571–1638).

**1625-6** Spends several months in Amsterdam studying with history painter Pieter Lastman (1583–1633).

**'25** Earliest dated painting, titled *The Stoning of Saint Stephen*.

**c. 1626** Establishes himself as an independent painter in Leiden.

Publishes his first etching.

**'28** 14 February: Accepts his first pupil, Gerrit Dou.

**'28** Completes his first painted self-portrait, *Self-Portrait as a Young Man*.

## 1630s

**'31** Moves from Leiden to Amsterdam.

**'32** Completes *The Anatomy Lesson of Dr. Nicolaes Tulp*.

**'33** Gets engaged to Saskia van Uylenburgh (1612–42).

**'34** Becomes a citizen of Amsterdam and a member of the guild of painters.

2 July: Marries Saskia.

**'35** 15 December: Son, Rumbartus, is born but lives for only a couple of months.

**'36** Working on five works, now known as the *Passion Series*, for the Stadholder Frederik Hendrik.

**'37** May: Moves to a house on Binnen-Amstel (now no. 41 Zwanenburgerstraat).

## 1630s continued

**'38** Members of Saskia's family go to court to complain that she is squandering her inheritance.

22 July: Their daughter Cornelia is baptized but lives for only three weeks.

**'39** 5 January: Buys a merchant's house in Sint-Anthonisbreestraat (now 4–6 Jodenbreestraat), which is now the Rembrandthuis Museum.

## 1640s

**'40** Another daughter is born, also called Cornelia, but dies after a few weeks.

Death of mother.

**'41** 22 September: Titus, the fourth child is baptized. He is the only one to survive childhood.

**'42** Completes *The Night Watch*.

5 June: Saskia is sick and alters her will in which Titus is to be the benefactor.

14 June: Saskia dies and is buried.

Geertje Dircx (1610/15–c.1656) becomes Titus's nurse. She and Rembrandt begin a relationship.

## 1640s continued

**'47** Hendrickje Stoffels (c.1625–63) is employed as Rembrandt's housekeeper. She later becomes Rembrandt's partner.

**'49** Geertje Dircx goes to court against Rembrandt. She is awarded 200 guilders in alimony.

## 1650s

**'50** 4 July: Geertge Dircx is committed to a house of correction.

**'53** Rembrandt receives a bill for arrears of payment for his merchant house. He borrows money to pay the debt, but is in trouble financially.

He paints *Aristotle with the Bust of Homer*.

**'54** Hendrickje is summoned before the church accused of 'practising whoredom with the painter Rembrandt'.

30 October: Hendrickje and Rembrandt baptize their daughter, Cornelia.

## 1650s continued

**'56** Rembrandt applies for voluntary bankruptcy

12 September: First public auction of some of his possessions takes place.

He paints *The Anatomy Lesson of Dr Jan Deyman*. Only a fragment survives.

**'58** 1 February: House is sold and the family move to rented accommodation in Rozengracht.

Paints *Self-Portrait as a monarch*.

**'59** 7 October: Rembrandt gives Titus power of attorney.

## 1660s

**'60** 15 December: Titus and Hendrickje create a company relieving Rembrandt of all financial control.

**'61** Rembrandt paints *Self-Portrait as the Apostle Paul*.

**'62** He paints *Syndics of the Drapers' Guild* and *The Jewish Bride*.

27 October: Rembrandt sells Saskia's grave.

## 1660s continued

**'63** Hendrickje Stoffels dies and is buried in Amsterdam's Westerkerk on 24 July.

**'66** 18 November: Rembrandt's son Titus is appointed Rembrandt's legal agent.

**'67** 29 December: Cosimo de' Medici (1642–1723) visits Rembrandt.

**'68** Titus marries Magdalena van Loo (1642–69).

7 September: Titus has died and is buried in Amsterdam's Westerkerk.

**'69** 22 March: Rembrandt's granddaughter and goddaughter Titia van Rijn is baptized.

Rembrandt paints three self-portraits in this last year of his life.

4 October: Rembrandt dies, and is buried in a rented grave in Amsterdam's Westerkerk on 8 October.

## FURTHER INFORMATION

Rijksmuseum – Rijksmuseum.nl
National Gallery, London – nationalgallery.org.uk
Rembrandt Research Project – rembrandtresearchproject.org
Complete Rembrandt Catalogue – rembrandtpainting.net
Rembrandt House Museum – rembrandthuis.nl
British Museum – britishmuseum.org

## SELECTED READING LIST

C. White and Q. Buvelot, *Rembrandt by himself*, National Gallery
Publications Limited and Royal Cabinet of Paintings Mauritshuis, 1999

G. Schwartz, *Rembrandt: his life, his paintings*, Guild Publishing, London, 1985
G. Schwartz, *The Complete Etchings of Rembrandt*, The Dover Edition, 1994
S. Schama, *Rembrandt's Eyes*, Penguin Group, 1999
J. Bikker, *Rembrandt Biography of a Rebel*, Rijsmuseum, 2019
C. Schneider, *Rembrandt's Landscapes Drawings and Prints*, National
Gallery of Art, Washington, 1990
A. Van Camp, *Rembrandt in Print*, Ashmolean Museum, University of
Oxford, 2019
A. Van Camp, C. Brown and C. Vogelaar, *Young Rembrandt*, University of
Oxford, 2020

## LIST OF ILLUSTRATIONS

**Page 6**
*Self-Portrait*, c.1628, oil on panel,
22.6 × 18.7 cm (9 × 7 ¼ in),
Rijksmuseum, Amsterdam. ©
Rijksmuseum.

**Page 8**
*A Feast of the Gods (with Seven
Deadly Sins)*, Jacop Isaacsz van
Swanenburg, c.1591–1638, ink
and wash on paper, 20.7 × 32.3
cm (8½ × 12¾ in), Rijksmuseum,
Amsterdam. © Rijksmuseum.

*The Last Judgement and the Seven
Deadly Sins*, Jacop Isaacsz van
Swanenburg, c.1600–38, oil on
panel, 28cm × 88cm (11 × 34½
in), Rijksmuseum, Amsterdam. ©
Rijksmuseum.

**Page 10**
*Orestes and Pylades Disputing at
the Altar*, Pieter Lastman, 1614,
oil on panel, 83.2 × 126.1 cm
(32¾ × 49½ in), Rijksmuseum,
Amsterdam. © Rijksmuseum.

**Page 11**
*Jonah and the Whale*, Pieter
Lastman, 1621, oil on panel, 36
× 52.1 cm (14¼ × 20½), Museum
Kunstpalast, Dusseldorf, Germany.
Wikimedia Commons.

**Page 12**
*The Leiden History Piece (History
Painting)*, 1626, oil on panel, 90 ×
121 cm (35½ × 47½ in), Stedelijk
Museum De Lakenhal, Leiden.
Wikimedia Commons.

**Page 13**
*The Stoning of St Stephen*, 1625,
oil on panel, 89 × 123 cm (35 ×
48 in)

Musée des Beaux-Arts,Lyon.
Wikimedia Commons.

*Coriolanus and the Roman
Matron*s, Pieter Lastman, 1622, oil
on panel, 81 x 132 cm (32 x 52 in)
Trinity College, Dublin. Wikimedia
Commons.

**Page 14**
*Musical Company*, 1626, oil on
panel, 63.4 × 47.5 cm (25 × 18½
in), Rijksmuseum, Amsterdam. ©
Rijksmuseum.

**Page 15**
*Tabit and Anna with the Kid*,
1626, oil on panel, 39.9 × 29.9 cm
(15¹¹⁄₁₆ × 11¾ in), Rijksmuseum,
Amsterdam. © Rijksmuseum.

*Tabit and Anna with the Kid*,
Jan van de Velde after Willem
Buytewech, c.1619, etching,
19.3 × 11.2 cm (7½ × 4½ in),
Rijksmuseum, Amsterdam. ©
Rijksmuseum.

**Page 16**
*Self-Portrait Leaning Forward*,
c.1627/8, etching on paper, 4.3 ×
4 cm (1¾ × 1½ in), Rijksmuseum,
Amsterdam. © Rijksmuseum.

**Page 17**
*Self-Portrait with Plumed Beret*,
1629, oil on panel, 89.7 × 73.5
cm (35⁵⁄₁₆ × 28¹⁵⁄₁₆ in), Isabella
Stewart Gardner Museum, Boston.
Wikimedia Commons.

**Page 19**
*The Painter in his Studio*, c.1629,
oil on panel, 24.8 × 31.7cm (9¾
× 12½ in), Museum of Fine Arts,
Boston. Wikimedia Commons.

**Page 20**
*Judas Repentant, Returning the
Thirty Pieces of Silver to the Chief
Priests and Elders*, 1629, oil on
panel, 79 × 102.3 cm (31 × 40¼
in), Private Collection. Wikimedia
Commons.

**Page 21**
*Portrait of Amalia van Solms*, 1632,
oil on canvas, 68.5 × 55.5 cm (27 ×
21¾ in), Musée Jacquemart-André,
Paris. © Tallandier/Bridgeman Images.

*Portrait of Constantijn Huygens*,
Jan Lievens, c.1628/9, oil on
panel, 99 × 84 cm (38.9 × 33 in),
Rijksmuseum, Amsterdam. ©
Rijksmuseum.

**Page 22**
*Self-Portrait in a Soft Hat and
Pattern Cloak*, 1631, etching with
drypoint on paper, 14.8 × 13.1 cm
(5¾ × 5¼ in). Location, Public
Domain.

**Page 24**
Portrait of Nicholaes Ruts, 1631,
oil on panel, 116.8 × 87.3 cm (46 ×
34³⁄₈ in), The Frick Collection, New
York. Wikimedia Commons.

**Page 25**
*A Self-Portrait*, Peter Paul Rubens,
1623, oil on canvas, 85.7 × 62.2
cm (33¾ × 24½ in), Picture
Gallery, Buckingham Palace.
Wikimedia Commons.

*Prometheus Bound*, Peter Paul
Rubens, 1612, oil on canvas, 244 ×
210 cm (96 × 83¼ in, Philadelpha
Museum of Art. Public Domain

**Page 26**
*Portrait of Marten Looten*, 1632,
oil on panel, 92.7 × 76.2 cm (36½
× 30 in), County Museum of Art,
Los Angeles. Public Doman.

**Page 27**
*The Shipbuilder and his Wife*, Jan
Rijcksen (1560/2–1637) and Griet
Jans (c.1560–after 1653), 1633, oil
on canvas, 113.8 × 169.8 cm (41¾
× 66¾ in), Royal Collection Trust.
Public Domain.

*Portrait of Aechje Claesdr (Portrait
of an 83-Year-Old Woman)*, 1634,
oil on panel, 71.1 × 55.9 cm (28 ×
22 in), National Gallery, London.
Wikimedia Commons.

**Page 28**
*The Anatomy Lecture of Dr
Nicholas Tulp*, 1632, 169.5
× 216.5 cm (66¾ × 85¼ in),
Mauritshuis, The Hague.
Wikimedia Commons.

**Page 29**
*Portrait of Marten Soolmans*,
1634, oil on canvas, 210 × 135
cm (82¾ × 53¼ in), Rijksmuseum,
Amsterdam. © Rijksmuseum.

*Portrait of Oopjen Coppit*, 1634,
oil on canvas, 209.9 cm × 134.8
(82¾ × 53¼ in), Musée du Louvre,
Paris. Public Domain.

**Page 30**
*Portrait of Saskia Uylenburgh*,
1633, silverpoint on prepared
parchment, 18.5 × 10.7 cm (7¼
× 4¼ in), Kupferstichkabinett,
Staatliche Museen zu Berlin.
Wikimedia Commons.

**Page 31**
*Saskia as Flora*, 1634, oil on canvas, 125 × 101 cm (49¼ × 39¾ in), State Hermitage Museum, St. Petersburg. Wikimedia Commons.

**Page 32**
*Saskia in a Red Hat*, 1633-42, oil on panel, 99.5 × 78.8 cm (39¼ × 31 in), Museumslandshaft Hessen Kassel. Wikimedia Commons.

*Self-Portrait with Saskia*, 1636, etching on paper, 10.4 × 9.5 cm (4⅛ × 3¾ in, Princeton Art Museum. Public Domain.

**Page 33**
*Rembrandt and Saskia in the Scene of the Prodigal Son*, c.1635, oil on canvas, 161 × 131 cm (63½ × 51½ in), Gemäldegaleri, Dresden. Public Domain.

*Bedroom with Saskia in Bed*, c.1635/1638, pen and brown ink with wash and bodycolour on paper, 17.7 × 24.1 cm (7 × 9½ in), Rijksmuseum, Amsterdam. © Rijksmuseum.

**Page 34**
*Studies of the Magdalen and the Virgin Mourning*, c. 1635–36, brown ink and red chalk on paper, 20.1 × 14.3 cm (8 × 5½ in), Rijksmuseum, Amsterdam. © Rijksmuseum.

*Jacob and his Sons*, c.1641, pen and brown ink with bodycolour on paper, 17.6 × 23.3 cm (7 × 9¼ in), Rijksmuseum, Amsterdam.

**Page 35**
*Reclining Lion*, c.1660, reed pen and brown ink on paper, 12.2 × 21.2 cm (4 ¾ × 8¼ in), Rijksmuseum, Amsterdam.

*Self-Portrait*, c.1628–29, pen and brown ink, with wash on paper, 12.7 × 9.4 cm (5 × 3¾ in), Rijksmuseum, Amsterdam.

**Page 36**
*Self-Portrait Wearing a Helmet*, 1634, oil on panel, 80.5 × 66 cm (31¾ × 26 in), Museumslandscaft Hessen Kassel. Wikimedia Commons.

**Page 37**
*Bust of a Man in Oriental Dress*,

1635, oil on panel, 72 × 54.4 cm (28¼ × 21½ in), Rijksmuseum, Amsterdam. © Rijksmuseum.

**Page 38**
*The Raising of the Cross*, c.1633, oil on canvas, 96.2 × 72.2 cm (37¾ × 28½ in).

*The Descent from the Cross*, c.1633, oil on panel, 89.4 × 65.2 cm (35¼ × 25¾ in), Both Bayerische Staatsgemäldesammlungen, Alte Pinakothek, Munich. Wikimedia Commons.

**Page 39**
*The Ascension of Christ*, c. 1636, oil on canvas, 92.7 × 68.3 cm (36½ × 27 in).

*The Entombment of Christ*, 1639, oil on canvas, 92.5 × 68.9 cm (36½ × 27 in). Both Bayerische Staatsgemäldesammlungen, Alte Pinakothek, Munich. Wikimedia Commons.

**Page 40**
*The Holy Family*, c.1634, oil on canvas, 183.5 × 123 cm (72¼ × 48½ in), Bayerische Staatsgemäldesammlungen, Alte Pinakothek, Munich. Wikimedia Commons.

**Page 41**
*Belshazzar's Feast*, c.1635, oil on canvas, 167.6 × 209.2 cm (66 × 82½ in), National Gallery, London. Wikimedia Commons.

**Page 42**
*The Blinding of Samson*, 1636, oil on canvas, 236 × 302 cm (92½ × 119 in), Städel Museum, Frankfurt. © Fine Art Images/Bridgeman Images.

**Page 43**
*Christ in the Storm on the Sea of Galilee (St Peter's boat)*, 1633, oil on canvas, 160 × 128 cm (63 × 50½ in), Stolen from the Isabella Stewart Gardener Museum, Boston. Wikimedia Commons.

**Page 44**
*Still-Life with Dead Peacocks*, c.1639, oil on canvas, 144 × 136.9 cm (56¾ × 54 in), Rijksmuseum, Amsterdam. © Rijksmuseum.

**Page 45**
*Landscape with a Stone Bridge*, c.1638, oil on panel, 29.5 × 42.5 cm (11½ × 16¾ in), Rijksmuseum, Amsterdam. © Rijksmuseum.

*Landscape with a Long, Arched Bridge*, 1638, oil on panel, 28 × 40 cm (11 × 15¾ in), Gemäldegalerie, Berlin. Wikimedia Commons.

**Page 46**
*Saskia with Red Flower*, 1641, oil on panel, 98 × 82.5 cm (38½ × 32½ in), Gemäldegaleri, Dresden. © Staatliche Kunstsammlungen Dresden, Bridgeman Images.

**Page 47**
*Self-Portrait Leaning on a Stone Sill*, 1639, etching on paper, 20.5 × 16.4 cm (8 × 6½ in), Metropolitan Museum of Art, New York. © Metropolitan Museum of Art

**Pages 48–51**
*The Night Watch (Civic Guardsmen of District II under the Command of Captain Frans Banninck Cocq.)*, 1642, oil on canvas, 363 × 438 cm (143 × 172½ in), Rijksmuseum, Amsterdam. © Rijksmuseum.

*Officers and other Civic Guardsment of the IV District of Amsterdam, under the Command of Captain Jan Claesz van Vlooswijck and Lieutenand Gerrit Hudde*, Nicolaes Eliasz Pickenoy, 1642, oil on canvas, 340 × 527 cm (134 × 207½ in), Rijksmuseum, Amsterdam. © Rijksmuseum.

Details of *The Night Watch*.

**Page 52**
*Self-Portrait in a Flat Cap*, 1642, oil on panel, 70.4 × 58.8 cm (27¾ × 23¼ in), Royal Collection. Public Domain.

**Page 54**
*The Shell (Conus marmoreus)*, 1650, etching, engraving and drypoint on paper, 9.7 × 13.2 cm (3¾ × 5¼ in), Rijksmuseum, Amsterdam. © Rijksmuseum.

*Self-Portrait at the Window*, 1648, etching and drypoint on paper, 15.5 × 12.8 cm (6¼ × 5 in), Rijksmuseum, Amsterdam. © Rijksmuseum.

**Page 55**
*The Adoration of the Shepherds*, 1646, oil on canvas, 97 × 71.3 cm (38¼ × 28¼ in), Bayerische Staatsgemäldesammlungen, Alte Pinakothek, Munich. Wikimedia Commons.

**Page 56**
*The Holy Family with painted frame and curtain*, 1646, oil on panel, 46.5 × 68.8 cm (18¼ × 27 in), Museumslandshaft Hessen Kassel. © Museumslandschaft Hessen Kassel/Ute Brunzel/ Bridgeman Images.

*The Windmill*, 1641, etching on paper, 14.5 × 20.5 cm (5¾ × 8 in), Metropolitan Museum of Art. Public Domain.

**Page 57**
*The Milkmaid*, Johannes Vermeer c.1660, oil on canvas, 45.5 × 41 cm (17⅞ × 16¼ in) Rijksmuseum, Amsterdam. © Rijksmuseum.

**Page 58**
*A Woman in a Bed*, c. 1647, oil on canvas, 81.1 × 67.8 cm (32 × 26¾ in) National Galleries Scotland. Wikimedia Commons.

**Page 59**
*The State Bed (Het Ledikant)*, 1646, etching and drypoint on paper, 12.5 × 22.3 cm (5 × 8¾ in, Rijksmuseum, Amsterdam. © Rijksmuseum.

**Page 60**
*Portrait of Jan Cornelisz Syvius, Preacher*, 1646, etching, drypoint and engraving on paper, 27.6 × 18.7 cm (10½ × 7⅜ in), Rijksmuseum, Amsterdam. © Rijksmuseum.

**Page 61**
Aristotle with a Bust of Homer, 1653, oil on canvas, 143.5 × 136.5 cm (56½ × 53¾ in), Metropolitan Museum of Art, New York. Metropolitan Museum of Art.

*The Three Crosses*, 1653, drypoint on paper, 38.1 × 43.8 cm (15 × 17¼ in), Metropolitan Museum of Art, New York. Metropolitan Museum of Art.

# INDEX